Belle de Jour

Belle de Jour

DIARY OF AN
UNLIKELY CALL GIRL

by Anonymous

WARNER BOOKS

NEW YORK BOSTON

Warner Books Edition

Copyright © 2006 by Bizrealm Limited on behalf of Belle de Jour
Originally published in the U.K. by Weidenfeld & Nicolson.
Material from the work has been previously published on the author's Weblog diary at
http://belledejour-uk.blogspot.com.

This Warner Books edition is published by arrangement with Weidenfeld & Nicolson.

Warner Books

Time Warner Book Group
1271 Avenue of the Americas, New York, NY 10020
Visit our Web site at www.twbookmark.com.

Printed in the United States of America
First Warner Books Edition: July 2006
10 9 8 7 6 5 4 3 2 1

Library of Congress Control Number: 2005929534
ISBN: 0-446-57725-1

Book design by Giorgetta Bell McRee

Dedicated to F and N

Prologue

The first thing you should know is that I'm a whore.

I don't mean that in a glib way. I'm not using the word as an analogy for working a desk job or toiling away in new media. Many of my friends will tell you how temping for a year or ending up in sales is equivalent to prostitution. It's not. I know this because I've been a temp, and I've fucked for money, and they are in no way similar. Not even the same planet. Different solar systems altogether.

The second thing is that I live in London. These two facts may or may not be related. It's not a cheap city. Like almost all of my friends, I moved here after university with the hope of getting a job. If not a well-paying one, at least something interesting, or populated exclusively by handsome, eligible men. But such positions are thin on the ground. Almost everyone is studying to be an accountant now, including my friends A2 and A3, who are respected in their academic circles. Good God—a fate worse than death. Accountancy trumps even academia in the unsexiness stakes.

Prostitution is steady work but not demanding. I meet a lot of people. Granted, they're almost all men, most of whom I'll never see again, and I'm required to fuck them regardless of whether they're covered in hairy moles or have a grand total of three teeth or want me to re-create a fantasy involving their sixth-form history teacher. But it's better than watching the clock until the next scheduled tea break in a dismal staff room. So when my friends pull out the tired analogy of corporate-employment-as-whoring yet again, I nod knowingly, and commiserate with them, and we down cocktails and wonder where all our youthful promise went. Theirs is probably taking a commuter train to the suburbs. Mine is spreading its legs for cash on a regular basis.

Having said that, the leap to full-on prostitution did not happen overnight.

I ended up in London like thousands of other recent graduates. With only a small student debt and a bit of cash saved, I thought I was set for a few months, but that was quickly drained by rent and a thousand trivial expenses. My daily routine consisted of poring over the job pages, writing enthusiastic and sycophantic cover letters for positions I knew I'd never be interviewed for, and masturbating furiously before bed every night.

The masturbation was, by far, the highlight of those days. I imagined myself employed as a testing engineer for an office supplies manufacturer, in which the job involved covering my inner thighs with bulldog clips as someone screwed me vigorously. Or being the personal assistant to a powerful dominatrix, chained to her desk and eaten out by one of the other slaves, who in her turn was impaled on a dildo. Or floating in a sensory deprivation tank as unseen hands pinched and pulled at my skin, gestures at first gentle, then painful.

London wasn't the first city I'd lived in, but it was certainly the largest. Anywhere else there is always the chance of seeing someone you know or, at the very least, a smiling face. Not here. Commuters crowd the trains, eager to outdo their fellow travelers in an escalating privacy war of paperbacks, headphones, and newspapers. A woman next to me on the Northern Line one day held the *Metro* just inches from her face; it was only three stops later that I noticed she was not reading but crying. It was hard not to offer sympathy and harder still to not start crying myself.

When work did come, it was always temporary, and usually paid badly. I did all the usual office drudgery, from answering phones (I never did figure out how to transfer a call without losing it) to filing (my alphabetization skills are probably surpassed by the average five-year-old; I always claim dyslexia, but am just lazy) to transcribing dictation (100,000 monkeys at 100,000 typewriters would do a better job). The day I came home with blistered fingertips from sealing envelopes was probably the worst. And even all this was better than the long, frequent periods in which I had no work at all.

So I watched my mean savings dwindle away as buying a Metrocard became the highlight of each week. And while I have a crippling lingerie-buying habit, even cutting down the intake of lacy things was not going to solve the problem.

Not long after moving, I had a text from an acquaintance, known through my friend N. This is N's city and he seems to know everyone. He's at least four of my six degrees of separation. So when he went out of his way to introduce me to this lady, I paid attention. *Heard you're in town—would love to meet when you're free,* the text said. She was a compactly sexy older woman, with a cut-glass accent and impeccable taste. When we had first met, I'd thought she was out of my league. But as soon as her back was turned, N indicated in half-whispers and furious hand gestures that she went like a train and liked women too. I dumped a gusher in my knickers instantly.

I saved that text for weeks as my imagination grew more heated and restless. Before long she had morphed into the latex-clad hell-bitch-boss of my nocturnal reveries. The wenches and sex-crazed office drones in my dreams were developing faces, and they were all hers. I texted back. She rang almost immediately to say that she and her new man would love to see me for dinner the next week.

I panicked for days about what to wear and splurged on a haircut and new underwear. On the night itself I tore my wardrobe apart, changing outfits a dozen times. Finally I decided on a tight aqua sweater and charcoal trousers—a little office-temp, perhaps, but modestly sexy. I arrived at the restaurant half an hour early, even after half an hour of trying to find the restaurant in the first place. The staff said I could only be seated when my party arrived. I spent the last of my money on a drink at the bar and hoped they'd cover the cost of the meal.

The sound of couples talking in the narrow rooms mingled with the burbling background music. Everyone looked possibly older than me, definitely better off. A few might have just come from work; others wandered in having been home to refresh. The door, each time it opened, let in a blast of chilly autumn air and the smell of dry leaves.

The couple arrived. We were seated at a table in the corner well away from the attention of the staff; I was tucked between them. He looked down the front of my sweater while she talked about art galleries and sport. As I felt his hand creep onto my right knee, her stockinged foot started to slide up the inside leg of my trousers.

Ah. That's what they're after, I thought, and hadn't I known it all along? They were older, libertine, gorgeous. There was no good reason not to fuck or be fucked by them. I followed their lead in ordering: rich, buttery dishes. A mushroom risotto so thick it could barely be torn away from the shallow bowl, so glutinous the only way to dislodge it from the spoon was with teeth. Fish with the head still attached and its heat-glazed eyes staring up at us. She licked her fingers and I had the feeling this was a purposeful gesture rather than a lapse in manners. My hand slid over her skintight trousers to her crotch, and she clamped her legs together around my knuckles. At that particular moment the waitress decided our table needed more attention. She brought over a sampler of tiny pastries and chocolate treats, and the man fed his girlfriend with one hand, gripping my hand in the other, while my fingers crawled in her lap. She came easily, almost silently. I brushed her neck with my lips.

"Excellent," he murmured. "Now do it again."

So I did. After the meal we left the restaurant. He asked me to strip to the waist and sit in the front passenger seat while she drove. From the back seat he grabbed my breasts and pinched my nipples as we traveled the short distance to her house. I walked from the car to the door topless and, once inside, was ordered on my knees. She disappeared into the bedroom as he put me through a few basic obedience lessons—holding uncomfortable positions, holding heavy things in uncomfortable positions, holding heavy things in uncomfortable positions with his cock in my mouth.

She returned with candles and whips. While I have had both hot wax and the business end of a riding crop applied to my flesh before, it was a new experience to have it done with my legs in the air and lit candles plunged into me, dripping over my torso. After two hours, he entered her and, using his cock like the domme in my fantasy, drove her face-first into my pussy.

We dressed, she showered. He walked me out to find a black cab. His arm threaded through mine. Father and daughter, any passing stranger might have thought. We looked a comfortable pair.

"Quite a woman you have there," I said.

"Whatever it takes to keep her happy," he said.

I nodded. He waved down a taxi and gave the driver directions. As I stepped into the back he handed me a roll of money and said I was welcome anytime. I was halfway home before I unfolded the wad of notes and saw it was at least three times as much as the cab fare would cost.

My mind made the calculations—rent due, the number of days in a month, the net profit from the night out. I thought I should feel a pang of regret or surprise at being used and paid for. But it was nothing like that. They'd enjoyed themselves and to a wealthy couple the expense of dinner and a taxi was nothing at all. And, truth be told, I hadn't exactly found it a chore.

I asked the driver to stop a few streets from my flat. The staccato sound of my heels on the pavement echoed off the housefronts. It was still summer, still warm at night, and the red candle-wax marks under my clothes glowed with sympathetic heat.

The idea of selling sex festered, it grew. But for a while I buried my curiosity about prostitution. I borrowed money off friends and started seeing a young man seriously. This was pleasantly distracting until the first overdraft statement from my bank arrived, suggesting I see them about a loan. The festering whispered and itched with every job application rejection and failed interview. I couldn't stop thinking how it felt, swept away in the back of a black cab in the middle of the night. I could do it. I had to see.

And it wasn't too long after deciding to do it that I started keeping a diary.

Novembre

Belle's A–Z of London Sex Work

A–C

A is for Agencies

An agency in London typically takes one-third of the fee off a girl, excluding travel and tips. The man is expected to pay for travel expenses on an outcall, and this can add another 30 to 40 pounds.

Agency commission covers advertising, arranging and confirming appointments, as well as some security when needed. Some agencies deduct photography costs from a girl's first appointments or ask her to pay up front. The agency I am registered with did not; photos and building a profile were free.

With luck, contact with the agency will be minimal. The last time I saw my manager, she criticized my lipliner. So much for feminine solidarity.

B is for Bad Hair

Sometimes the lead-up to an appointment leaves no time for the three-act fluffing and primping in a girl's regime. The hair is usually the first to suffer. If I hurry, it tends to come out a bit limp and flat, a touch on the greasy side. There's an emergency one-time, one-hour-only trick a girl at uni taught me: shake a light dusting of talc through the hair, then comb lightly. It'll look good enough for long enough. Avoid moisture, though, or you risk gluing your head to the wall.

C is for Cash Only

I don't take cards. Where would I put the swipe machine?

C is also for Chatter

Keeping up your own end of the conversation is not only useful, but probably the most relevant skill for the job. Pretend to be interested in everything. Be vague about political tendencies and other potentially inflammatory opinions. In other words, lie your head off. Think of it as proving ground for a future political career.

samedi, le 1er novembre

A client was latched on to my nipples like a bulldog clip. "Careful there, premenstrual," I said, gently guiding his hands elsewhere.

"Tell me something you fantasize about," he said.

~~Not having to wear open-toed sandals in winter.~~

~~A sailing holiday with the Boyfriend.~~

~~Saturday nights off.~~

"I'm abducted by four men, stripped and tied up in the back of a car. They park the car and get out and masturbate on me through the open windows."

"Are there horses nearby?"

"There are a lot of horses nearby. We're in the middle of the country. We're on a farm. They're farmers."

"Can you smell the horses?"

"I can smell the horses, they're making noises in their stalls and getting very excited. Horses have giant cocks, don't they?"

"Oh yes. Yes, they do."

"When the farmers are finished, they take me to the stables."

"Don't fuck the horse."

"Oh no, I don't even get close. It's too big! And the horse . . . the stallion . . . is out of control, too excited. I think it's far too big. It sounds like it's going to break down the stall door."

"Urrrrrrrr . . ."

dimanche, le 2 novembre

A few things I have learnt on the job:

Fact. In a world of twelve-year-olds in sexy boots and grannies in sparkly minidresses, the surest way to tell the prostitute walking into a hotel at Heathrow is to look for the lady in the designer suit.

The buildup to an appointment is almost always the same. The clients contact the agency after seeing the website. Then they ring, the manager rings me, she reconfirms with them, then they wait. I usually need two hours' notice. One hour of plucking, showering, making up and hair; one to call a minicab and get to the meeting point. The makeup sits apart from the rest of my toiletries on its own shelf. I stand in front of a full-length mirror as the layers go on: powder and cologne; knickers, bra, and stockings; dress, shoes, makeup, and hair. Three outfits in the rotation—a modest but slinky gray jersey dress, a white-on-white checked suit, a tailored black linen dress with smart jacket. An infinite choice of underwear and shoes.

The last three seconds before entering the hotel are vital. Are the doors glass? If so, scan quickly for the lifts. Don't go in and just stop; don't ask the staff for directions. Sweep through, acknowledge them with a slight nod. If the lifts or toilets aren't obvious, go for the nearest hallway, then get your bearings. If you leave an impression at all, it should be of a well-dressed lady. You are a businesswoman.

Not strictly untrue.

Lifts are useful. Time to dig through the purse for a phone, text the agency—they'll want to know you arrived on time. If you've been running late, they'll let the client know to expect you. Freshen lipgloss if needed; arrange clothing. Never be sweating or looking rushed. Find the door and knock briefly, firmly. "Darling, hello, pleased to meet you," you say on entering the room. "Sorry to keep you waiting." Whether late or not. Even if you make it bang on time, the customer will have been counting the minutes. If anyone in the room is nervous, it mustn't be you. Coat off, sit down. The client usually offers a drink. Never say no. If nothing else, have a sparkling water.

Collect the money before anything starts. One time I forgot to do this. The client laughed. "You must be new to this," he said, and when I went in the toilet to clean up afterwards, he stuck the notes in the toaster in his flat. Don't count it in front of him; there'll be time later if you're suspicious. Leave on time. If he wants you to stay longer, he has to ring the manager, arrange the price, and pay you right then. On leaving, a quick kiss. "An absolute pleasure. I hope to see you again." Out the front, nod to the staff, as quickly gone as you arrived. Text or ring the agency once out of the hotel. If the manager can't get through, she'll ring the client, then the hotel, her own security if they're nearby, then the police. She knows. She's been in your shoes too.

My manager is sweet, an absolute doll. When she asks how it went, I always reply that the client was lovely, a gentleman, even if it's stretching the truth. I wouldn't want her to worry.

And sometimes it doesn't go off quite right—like the time I inadvertently waved goodbye to an underendowed client by waggling my index finger. Cringe. That's okay, perhaps he didn't notice, and there's always next time.

lundi, le 3 novembre

The traffic close to the city center is unpredictable, and it's better to be early to work than late. I had a meeting yesterday near Leicester Square. Arrived half an hour early and went into a record store to kill time.

I like record stores; I like music. This was a chain store, though, its lower level full of DVDs and books about music. The few racks of actual albums were heavy with chart-toppers and low price deals. I stole upstairs to the jazz and blues section.

Most of the other customers were kids killing time just like me, though not caked in quite so much makeup. Would the client be at the appointed meeting place, I wondered, or was he out too? Perhaps he was even in here? I looked round. There was one man, blond and thin, leaning over the end rack. Attractive in a sort of corruptible-young-lecturer way. I sauntered by and glanced over his shoulder.

His slender fingers played with the corner of an Isaac Hayes disc. "Good choice," I murmured, and he almost dropped it in surprise. I must have looked a sight—overdressed, bulging coat, and face like a fright mask of makeup. Idiot, idiot, idiot. I made for the ground level, shoes clattering on the stairs.

When I met the client, he was, of course, not the man from the shop.

It was an overnight job: staying until sunrise. The manager has received such positive feedback about my skills as a disciplinarian that she lists it prominently in the website portfolio. I'm not naturally dominant, but I don't mind doing it. Now it seems all clients want the treatment.

He: "There's nothing quite like the buzz from fucking strangers."

Me: "Can I quote you on that?"

"Yes." (pauses) "What are you doing with your hands?"

My fingers were tented, bearing my weight above him. "I don't want to knock the paintings off the wall." I gritted my teeth.

"Good idea. Try not to, then." Cripes, mate, it's not as if it's your own house. Hmph. Pretty demanding for a submissive, I thought.

(later still)

He: "You're a class act, my dear."

Me: "I didn't know anyone actually said that, outside the movies."

"Have to get my lines from somewhere."

N met me outside the hotel just before sunrise. He's a close friend, we used to date, he knows what I do, and can double for George Clooney in the right light. As in, pitch black. N was smirking. "Have fun in there?" I opened my coat to show him two whips tied to the inside lining. "You brought the Persuaders. So you were having fun."

"Sort of. Yes. He couldn't stay hard, so we drank the minibar and watched Channel Five for the last hour." We got into N's car, which was parked on the pavement. "And he gave me a silver bubble blower." I took the gift out of my purse. It was in a wooden box wrapped with gold and black ribbons, and shaped like a tiny champagne bottle.

I wasn't feeling tired and neither was he. "You want to blow bubbles?" N asked as we drove over Tower Bridge. We turned and drove up the leafy Embankment, and the growing light of the morning made the water glint darkly. N knows about the tides of the Thames; he's seen bodies dragged out of the river; he knows where the terrapins and seals go when the weather is warm. He pointed to a building with a swimming pool in the basement, said he used to swim there when he was at school because it was the closest one. And that bridge, he remembers the woman who threw herself off it, pockets full of pebbles, but who didn't realize the air would catch in her layers of clothing so she couldn't sink. When the rescue boats came to drag her out, she fought them off—"Put me in, put me in!" I sat back, eyes half closed, as he told me more of the city lore. We ended up at Charing Cross station at sunrise, blowing soapy scraps of bubble juice diluted with manky Thames water onto the first commuters of the day.

mardi, le 4 novembre

Small handbags, bah. The magazines can tout this or that tiny purse of the season. But considering what I typically leave the house carrying,

a pair of folding scissors (stray threads are the enemy)
a pen (my memory is good, but not that good)
phone (phone agency on arrival and leaving)
condoms (polyurethane as well as latex—some people have allergies)
a spoon
bottle of lube
lipgloss (reapplying lipstick after a blowjob is too complicated)
compact and mascara
small vial of scent (anything citrusy is nice)
tissues
spare knickers and stockings
keys, bankcards, other normal detritus
and sometimes, nipple clamps, ball gag, and a multitailed rubber whip,

a capacious holdall is the order of the day. Packing all that into a Fendi baguette is a black art not even Houdini could master.

mercredi, le 5 novembre

I was reminded of a phrase I had forgotten existed—*turning tricks.*

Turning tricks! What an intriguing concept! I imagine a Vegas dealer turning over the flop, an Edwardian society belle sifting through a silver plate of calling cards, a dominatrix flipping bound captives like so many grilling sausages.

vendredi, le 7 novembre

My parents are quite nice. I know I'm biased, but it's true. In spite of having left home years ago, I'm still in contact with one or both of them on an almost-daily basis.

They don't know, officially, what I do. They know I'm in the sex trade but that's it. Knowing my mother and her middle-class sensibilities, she probably tells her friends I'm a sales rep for Myla or something.

So while they officially don't know, I suspect they unofficially do know. Or at least have a clue. Mum and Dad, they're not stupid people.

I rang home for no particular reason. "Hello, honey," Daddy said. "Still beating the streets? Ha ha ha."

"Ha," I bleated flatly. "Mum there?" He grunted and handed the phone over.

"When are you coming home?" she asked. No hello. No asking after my health. No one in her family has bothered with polite pleasantries since antediluvian times. Straight to the point, that's them.

"Couple of weeks?"

"How's the job search going?"

I ummed and erred. I couldn't remember what I'd last told her. That I was looking for work, or starting on a research project? Thinking about postgrad programs, or applying to some? "Not bad, a few things out there, no interviews yet."

Actually, it's not quite all lies, I had a job interview.

Don't get too excited—it wasn't a real one. I was instructed to meet a client at a hotel, and was e-mailed his specific requirements for my interview technique. He required a shy, almost virginal secretary who would be powerless under his persuasion. Needless to say, A levels (not the academic sort) were required.

We finished early and snapped out of character. I found a lime-scented cream in the bathroom and massaged his tense shoulders. "Do you find my fantasies odd?" he asked.

"Odd?"

"Do you think it demeans women?"

I chose my words carefully. "I think this is the appropriate outlet for it." We talked a bit longer. Interestingly, his background was very similar to mine—his mother comes from where my father is from, and vice versa. The conversation strayed to places, attitudes, foodstuffs, sport. As we spoke homesickness hit quickly and hard, and I was suddenly looking forward to the holidays.

My mother seemed satisfied with the evasion of her question. "Let me know when you're visiting, yes? And if you're bringing anyone, yes? So I can make up the rooms."

"Of course," I lied. Setting a date would have been pointless, because she inevitably forgets. On the day I turn up at home, suitcases in hand, she can always be counted on to exclaim, "Oh, was it today you were coming home? I thought it was tomorrow!"

She put Daddy back on the line. "Tell that nice boy of yours with the glasses I said hello!" he chirruped. That was a boy called A4, a lovely young lad who was very clever and always smiled. My father still says from time to time that he hopes we'll marry. I don't know if this is a sign of senility or a misguided attempt at matchmaking. A4 was three relationships ago. We're still friends, though. I sighed, and wished them a pleasant weekend, and rang off.

dimanche, le 9 novembre

Prostitution isn't my first foray into sex work. Not that I'm equating standing behind an attractively arranged display of dildos to real live wetsex. I can't brook the sanctimonious tut-tutting of shop assistants who don't even have wankbooths to empty. Checking stock of rubber dicks is all well and good, but not an exalted position from which to crap on strippers, porn actresses, and prostitutes for not doing their part for the sisterhood.

Anyhow. Perhaps my odd CV did lead to the current job. Here's the executive summary:

- as a student, was rather short of money
- someone suggested stripping. By "someone" I mean my then-boyfriend Al. By "suggested" I mean "used to date a stripper and would take me to the fleshpots with his friends, which I rather liked"
- it was not terribly hard work, the girls were frightening
- couldn't stop giggling at the men talking to me between sets. Who wants to go over the finer points of Greek tragedy with a girl in a see-through bra?
- scratch that, I completely see the appeal, BBC 3 take note
- but it was a stopgap and I was dead scared of a tutor walking in. I left.

Then, a couple of years later,

- was at a vaguely witchy party with a housemate
- dressed in black and carrying a whip (mine). The housemate was dressed as Miss World, which is not relevant, but interesting

- a woman approached us, talked to me a bit, she had a dungeon, and plenty of equipment
- it paid far more than stripping, I managed to control the impulse to laugh
- stopped when I landed a "legit" job in a bookshop on weekends, less well paid, but access to loads of free books
- in retrospect, did not choose wisely.

But enough backstory. Today's my birthday, and I mean to celebrate in style.

lundi, le 10 novembre

9 p.m. yesterday: Whilst readying ourselves for a birthday night out (all shaving shaven, all brushing brushed, all scrubbing scrubbed), my boyfriend and I finished off a sex quiz from a glossy women's magazine.

Yes, as you have probably picked up, I am a call girl with a boyfriend. A boyfriend who knows what I do. We've been together about a year. He doesn't live in the city, though.

Yes, it causes friction. Mmm, friction. Not always a bad thing. Especially in bed. He doesn't like my job but he has some abominable social habits too, like sneaking rum into people's drinks when they're not looking and voting Conservative.

He buttoned up a soft dark blue shirt, a gift from his mother. I sat at a dressing table, crossed my legs, and read out the questions in my sauciest voice. "At what time is a man most likely to be aroused—A, morning, B, midday, or C, night?"

He raised an eyebrow at his reflection in the mirror. "Is there a D, 'all the time' option?"

10 p.m.: Met A2 (one of my exes), A4 (the clever boy), and other friends at the Blue Posts, commandeered the big leather

seats by the fire (also blocking the cigarette machine and the stairs, which makes one wonder about the people who devised this layout). Set about attempting to fill the greater percentage of my stomach with alcohol.

Midnight: A club nearby, I think. It all grows a bit hazy. Multiple shots imbibed containing schnapps, which is evil. I lost a pair of gloves.

2 a.m.: Emboldened by recent gym-going, asserted that I was strong enough to pick the Boy up. Wobbled on my heels and we both fell back on the floor. Certain if I wasn't so drunk, I would have felt a right twat.

3 a.m.: Oxford Street, everyone marching along and singing "Seven Nation Army" in unison. No one can remember all the words, except for the part about Wichita. We lose the few celebrants who haven't begged off yet to bus stops along the way.

Sometime after that: Minicab. We collapse in the approximate location of my bed twenty minutes later.

9 a.m.: I get up to use the toilet. When I come back, the Boy is standing in the door. "Close your eyes," he says. I do. He puts one arm under my arms and one under my knees and carries me to the bed. Gently, he sets me down. I feel the softness of fleece under my back and toes. "Open them," he says, and I see that he has spread the bed with a soft white sheepskin blanket identical to the one on his bed. "Happy birthday," he whispers, and we make love three times.

A happy birthday indeed.

mardi, le 11 novembre

So much for a relaxing break from work—every morning I wake to missed texts and calls from the agency.

The benefits of taking a few days off—aside from the chance to catch up on laundry—are largely spiritual. But one learns a few mundane things as well. Such as that it's nice to let hair grow out a bit to get a good, clean waxing. Also, you remember what the hair was there for in the first place. Lubrication. No, really.

Pity the clients will never know this.

mercredi, le 12 novembre

The manager of the escort agency rang. "Darling, is verrrry nice gentleman who loves your pictures. Are you free?"

"I'm afraid not, no," I say, hoping the Boy doesn't overhear.

"But he is verrrrry nice."

"Sorry, no."

A few months after the encounter with the older woman and her boyfriend, I located what sounded like a small, discreet agency on the Internet. The miracle of information interconnected by technology means that any site is only three clicks away from an escort service, really. The website was modestly designed compared to some others, but the girls were attractive and straightforwardly described. Most of them looked extremely normal—not scary robe-women, and not shudderingly unattractive amateur cam girls, either. Just reasonably normal women, but, you know, naked and straddling a garden wall. After e-mail contact and sending my photos, I finally rang to make arrangements to meet the manager at the dining room of a central London hotel. She sounded very young and had a very strong Eastern European accent. Polish, maybe? Should I ask?

"How will I know you?" I asked. "What do you look like?"

"When I was younger, everyone used to say I looked like Brooke Shields," she said.

"Ah, you must be very beautiful then."

"No, I am old and decrepit. Now people say I look like Daryl Hannah."

I ended the call feeling disloyal. After all, my relationship with the Boy at that stage was fairly new, and here I was arranging to meet a madame and work as a whore. Would he have a problem with it? Stupid question, girl. My mind worked through the possible outcomes.

- He chucks me instantly, and tells all his friends.
- He chucks me instantly, and is too embarrassed to tell his friends.
- He doesn't chuck me, but becomes scary and unbalanced as the result of dating a whore.
- He doesn't chuck me, but becomes scary because he actually likes the idea.
- He offers to join in, pro bono.
- He offers to join in, and earns better money than I do.
- He's okay with it and things go on as normal.

The first three seemed likely enough, while the last four varied in credibility from "no way" to "really no fucking way."

I could have backed out at any time before meeting the manager, of course. A few days passed between making first contact through e-mail and the interview with the escort agency. I went out and restocked makeup supplies. On the day of the appointment, I spent all morning getting ready. This involved no small amount of eyelash curling, hair straightening, and wardrobe panicking. Sexy but not slutty? You'll be wanting the dark silk top, then. Young but serious? Well-cut coat. As much cleavage as I could muster. Boots, of course—it is autumn in London after all. My nails are an acrylic nightmare but there was simply no time to do anything about them. I have a horrible habit of chewing the cuticles, and it wreaks havoc with anything manicurists try to do.

On the way to the meeting point, I passed a movie poster and convinced myself that I looked not unlike Catherine Zeta-Jones.

Right. Now pull the other one.

I arrived early and went to the toilet. Makeup was already coming off in some places, cakey in others. Turning the cold tap on, I flicked a few drops of water on my face, dabbed, and reapplied lipgloss. Better. Little did I know this mini-ritual would become a central theme in my WG experience. Poking my head into the restaurant, I could see it was deserted on a weekday lunchtime. The single bored Asian waitress walked round and round the planters of fake flowers. I wouldn't want to be there either.

The manager rang and asked me to take a table near the window. Was this so she could spy on me and run off if I didn't fit the bill? Was it an elaborate setup, some kind of sting? More likely, she was just covering her back. I ordered coffee and waited.

She arrived, as described. Long blonde hair. Horsey face. Tight dress and killer brocade boots that matched her handbag—my chocolate High Street clompers were dull in comparison. "Darling, hello." Air kisses.

She had to take a few calls during lunch, where I learned she speaks fluent German and Arabic. Domineering. God, the punters must love that. She asked about my experience. Some dominatrix works, some stripping, no sex with clients, all ages ago. She nodded. She asked if I had a partner; I said yes. She told me about hers, and how he didn't know what she did for a living. I found that incredible—her phone had gone off three times already.

She ordered herbal tea. I had a coffee. I could feel the full weight of her gaze as I tipped a spoonful of sugar into the cup. Whether hunger or disapproval, I wasn't sure. "So now we have to talk about services." She pronounced the word like it had twelve vowels: *suuuuuuuurvices.* "Have you done A levels?"

A levels? Well, yes, but that was years ago. Who knew that academic fluency was a prereq for the job? Maybe the customers were more discerning than I thought. "A levels?"

"You know"—her voice dropped to a whisper—"anal." I'm quite sure the waitress didn't need to refill my coffee right at that moment. Weren't there some decorative olive oil decanters she could be rearranging elsewhere?

"Oh, right. Yes, I can do that. Provided I haven't been out for a curry the night before." We laughed.

She asked if I would do incalls or outcalls. On incalls a girl sees her clients at her own flat (or one rented by the agency); outcalls take place in a hotel or a client's home.

I chose outcalls only. The idea of someone knowing where I lived was uncomfortable. Hell, they wouldn't even know my real name. Also, outcall girls earn more per hour—presumably for the convenience—and the client covers any travel expense.

The fee would be £300 per hour, more than thirty times what I would have made doing anything else. Of the fee, I would keep £200 per hour, plus the entirety of any tips or travel expenses.

The manager said she needed more up-to-date photos for her portfolio. The ones I had sent were fairly unsuitable, as they were nothing like the usual glamour shots, showing me in various states of inebriation at clubs and, in one, with something that looked suspiciously like vomit down the front of a silky black vest. All class. More air kisses and she was away, sticking me with the bill. Luckily it appears we have similar attitudes to food, i.e., admiration from a distance, so it was hardly a burden. Two pots of tea and an untouched stale pain au chocolat: 8 quid. Probably a bargain at the price.

dimanche, le 16 novembre

I packed the Boy into his car and waved until he reached the end of the street. Before he even could have reached the motorway, he texted a kiss.

It's been the better part of a year since starting this work, and he's still with me. Not that it was easy at first, especially when I had to tell him.

The Boy came up to London for the day. He was having a job interview. I was unsure how to bring up the subject of my new employment. Gently, blurring the edges of truth if necessary? "Darling, I want you to know, I've been seeing men for money, but I do it fully clothed and they come in aluminum foil in another room. Every time. Did I mention I love you?" Or, be blunt and see what happens. "My dearest one, I'm a ho. Did you somehow fail to notice the bling?"

He gabbled about his family and work through sandwiches, coffee, our walk down the road to buy a pastry. Over a morsel of baklava I finally blurted it out. He didn't say anything, just pursed his lips and nodded. But he didn't object outright. I took a deep breath. "Of course, if ever you want me to stop, I will."

He still didn't say anything. We left the shop and walked in the sunshine. Falling leaves spiraled on the pavements; crunching underfoot, they smelled of earth and dust. My step fell in with his: we used to run together and are accustomed to the same length of stride. He put an arm around me, started to speak, but stammered. He tried again. "You'd be surprised. I've been thinking about it and I think it's okay."

I kissed him. We walked up to the British Library together, to look at the Lindisfarne Gospels. The Boy told me they were portions of the Bible in Gothic style written on skins. I'm not terribly au fait with the finer points of Christianity, but suspect the

King James is not usually published on abbatoir by-products. The raw craftness of these sounded appealing. In the dim exhibit rooms the gold and painted vellum seemed to glow with animal intensity. Brutal ends to saints and the devouring of virgins always seem to feature strongly in the European arts of that period. The Boy told me of his visit to the Lindisfarne island, where he almost drove a car into the surf. I laughed, the sharp noise shattering the reverent quiet. We went home and watched television, cooked a meal together, and played lion attacking the Gothic maiden in a big white bed. He was the lion, of course.

lundi, le 17 novembre

Client: "So why do you do this?"

Me: "I'm not sure I have an answer to that."

"There must be something that you at least tell yourself."

"Well, perhaps I'm the sort of person apt to do something for no good reason other than I can't think of a reason not to."

"So if someone told you to jump off a bridge . . ."

"Depends on the bridge. Depends if they were paying. Why?"

"Oh, no reason. Will you suck me now?"

mardi, le 18 novembre

One of my more potent fantasies is of the Boyfriend fisting me. This is not because he's done it, but because he hasn't. For one thing, he has the most gorgeous hands I've seen on anyone, male or female. Artist's hands, I say, and he splays out this wide paw for me to admire. They ferret under my clothes when we're in public; I rarely feel safe from manhandling. But I don't mind. I want to feel planted on the end of his arm, an extension of him, controlled.

Even with regular erotic exercise I prove a bit too constricted for the Boy's fist. The manuals say this will come with time, but let's face it, I'm a busy girl and sitting around working his greased digits up my fluffy bits is the anathema of romance. I know the women in the shiny magazines all seem to be able to manage it these days. Back when oral sex was considered the height of depravity in the mainstream, the hard-core magazines were all showing nothing but anal sex. Now that anal sex can practically be broadcast on prime time telly, fisting is where it's at for the truly sick. So much so that I wonder if I shouldn't stay ahead of the curve by just skipping ahead to anal fisting instead. But the ladies capable of such things are probably either possessed of a far greater pain threshold than mine or descended from a train tunnel. My own history with the practice of fisting can be broken down thus:

First, a teenage boyfriend. He wanted it, I wanted it. He had narrow hands, I was dripping wet. Young, foolish, and incapable of getting more than twenty minutes' privacy at either of our parents' homes, we went out of town for a dirty weekend at a hotel. We were hardly in the room before I was stretched across the bed and he was concentrating manfully on the progress of his fingers inside me. Then his fingernails hit my cervix: ouch. Much fantasized, but never attempted with him again.

Second, N. Years ago, when we were still an item. He wanted it, I was dubious. It had been a long time since the teenager who tried to scratch me out, but I could still imagine the gritting pain. But N was experienced, he knew about the finger-curling wrist thrust necessary to get a whole fist in without the woman experiencing involuntary hysterectomy. Unfortunately, N also has hands that can span my waist. His last girlfriend had taken the fist many times, often whilst being buggered. She was also six feet tall and about twice my weight. We tried, many times, but never quite got there. I practiced with all manner of widening tools: vegetables, dildos, an extremely large-handled flashlight. No luck.

Third, my hand goes where no hand has gone before. Namely up a woman who is on the phone to her boyfriend in Italy. He's paying me to make her come as many times as we can in an hour. This is also the day I discover you need to break the internal vacuum to take the fist out again, unless of course your intended is into suction. And I don't mean the Jenna Jameson kind. Yeeks.

Fourth, one night, with a customer. And I discover that while someone else's hand might be out of my reach (so to speak), my own is slender and small enough to make it in. Contortionally awkward, but successful nonetheless. Finally, a perfect fit. Only then do I discover the black art of fisting is not getting it in; it's getting the damned thing out again.

I rang the Boy when I got home to let him know. I didn't mention it was with a client. "Can you do it now?" he said over the phone.

"Probably," I said. In pajamas, in bed. Under the duvet. "I'm just about asleep, though."

"Oh." There was a silence. "Can you just describe it now, instead?" he asked. Of course I could. "And then show me next time you see me?" Yes, of course, anything, love. I do not grow weary of you. Come see me, come take me away.

I woke to a missed text message from him:

the best things in life r still free. i miss your cuddles most of all xx

mercredi, le 19 novembre

I crouched between the man's legs. His inner thighs were smooth and I brushed the skin with my fingertips. "How was your holiday?"

"Good, good. Japan is an interesting place. Have you ever been?" he asked, leaning back on the bed.

"No." I took the hardening cock in my hand and pulled on its foreskin gently. It stiffened and lengthened in my palm. "What is your favorite thing to do there?"

"They're an odd people, they have these places," he said, pausing slightly as I took his member between my lips. "Simulating a crowded underground carriage. Where people's bodies rub up against each other . . ."

He slipped out of my mouth; I began pumping the shaft with my fist. "I've always had a fantasy like that," I said. "A crowded student pub, short skirt, leaning over the bar to get a drink, someone comes up behind me. And there's no space to move, so not only can I not get away, no one else can tell it's happening."

"Mmm, that sounds good."

"Will you promise me something?" I asked. "If you ever see me after this at a bar, will you just come up and do that?"

"You have my word," he said, angling his erection back into my mouth.

jeudi, le 20 novembre

The Boyfriend is in town, so I saw no clients. We went to the gym, ostensibly so I could show him off, but mostly so he could show himself off.

First event was the rowing machine. I hate the rowing machine.

Hate hate hate it. It is the Devil's Bicycle. It is my nemesis and wants me dead. However, I will gladly sit alongside the Boy as he thrashes the metal beast into flywheeled submission. After five minutes, droplets of sweat appeared on the back of his neck. After ten, the rippling ribbons in his forearms were driving me to distraction. A glorious half hour later I was aching to jump his bones.

Suitably panting, we headed for the bench press (which I can't do) and the bench pull (which I can). Suffice to say I am not fit to hold the man's towel.

For the pièce de résistance I goaded him into chin-ups. Four sets of six, shirt off, ensuring that even the resident thick-necked gym bunnies were suitably humbled. Cower in the wake of his manly pheromones, you six-packed Narcissi!

In order to reassert control, we did something I am good at—stretching. A cliché perhaps, but I have always been able to put my legs behind my ears. A long session of contorting hamstrings ensured that, fragrant with sweat and lusting as only long-distance lovers can, we never got past the carpark.

Well, we did. But our clothes didn't. And our dignity came nowhere near.

Ah, young love.

samedi, le 22 novembre

Special Film Edition! As I've been staying in with drinks and videos all week, we've been having a little North London Prostitution Film Festival. Sorry, darlings, but the event is *muy* exclusive—guest list runs to two. And the paparazzi have been, frankly, disappointing.

Women who are not working girls but should be:

Elizabeth Hurley

Gillian Taylforth
Laura Dern
Sue Barker

Women who have played WGs, but shouldn't have:

Julia "Sexless" Roberts
Jodie Foster (no one must defile the goddess)
Jane Fonda
Elisabeth Shue

Perfect casting:

Laura San Giacomo. The Boy says, "Rowr!"
Patricia Arquette
Louise Brooks
Mira Sorvino

Special Award for Services to Tongue-Manipulation Ability During a Scene in *Twin Peaks* in Which She Is Interviewing to Become a Prostitute:

Sherilyn Fenn

The Is She or Isn't She? Obfuscation Award:

Audrey Hepburn

Acceptable as a robot whore, but only just:

Daryl Hannah

My favorite movies about prostitutes:

Le Notti di Cabiria
Belle de Jour (obviously)
Frankenhooker

Live by the phone, die by the phone, but never again will I leave it on during dinner! Between the Great Portland Street station and when we left the restaurant on Marylebone High Street, it must have gone off twelve times. Say what you will about springtime and a man's fancy turning to romance, I believe there's something about the impending holiday season that really sets libidos on eleven.

Back in business by Monday—even I can't spin out birthday celebrations indefinitely. And there'll be all sorts of good things in my stocking, promise.

samedi, le 22 novembre

I noticed that of all the services the manager and I had discussed, there was one neither of us had mentioned. Oral. And there on the website for all to see, I was advertised as OWO. Oral Without. Without condom, that is.

To tell the truth, if she had asked, I would have said yes. I've done the deed with condoms in the past and my lips react badly to the latex and spermicide, swelling and tingling. And like all other sex acts, there is some risk involved, but nothing near what most things entailed. I wouldn't do it if I had cold sores, for instance. Or if I was especially concerned about the staying power of my lipstick.

But I'm a swallower and always have been. Once it's in there, it doesn't taste any better to spit it out, and to be frank, it's no worse than the taste of a woman. A girl I went to school with once described semen as tasting of "an oyster on a 2p piece." I wouldn't know, having never eaten either, but she's probably not far off the mark.

dimanche, le 23 novembre

Last night I was walking down the fag end of Fulham High Street looking for a cab. There is a bookstore on the corner—not the horrible kind assaulting you with endless stacks of remaindered Michael Moore and lattechinos to go, but the wonderful quirky kind. The sort of shop where the proprietor—who can remember your tastes, previous purchases, and make appropriate recommendations even if you've not been there in years—appears to live on site, and either owns a collection of identical outfits or never changes his clothes. The proprietor of such a shop is always a man, always.

Unfortunately, the shop was closed. Or perhaps fortunately—I had a wad of notes on me, some time to kill, and a distinct inability to refuse fusty booksellers. When I was a student, I calculated I spent more per term on books—and not ones related to my course, either—than I did on food. But the shop was locked up and dark. Outside the door a plain white shelving unit held a few paperbacks. Whether these were donations to the public or from the public I didn't know. Being curious, I perused the titles. This is how I ran across the best thing I've ever read on a paperback cover: *A girl can go anywhere if she believes in herself and has a mink coat.*

Well, yes! Indeed! How true, and wonderful! How very Holly Golightly! Uncertain whether the books were for sale or not, but certain this novel was destined to be mine, I deliberated a moment before dropping a pound coin through the post slot.

(Now is a good time to point out that I do not actually have a mink coat. I have a fairly nice watch, and suppose it is the most politically correct luxury item one can get away with wearing. I wouldn't want to be accused of either animal torture or funding cartels in the developing world. The possible exploitation of Swiss craftsmen is not a daily burden on my soul.)

The book, in case you are wondering, is *B. F.'s Daughter* by John P. Marquand, he of the Mr. Moto novels. It is the most delicious trash. Think Mickey Spillane meets Françoise Sagan in the lobby of Saks Fifth Avenue. In 1946. Shopping-and-fucking chicklit really has nothing on this.

lundi, le 24 novembre

Does it seem like Christmas begins earlier every year? I think I saw someone hanging Christmas lights last week and I swear my next-door neighbor has had red tinsel in her window since July. Now everyone's at it, and even though the day is a month away I'm sick of it already. Granted, not being Christian, my tolerance is fairly low.

Rubbish "holiday" occurrences:

- Being asked to wear red, fur-trimmed lingerie, which serves to confirm that only men think this is a good idea. Further, that they must have had very strange childhoods indeed to find Father Christmas a turn-on. Perhaps it is a relief to know that this is a perversion that must be paid for.
- People who use the word "Crimbo." That's just wrong.
- The drone of fervent Christians begging us to remember what "this season is really about." It's about the blessed appearance of Our Lord Harvey Nichols, right?
- People who are impossible to shop for. In this category is

A3, whose only extravagance is a Manchester United football season ticket each year. What to buy the man who thinks he has everything? I ring A4, who helpfully suggests socks.

- Customers who ask what I'll be doing for the holidays. Simply because I can't decide what would be a suitable answer—a glamorous lie (pulling Donovan Leitch's cracker) or the mundane reality (schlepping up north to light the menorah).

But the holidays are great because:

- Whether by divine right or unspoken charter, the entire country decides to piss off work. As a result, no one really expects reliable communication.
- The smell of mince pies. Complicated, passionate discussions involving mince pies. Shopping trips consisting largely of the need to purchase mince pies. Forgoing meals in favor of mince pies.
- End-of-year anxiety equals a spike in workload for me. I feel like the Samaritans of sex.
- Getting to see the people you know and love. Getting to see the people you know and love drunk.

This year, I actually want the terrible gifts from ancient aunties. Bring on the woolly socks and embroidered handkerchiefs, please!

mardi, le 25 novembre

I had two customers one hour apart, located only several blocks from each other. The wind and rain were too heavy to do anything but hole up for the duration. So, finding a conveniently located pub near Southwark, I popped in for a drink.

Walked up to the bar and ordered a double rum and soda. One does not often see a stiletto-clad blonde midweek in a pub, but I am accustomed to tumbleweed moments when entering a local. The large screen precariously mounted above the (real) fire was tuned to football. Everyone was watching it, and so did I.

The septuagenarian barmaid aside (or should that be bar-matron?), I was the only woman in the room. But the looks I got were neither contemptuous nor salacious. Everyone paused, saw me, then turned back to their drinks and football. The match was clearly an important one.

The ninety minutes ended in a draw. A few men came up from the back table to order fresh pints. One of them stood next to my seat while waiting for his lager.

"When we saw you come in, we thought maybe you were the mascot."

"Is that so?" I said, rather confused.

"Ah well, it doesn't matter much, Celtic are still at the top of the group."

"So they are. I did my best, anyway."

He laughed and returned to a far corner. It was then I realized my hat, which I'd left on the entire hour, was green-and-white striped, just like the Celtic colors. Some mascot. I drained my glass and left to make the next appointment.

mercredi, le 26 novembre

It's a public health issue, I know.

I understand such feelings perfectly. This job I do, the number of people I come in contact with. Living in a city where disease flies in from all over the world. And the time of year—the festive season when people are out partying, splurging, doing things they wouldn't normally do because they think, hey, it's the end of another year, I deserve a treat. Then they wake up the next morning unsure of what they got and whom they were with. And even if you do remember, you never know at the time who has it and who hasn't.

I'm a disease-spreading vector. No one is safe, sure, but some of us are more at risk than others, even with all the precautions available these days—the free clinics, the vaccinations, the public awareness campaigns.

And it's important to me. There's no such thing as paid sick leave for call girls. And God forbid you end up in hospital.

So I want to set your minds at ease as much as I can. I want you to know.

I have had a flu shot.

jeudi, le 27 novembre

A late text from the Boy last night:

We were taken out for free drinks after work. Am now in a tree.

It's cold out there. I hope his rapidly shrinking boyparts make it home safely and are up for warming again soon.

The first time we met, it was his birthday, about one year ago now. He was tearing up the dance floor in a club, almost literally—the bouncers had their hackles up the moment he and his equally large, drunken friends came in the door. They weren't the only ones. I couldn't take my eyes off this man who moved like water and threw his limbs around like they were only nominally attached to his body.

The otherwise crowded floor cleared a wide circle around their group. They took turns chucking each other around, laughing, like little boys. His eyes were shining, probably from alcohol. His curly hair and freckles stood out in a room of pale poseurs. I demanded a mutual friend introduce us. The club was too loud—he looked down and smiled at me, but didn't hear a word we were saying. I stayed on the fringes and waited. When he went out in the hall to join the queue for the toilets, I followed him.

"Happy birthday," I said.

"Thank you," he said, and smiled. He didn't appear to recognize me. He did seem quite interested in staring down my top, though. Hey, I thought. It's a start.

I stood on tiptoe and kissed him. He seemed puzzled but didn't resist. I pulled at the sleeve of his shirt to drag him to the smaller, quieter room. We found a corner of a red velvet sofa and snuggled together.

"You can't do this," he said.

"Why not?"

"You don't know me at all," he said. "My name, where I'm from. You know nothing about me."

"I want to know you," I said, squeezing my hand around his arm, which was roped with thick muscles. His hands, resting lightly on my waist, were easily the largest and finest I'd ever seen on a man.

Just then another woman—maybe biologically not female, it was difficult to tell in the dark—interrupted us. "Love the boots, honey," she said.

"Cheers." I was wearing knee-high leather shoes with vertiginous heels. They were practically hobbling me, but worth it.

The Boy looked down. "They are actually rather good," he said, fingering the skin just under my knee. I melted. "But I don't think we should go back to the others. You'd likely break an ankle dancing in those."

"Guess we'll have to find something else to do?"

"I suppose," he agreed, and we groped a bit longer, until I caught a glance at my watch. It was time for Cinderella to make her escape. "Come home with me," he growled in my ear, fiddling with the zip of my left boot. It was the kind of order a woman dreams about. Irresistible.

"I have a boyfriend," I said. It seemed only fair to mention it. The Boy said he didn't care. I was technically in an open relationship, but knew this man was not one-night material. He was far more interesting than that; there was too much crackling energy around him. "Well," I said, "you can have me one night or see me again. Which will it be?"

"I can't not see you again," the Boy said. I shrugged—*tant pis.* "Shameless trollop." But he was smiling, and took my phone number. He followed me as far as the bouncers. The rest of his friends were still inside. There was a pause. I could have invited him back and wanted to, but also knew, as I walked out the glass doors, he'd be watching me go.

I went home and told the housemates I was in love. The fact that I was also blind drunk and trying to balance four candles in a fir wreath on my head is by the by.

The Boy and I met for drinks later that week but nothing happened. I felt uncomfortable following up on the promise of that first meeting. He did try at first—a lingering glance here, a trailing hand there—but soon learned the boundaries. He may have been a fully paid-up member of the bon ton, but he was no cad. Or perhaps he was biding his time. The relationship I was in was clearly not healthy. By the time I split with that boyfriend and moved to London, the Boy had new digs in Brighton. He drove up to meet me and moved everything into my new flat. We fucked for the first time among the scattered boxes and suitcases and piles of books on the floor. Wooden planks. I had friction scars for weeks after.

samedi, le 29 novembre

I was cleaning off the makeup shelves, discarding crusty bottles of drying nail varnish and foundation-sodden sponges. I thought this job would just be a stopgap, but it's been absolute months now. It's become almost routine now but didn't always seem like that.

Preparing for my first appointment had felt like making up for the stage. I remember laying out a liquid base and a stick one; eye shadow, liner, and mascara; lip liner, gloss. Preparation had started early. Too early. But I had no inkling of how to put it all together, how long it would take.

I showered and dried myself carefully in the white-tiled bathroom, looking for stray hairs missed by waxing and shaving. A quick blast of deodorant. Applied a drop of cologne to my cleavage and inside elbows. Put on a white lace bra and knickers, stockings, dried my hair. Part it here or there? Which way should it fall? Hair up or hair down? Fluffy or straight? I straightened the ends so they wouldn't curl in the damp night air but otherwise left it alone. Small pearl earrings.

I put the dress over my head, then started on makeup. Foundation, no powder. A damp tissue applied lightly to take the excess off. Violet eyeshadow—only a touch. A dab of silvery white eyeliner just at the inside corner of my eyes. Cat eyes or not? Vamp or girlish? My hand was shaking slightly. Unwound the mascara, wiped the excess on a tissue, let it sit in the air a moment. Brushed on one layer. Then a second.

My eyes in the mirror stood out a mile from the rest of the face. I lined my lips, wondering how much to use and how much would come off on him. What would I have to take with me, would there be time to reapply? With the tip of my little finger I dabbed a liquid blusher on as lipstain. Gloss. More gloss. I thought of the manager's advice: men love glossy lips. I suppose it doesn't take a genius to think why.

A touch of gel to keep the hair off my forehead and cheeks. A clip to keep it back. I put the shoes on and buckled them at the ankles. Black, patent-leather stilettoes showing a long stripe of instep. Incredibly high heels, but once I'd run for a bus in them. I had danced till morning in these many times. Fuck-me shoes.

Then my coat. College scarf or fluffy blue one? The blue would leave fibers on the coat; I decided against it in the end. It was a cold night. Navy gloves with tiny buttons along the wrist. I stuck a pin with a butterfly in the coat lapel. Nervous; took deep breaths. Still a quarter of an hour to wait.

My mouth had gone dry. Went to the kitchen and poured a drink. Was alcohol a bad idea? Didn't know. One couldn't hurt. My lips left a crackling pink half-moon on the rim of the glass. Packed a handbag. I was sweating inside the coat and scarf and gloves. Still ten minutes until the taxi. Looked at the location for the appointment again on a map. Didn't want to carry it with me. It was near a tube station. If I could memorize the directions from the tube station, I should be fine.

Went downstairs and stood outside. The cold wind tickled the damp hair at my neck. Looked down my road. No one was out walking. Very few cars came by. A bus paused at the bus stop, no one was waiting, it drove on. A small car came up behind it. A man looking out the window. That must be the cab, I thought. Focus. I'm working as of now. Smile, wave, give him the address. From here on, I am not me.

We found the house. Paid the driver. Up the walk, brass knocker on the door. A light on inside. My hair was falling in my face. I took the clip out and shook the hair loose. Smiled. Rapped at the door. No turning back.

The next morning I woke up in my own bed. Held my hand up, stared at it for ages. Was something supposed to be different?

Should I have felt victimized, abused? I couldn't say. The finer points of feminist theory didn't seem to apply. Things felt as they always had. Same hand, same girl. I got up and made breakfast.

dimanche, le 30 novembre

The Boy has been casting around for a new position for some time (working position that is, not sexual, though all offers gratefully received). He's been unhappy at work for so long, but it's secure, but this, but that, well, and so on, and so forth. His workmates are the same crowd he ran with at university. But now one of them has been made redundant and he's starting to feel the full focus of the upper echelons of administration looking carefully at what he does. I keep suggesting military service, and not just because I think he would fill out a uniform in a most attractive manner. So he e-mailed his CV to see if there was anything I could do.

I returned it within the half hour. Almost immediately the phone rang. It was the Boyfriend, and he was laughing.

"This is great stuff, kitty . . . but I don't think I can use it."

"No?"

"For one thing I don't think the Army cares either way about the size of my member."

"You don't know that for sure. You could get anyone interviewing you." I hear the services are really very modern these days.

"Nice thought." I heard him scrolling down the e-mail from the other end of the phone. "Recovery time between ejaculations should not be in the Other Qualifications section."

"It's important to me, sweetie."

"Doubtless. And 'Oral sex: giving and receiving' under Interests and Activities?"

"Are you saying they're not?" We laughed.

It occurred to me to recommend my own line of work, not that he'd ever bite. The Boy is as straitlaced as a whalebone corset. I, by contrast, am widely considered among our acquaintances to be amoral. Even by the ones who don't know what I do for a living.

Décembre

Belle's A-Z of London Sex Work

D-G

D is for Disasters

For me, there's no such thing as an insurmountable disaster. If it all goes horribly wrong, console yourself with the knowledge you'll probably never see the customer again. Even if it goes right, you will probably never see the customer again.

That said, always be certain your phone is fully charged and within arm's reach if needed. And keep a travel pack of baby wipes on hand for cleaning up all messes of biological origin.

E is for Eating

Whoring is like exercise: you can't eat too soon before the appointment, or you risk blowing chunks at an inopportune moment. The usual timing of non-dinner dates means that normal meals are almost always out of the question. Have a generous lunch. Take a snack to nibble on the way home. Carry a spoon just in case.

E is also for Exercise

Someone once told me that girl-on-top positions can burn as many calories per hour as one of those gym stepper machines. Note that the gent is apt to give out before you have achieved a fat-burning workout, though.

F is for Forgetfulness

Always reconfirm appointment details with the agency. My memory is not worth relying on, and knocking on the door of room 1203 instead of 1302 can have unexpected—and probably not hilarious—consequences. I keep a small pad of paper handy.

That said, don't write the details on the back of your hand, either.

G is for G-spot

You won't need to know where this is at work. Tuck it away in the cupboard at home and save it for best.

lundi, le 1ᵉʳ décembre

The client's hands were square, long-fingered, and wandering. They reminded me of my boyfriend's. He pawed my breasts, my thighs, and ventured inside.

I jerked suddenly. "Sorry—did I hurt you?" he asked.

I was on my side, he was spooning me, the offending fingers resting between my legs from behind. "Only a little." I picked up his right hand and examined the nails. Clean, but longer than most. And rather jagged. "Do you bite these?"

"Yes."

I rolled over the edge of the bed to reach my purse on the floor. "Hold on." Brought back a small silver cosmetic bag and pulled out an emery board.

He shuddered. "I can't take files," he said. "It's a nails-on-chalkboard sort of thing."

"Trust me," I said, and sanded his edges smooth. He ran his thumbs over the polished ovals, commented on the difference. "You're far too nice for this job," he said softly, which I took to mean either that he'd had bad experiences with escorts before, or most escorts are nice and I was just the first. Hoped it was the latter.

mardi, le 2 décembre

So what's a girl to do with a day off?

Besides shopping for knickers, naturally.

Booked in advance, plenty of warning. Boyfriend out of town, no gym session with N. Tried arranging lunch with A1, A2, and A4; no luck. No illness, no customers. A good proper lie-in. No errands, no appointments, and no laundry. Time to cook (and maybe leave the washing-up for another day). No cleaning lady and no calls from the manager. Nowhere to be, nothing to be. Just me on my own.

Best find that vibrator, then.

jeudi, le 4 décembre

There is someone in London who just paid to lick the pucker of my arse for one hour. Isn't that what everyone really wants in life, someone who'll kiss your grits and enjoy it?

If someone had only told me from the outset such perfect clients existed, I would have jumped in straightaway.

vendredi, le 5 décembre

"Have you ever been with a woman?" the client asked, stroking my breasts.

"Yes," I said. He sighed. "Many. Outside of work." It has been a while since the last. The Boy grumbles and pouts sometimes, because he knows about my past and has never had a threesome. I am wary of the problems that picking up a spare girl can introduce to a relationship. Better to go pro, I think. Maybe sometime in the future. Not now.

"Are you gay?"

"No, I just like women." Probably equally to men for sex. But I would rather be in a relationship with a man, which I think reads as essentially straight. This was a conclusion won over much heartrending identification nonsense during university. Women: I'll fuck them, but I don't want to go home to one.

"Any woman?" Perhaps he had one in mind. I hoped not.

"Not all women."

samedi, le 6 décembre

I've been looking through the site again. The manager rearranges the profiles from time to time, to give this or that girl a lift in business, or to emphasize a new arrival to the agency.

My own profile compares reasonably against the other girls on the site and pictures around the Web. Nothing to stand out particularly; just like hundreds of others. It was a bit stunning to see just how many call girls were working in London. There seemed to be a leggy blonde or brunette sex goddess for every potential horny businessman on earth, with maybe a MILF or two to spare.

I remember the first time I saw myself on the site. The profile turned out decently enough. I wouldn't have thought so, considering the way the photo shoot went. There had been some selective cropping and Photoshop magic, but the woman in the images is very definitely me. Would someone recognize me? Don't be silly, I scold myself. No one who knew you and spotted them perusing escort sites would ever confess to it. Or would they go one worse and book an appointment?

The photographer for the escort agency met me at a hotel. Cute until she opened her mouth. She started in on me straightaway. "Hair—not big enough," she said, and pulled out a teasing comb that looked as if it had served time in some of the country's finer dog-grooming facilities. Her own pink lipliner was enlisted in the quest to make my lips look fuller, poutier. The lingerie I had brought, still in their store wrapping, were judged unsuitable—

which is to say they were far too tasteful. "You would suit something . . . purple," she said, throwing a cheap lace vest at me. At least it was unworn; it still had the tags on. This is how I found myself in colors I'd never wear, with makeup I'd never use, hair ten times normal size, writhing on the hotel furniture. "Keep those legs straight up in the air," she said as my thighs shook from the exertion of holding pose after pose. "And . . . relax!"

We worked through a dozen standard glamour shots. "Are you getting bored yet?" she joked.

"Yes."

She looked hard at me. "You're bored? That's terrible."

"I was being ironic. Actually, I'm not bored at all," I said, cupping my own breast for the thirtieth time.

"Pity about the bikini lines. So seventies porn star." This from someone who put me in pink latex hot pants? She changed the film and shot through another roll. I couldn't imagine there were any more impossible contortions to exact. After an hour I'd had enough and got up to change back into my civvies.

"Next time we see you, I will give you the name of a salon I know, where they do miraculous facials," she said, a parting shot on my way out the door. Subtlety is not a strength in this woman.

The verdict came back within hours. Surprisingly, the manager seemed far more pleased with the results than either the photographer or I was. "Darling, the pictures, they are fabulous," she purred on the other end of my phone. I've noticed she never introduces herself on the phone but launches straight into conversation. Must be a graduate of the same charm school as my mother.

"Thank you, I was worried about not looking relaxed."

"No, they are perfect. Can you do something for me? Can you write something about yourself for the portfolio? Most of the other girls, I write something for them, but you should do this very well." She seemed pleased to have bagged another graduate for the agency; perhaps they make commission on educational level?

Cripes. I am a tall, luscious . . . ah, no. *Amusante*, savoir faire? Save me. Self-motivated, works well in group . . . perhaps closer to the truth. I wondered, where are the CV clinics for whores?

In the end I was pleased with the result. I had liked the look of the agency's website from the beginning, and especially the descriptions of the women. They seemed more honest than most—there was no messing about a girl's size and what she did—but also less pornographic. Not a one contained guarantees that the girl pictured could swallow hosepipes, was a raging sex machine, or had last been featured in the pages of a top-shelf publication. The tawdry outfits from the photographer's wardrobe looked unexpectedly sexier and more subtle in a picture than they had in person. I wouldn't have admitted this to her for the world, of course.

And I wised up to the tricks the photographers used. After seeing the poses echoed in hundreds of pictures, the contortions I had been put through looked familiar.

There is clearly an art to the glamour shot. On the one hand, perfection is expected and nothing less is tolerated, so who wouldn't consider pixel manipulation her best friend? On the other, those of us who do like the way our bodies look feel at a distinct disadvantage to those who would airbrush their way onto a catwalk if they could. Perusing the pictures revealed these trends:

- *The bending-over bumshot.* Everyone looks good like this. Roseanne probably doubles for Heidi Klum in such a pose. If you don't see the full-on wobbly face-up, don't be surprised if it turns out to be rather less (or rather, more) than you expected in the flesh. Also applies to *the all-fours crawl* and *the face-down spread eagle*.
- *The tit grab.* A double-A could take on Dolly-Partonesque

proportions given the right tilting of the chest-flesh. What is the point? Many men like small breasts. As someone once said, more than a mouthful's wasted (mine are a perfect handful, but you'll have to take my word for it. And I'm not saying whose hands either).

- *The deep-cleavage angle from above.* See previous.
- *The toe point.* She's not a trained balletist; she's trying to make her legs look longer. I reckon if God had meant us to point our bare feet in midair, he wouldn't have invented stilettoes.
- *The evening wrap/well-placed fur.* Fat arms, okay?
- *The turned-up collar/long hair obscuring the cheek.* Double chin, or lack of any at all.
- *Knee-high boot and pencil skirt combo.* In real life this is immensely sexy. Who hasn't wanted to stroke the milky white strip exposed on a lady's leg? In sexy photos, anyone willing to show only an inch of thigh at a time has issues.
- *Bubble bath.* Good for hiding a multitude of sins.
- *Bending backward.* Like the bending-over bumshot but in reverse. Poochy tummy extremely likely. Personally I'd rather see an inch to pinch than force someone to suck it in for an hour on the trot.
- *Crossed legs.* Hasn't waxed. Ankle socks, ditto.
- *Girlish pigtails and teenage clothing sense.* Is actually thirty-four.

dimanche, le 7 décembre

N, the hub of all gossip, was meeting me at the gym and coming back for supper afterwards. He has a keen interest in porn and the magazine collection to prove it. He told me about his plans for a trip to Amsterdam with a friend from work.

"Why not pick up some girls for a threesome while you're there?" I asked, leaning forward over the handles of a stationary bicycle. The threesome is his longest-standing fantasy. After the grannies and horses, naturally.

I feel bad for N. Having tasted once or twice the fruits of group sex, it has become a full-time obsession. He was the one, for example, who demanded I go over my night with the posh woman and her boyfriend in detail, even to the point of providing illustrative diagrams. "Why, do you think Dutch women are any more willing than the English?"

"No, I mean you could hire some."

"Mmph," he said. He's an attractive man. While supportive of the concept of prostitution, I don't think he'd actually dip a toe into sampling the professionals. He started a slow jog on a treadmill while I pedaled. "If there were legal brothels, I could hire out all the girls," he mused.

"Now you're being greedy," I scolded. "If I remember correctly, once is usually enough for you." With a few exceptions. Once in the distant past he and I had a threesome, and as far as I know, he hasn't had another shot since.

"Ouch." But he was smiling. And when he smiles, I think how sexy I find him, how his eyes crinkle like a film star's. "Any chance you might—"

"Sorry, darling, that train left the station years ago." Eww, friends hiring me for sex. The thought hadn't even occurred. Must make a mental note to nip all future suggestions in the bud. Especially as they are not all at the same level of knowledge about my work. A2 knows outright, A1 and A4 know the general outline but not the details, and the less A3 knows, the better. N, of course, gets the full skinny, warts and all. Literally.

The belt of the treadmill squealed and buckled under N's bulk. "Are you done torturing that machine? Because I'm getting hungry."

He drove us back to my house. It wasn't late, but the city was already as dark as midnight. N was born and raised in London, and guided the car around back roads and alternate routes I didn't know existed. The night air was still moist from rain in the afternoon, the streets shining with long red and white reflected lights, and I rolled down the passenger window to listen to the gentle *shrr* of tires on the road. "How much do you tell that man of yours?" he said after a long silence. N and the Boy know and don't approve of each other, but since they live in different cities, rarely meet.

"Enough."

"Can't imagine he's happy with it."

"Can't imagine he has a choice," I said, affecting more bravado than I felt. If he turns out to have major objections, I thought, I'll find something else to do.

Probably.

lundi, le 8 décembre

Booking with a banker at a hotel near Bond Street. We drank some coffee, chatted about New York briefly, then got down to business. And, as they say, business is good.

He: "That was my first anal."

Me: "Really? I'm surprised." Perhaps not that surprised, since there have been more than a few first-time anals in my past. But surprised he didn't mention it, and surprised at the spatial imagination of someone who manipulated me around his member so fluidly.

"Well, I enjoyed it."

"I would tell you it's my first time too, but you'd know I was lying."

He (laughing): "So how did I do?"

"Excellent—just remember, lots of lube, and use fingers first. As you did."

"Thanks—you're too nice."

"Well, you did all the hard work. So to speak."

(later)

He: "I don't understand why my colleagues would have an affair with some girl in the office, and risk a marriage, when they could have someone like you."

I nodded, didn't have anything to add.

"It must be a power thing, or to show off to other men. Still"— and he shuddered slightly, in the manner of a man whose faint tan line from a removed wedding band is still visible, and he knows it—"I just couldn't risk some little temp ringing my wife up weeks or months afterward."

We had time before both of our next meetings and talked about Lebanese restaurants in London (good, on the whole) and Italian ones (uniformly rubbish). Later he let slip that he had tried to book me before, when I was away. I'm glad his persistence paid off.

"Do you have a boyfriend?" he asked.

"Yes," I said.

mardi, le 9 décembre

I walked into the hotel, large coat bundled tight around me. It was more insurance that none of the tools of the trade would fall out than protection against the sharp weather. The client undressed while I laid out the things he had requested: blindfold, the Persuaders, choke chain collar, and nipple clamps.

"I've never done this before," he said, eyeing the whips.

Doubtful. Still, his fantasy, not mine. "I'll be gentle with you then," I said. I was lying, and we both knew it.

We were finished in exactly an hour. Sometimes the job seems too easy to be believed.

mercredi, le 10 décembre

Grumpy; nothing coherent to write. Have a list instead.

LOVE: A SPOTTER'S GUIDE

- *Love at First Sight:* the overwhelming desire to see the inside of the nearest closet (pub toilet, friend's back garden, the alleyway over there, et al.).
- *True Love:* can be introduced to the family without unreasonable fear of embarrassment. On the part of the family.
- *Everlasting Love:* a polyamorous couple who haven't had sex with each other in years.
- *Love Match:* an alliance between kingdoms.
- *The Love of Your Life:* the indolent boy from your last year at uni who spent eight-plus hours a day online and ate all the Nutella, the memory of whom somehow improves with time.
- *In Love:* a momentary instance of being almost as interested in someone else as in oneself.
- *Loving:* capable of untold amounts of suffocation.
- *Motherly Love:* capable of untold amounts of suffocation.
- *Brotherly Love:* forbidden by the moral laws of most world religions.
- *Lover:* the one who comes round when your partner's "out of town on business" (read: seeing his lover).
- *Lovable:* cuddly. In the pejorative sense (similar to the concept of "shapely legs," which is code for chubby).

- *Lovely:* only just bearable. "That was a lovely party! I do hope you take me to Kettering again!"
- *Love Potion:* About the only thing, at this point, that might incite the Boy to call. I'm getting lonely up here.

jeudi, le 11 décembre

N gave me a lift home. He had already eaten and I was beyond tired. I made a sandwich for myself and cups of tea for us both while he read to me from the paper.

Later I tried to kick him out of the flat so I could have a bath. It's been too long since I indulged in a long, bubbly soak. "I'll wait," he said. He's an odd one and stubborn as well, and I was too tired to argue, so I let him.

When I came out of the bath, he rolled me over on the bed and kneaded my back from neck to ankles. I would have thanked him—I imagine the satisfied sighs got the message across. On his way out the door he paused. "Next time, of course, I want at least a blowjob for that," he said.

"That's only funny because I know you're not kidding, sweetheart."

Some people wouldn't ask. I can think of one in particular. I've always been attracted to strong, tall men. And they have not ever forced anything on me. Except for one. But I begged him to do it.

It was assault with kissing. I'll call him W. When we met, we were both in love with other people, but it didn't matter. What we did could only loosely be called sexual congress anyway.

W was tall and nicely built, the result of a career in sport. We flirted over the course of a week and agreed to go out on the Friday night. I dressed and thought about W, his long, thick limbs and large hands, knowing something odd was happening. I couldn't imagine myself in this man's arms so much as on the end of his fist.

He looked capable of breaking me into small pieces, and crushing those pieces into a ball. I could not stop thinking of him hurting me, and the thought made me sick. It also turned me on.

Our meeting place was just south of the river. We stood at the crowded bar of a pub for a while before going on to a comedy club where I got legless on gin and tonic. The acts ranged from bad to criminally awful. I began fantasizing about having W's bulky shoulder rammed into my face. I went downstairs to the ladies'. W followed me in.

"You're not going to corner me in the loos, are you?" I asked, pawing his shirt. My head came to not quite the middle of his chest. I could smell the sour waft of a day's sweat on him and was aroused.

"I'm not stalking you," he said. "Much."

I bit him as discouragement. The layers of fabric felt fuzzy on my tongue. My teeth closed just hard enough to make it hurt. But he didn't flinch. "Now then," he said, taking my face in his hands, "you'll pay for that. I'll see you outside."

I was unstable on my heels, leaning heavily on his arm all the way to the corner of my street. We stopped and I looked up. He lifted my body easily, standing me on a bench. From that height we had our first kiss.

"Get a room," yelled some teenagers from the other side of the road.

We didn't. Not that night, anyway. The night after.

The location was a pastel-decorated chain hotel in Hammersmith. I didn't even take an overnight bag. He pushed me down on the bed as soon as we were inside and straddled my waist. Pulling out his cock, he aimed it not for my mouth or my cleavage but at my cheek.

So it began. After that first time, when he hit the side of my face so hard with his erection that there were blisters inside my mouth afterward, there was no going back. "I've never made a woman cry before," he said. "I liked that." No pretense of romance. Just us, anywhere we could be together alone, and his open palm. On cold days in parks where the biting weather would make it sting all the more, he'd stop the car suddenly, and we'd get out and he'd smack me one. My knickers were always sopping wet after.

I couldn't explain the bruises. I didn't. "Ran into the door," said with a shrug. "Hard session at the gym." Or, "A bruise? Where?"

There was the weekend W reserved a room at the Royal College of Physicians. Visiting medics can stay there when in London; I don't know how he blagged his way in. We sat on the narrow single bed, watched a porn documentary and ate pizza. I had too much to eat—when I went down on him, his member was too big and it choked me. I coughed up Meat Feast and diet cola on his thigh. His penis grew even harder. He pulled my hair until I cried as he masturbated on my tear- and vomit-covered face. The bathroom was shared with the next bedroom. When I stepped into the hall, a young Indian doctor left the room opposite. He glanced up and froze, shocked to see me. The young man must have been able to hear us carrying on, though perhaps not the detail of it, as he seemed puzzled at the vomit on my chin and shirt. I lifted my hand in a small wave. "So, then, which one of you is the physician?" he asked awkwardly. "I am," I lied, and walked past him to the toilet. The doctor's jaw plummeted.

W was as mystified by the attraction as I was. "What do you think when I'm hitting you?" he asked one afternoon. We were sitting on a bench in Regents Park watching the geese and swans. Every few minutes, satisfied no one was coming down the paths, he'd hit me again.

"Nothing," I said. There was only the moment when his hand would stop stroking my cheek and I knew the smack was coming; the first hard impact of his palm against the side of my face; the eye-wetting sting of pain; the warm glow of heat there afterward. It was perhaps the only time when there was nothing else in my head. It hurt, but the pain was neutral: there was no hate or disgust behind it. It was pure and exhilarating like any other physical experience. Like the moment of orgasm where you forget yourself, your partner, the world.

"Do you get angry with me?" he asked.

"No."

W visited my house only once. He whipped me through a shirt, then topless, stopping only when I started to bleed. In the shower at the top of the stairs, he covered me in piss, then forced my face down in the puddle as he beat the back of my thighs. After he spent his load on my face, he held a mirror up. "You are such a picture," he sighed. Eyes stinging with come, I half-opened my lids to see a red-cheeked girl squatting in a white tiled bath. And he was right. It looked good. Not in a cover-of-*Glamour* way, mind. I smiled broadly.

Once on holiday in Scotland I furtively sent W letters. "Ate a packed lunch and contemplated the dimensions of your hands," read the first, tentative one. Later: "Next time you see me, don't forget to bring a torch and those ropes."

And the last, written a day after I stood out in the cold night air while the midges chewed me alive and W outlined in detail exactly what he wanted to do to me: "After you told me how you would beat and defile me, I came back inside dripping wet." Yes, I was still in love with someone else, but that was a model-gorgeous, gentle lad, who would never even hear me on the toilet, much less contemplate painting my face with his feces.

The relationship felt too tightly wound to survive, destined for a breakup, a spell in prison, or, worst of all possible worlds, a suburban marriage with occasional light S&M. W couldn't bear the thought either, and one night we engineered, on the flimsiest excuse, the demise of our affair. And I—polite yet firm, like a woman in film noir—smacked him.

"You've been wanting to do that since we met," he said.

That never stopped me wanting him. Two weeks later I sent a note. "There are still marks on my left breast from your fingernails. I miss you."

vendredi, le 12 décembre

Phone call from the Boy last night. It consisted of the usual moaning and gnashing of teeth, both in a sexual way and at our fate of being star-crossed lovers with the A23 betwixt us.

Toward the end of the conversation, things turned a bit more prosaic. "My dad's going to be in London a couple of nights this week."

"Why's that?"

"Retraining courses for work," the Boy said. "I know he's dreading it. He hates London. I mean, what is there to do when you're stuck in the city by yourself and don't know anyone?"

One thing came to mind immediately. Dear God, I hope he doesn't call an escort. "Oh, I'm sure he'll be fine. Your dad's a smashing chap, someone's bound to take him out on the town one night." Please, don't let him call an escort. And please, I know it's a lot to ask . . . please don't let it be me. "Maybe your mum could go as well?"

"No, she's busy this week."

Fuck. My logical mind knows it's statistically unlikely. Still, I have three hotel visits in the next two days and can't help wondering. If time has taught me anything it's that (a) cheating is a common human condition and (b) the stars always align against me.

samedi, le 13 décembre

Went to Bedford for a booking last night and caught a late train back. There was almost no one on the platform: a youngish professional wearing sneakers and headphones, a few lone women. I wondered if they were going home from work, and if so, why this late? The trains were running behind and it seemed we were waiting ages.

A clutch of teenaged boys jumped on, drunk and raucous. One of them eyed me up whilst the others harassed the fat boy in the group. They took one of his shoes and played an increasingly violent game of keep-away which culminated in his loafer being chucked out the window at another train. He began screaming and tackled two of the other boys. They got off at Harpenden, unsurprisingly, and the carriage was mine alone as far as Kentish Town.

I felt inexplicably happy and walked home instead of taking a cab. Neither high heels nor drunken idiots frighten me much—when you spend a life in stilettoes, pavements are no hardship, and I've shrugged off enough come-ons that I could write the book on losing losers. I sang aloud, a song about lovers who want each other dead. Several empty night buses rumbled down the road. A man on a bicycle passed me and said, "Great legs!" He slowed down and glanced over his shoulder to gauge my reaction. I smiled and thanked him. He rode on.

It was cold and clear. I looked up, and was surprised at the number of stars.

dimanche, le 14 décembre

The manager rang to deliver the details of a client to meet near Waterloo. "This man, he is verrrrry nice," she said. I decided on top-to-toe white, mainly because I had a new lace basque that had never seen the light of day (or night, for that matter), also because all my other stockings had runs. He'd booked two hours, which I took to mean that he wanted something odd or that he wanted conversation.

This was the latter. I rattled the brass door knocker and a short-ish man answered. Older, but not ancient. Deep characterful grooves on either side of his thin-lipped mouth. Charming house and nicely decorated. I tried not to look too much like I was as-sessing the interior. We drank our way through two bottles of chilled chardonnay, discussed the Sultan of Brunei's gambling habits, and listened to CDs. "I suppose you're wondering when we're going to get down to it," he said, smiling.

"I am." I looked up at him from the floor where I was sitting barefoot. He leaned down and kissed me. It felt like a first-date kiss. Tentative. I stood up and stripped the dress over my head.

"Just like that," he said, running his hands over my hips and thighs. The thin fabric whirred against his dry palms. Standing up, he turned me around and bent me over a table. His mouth pressed to the gusset of my knickers and I felt the hot steam of his breath through the fabric. He stood again to slip on a condom and, push-ing the gusset to one side, took me from behind. It was over quickly.

"I'll take you on my next holiday, baby," he said. "You deserve to get out of the city." I doubted this, but it was nice to hear.

He had loads of fluffy towels and a giant bath for afterward, and we ate crisps and drank wine a full hour past when I was supposed to go. It was odd; I felt the cab turned up far too soon. He asked for my real name and direct number. I hesitated—against agency policy. Then again, the manager herself had indicated that more than a few girls do this. I gave it to him and texted the manager to let her know I was on my way home.

It was cold outside, even the few steps from the door to the cab. I had a long coat and woolen scarf on and was secretly pleased I wouldn't even be going as far as a tube station or bus stop. The cab driver was from Croydon, and we chattered about Orlando Bloom, New Year's fireworks, and Christmas parties. I told him I worked at a well-known accountancy firm. I don't think he was fooled for a second. Instead of going home, I directed him to a club in Soho. The cash, when I pulled out the bills to pay him, made an unfeasibly large lump in my hand.

N is a bouncer at a gay club. Among other things. I popped in to see how he was getting on with his cold, and hopefully to raise his stock a little. This ploy might work if we ever met in a place where straight people go.

"Darling, is it wrong to be jealous of a drag queen?" I sighed, as the very image of Doris Day slid past me in a white fur capelet.

"Who's the object of your envy this time?" he asked. I nodded toward the blonde goddess. "Oh, don't be," he said. "I hear she spends three hours every day just removing hair."

It got me to thinking about my own trials and tribulations. There is no optimal method of depilation. Razors leave terrible stubble, worse when it's winter. I have clocked the time between smooth skin and goosepimpled hell at about three minutes. Cream removers smell terrible and never quite get all the hair anyway. Those vibrating-coil epilators should be marketed to masochists only, and waxing is usually administered by a sixteen-stone Filipina woman named Rosie. Also, it leaves the most horrible rash for the first day.

This is not a complaint—it is a statement of fact on the condition of being female. Probably something to do with the Tree of Knowledge. In return for all this suffering, we do get a few benefits. Baby-soft nether regions. Easy cleanup. Increased sensitivity. I have to stay on top of it, being blessed with a follicular thickness that is the envy of most arctic animals. My mother by contrast used to joke that she shaved her legs once a year "whether they need it or not." I struggled with a razor as soon as I could get my hands on one and flirted as a teenager with the notion of shaving the hair off my arms, too.

My hair removal regime involves a combination of waxing and shaving, largely because of an aversion to having things ripped out of my armpit. Crotch, though, that's no problem. Go figure. "I know how she feels," I joked as N stepped to the side and let a group of hooting students through.

"So how did it go?" he said, looking back out at the street.

"Fine," I said. "Nice man."

"Single?"

"Could be divorced." I shrugged. "Photos of his wife or ex-wife everywhere."

"Children?"

"Two, both adults."

"Man, I would never," he said.

"Liar."

lundi, le 15 décembre

We sat in the car, silent. The light was on inside.

"I thought he was supposed to be out," I said.

"He was," the Boyfriend said. "At least, I thought he was." He looked like he might start crying. "Please, come in. You're my guest. I want you here and I'm sure he can stand it for a minute if he's on his way out anyway."

I knew there was a reason why the Boy always comes up to see me instead of the other way round.

When the Boy last visited, we met his friend S for breakfast. Now, S had been recently dumped by H. What S didn't know was that H had been sleeping with the Boy's flatmate for several weeks beforehand, and we agreed not to tell him. S seemed fairly chipper though and is commencing motorbike lessons now that there is no girlfriend around to forbid it. S already planned to christen the bike he will buy "the Crotch Rocket." I promptly offered to test-drive his giant machine once it's up and running. Anyway, that same housemate who was sleeping with S's ex was simultaneously two-timing his own girlfriend, E, who lived in the house, with an average of three girls a week. And while E had no idea, the Boy and I harbored no illusions about what sort of a man his housemate was.

And in such situations, what can you do but hold your tongue?

Taking my bags, we went to the door. The Boy opened it and put his head round the corner carefully. "Why, hello, you're still in situ?" he cheerily queried of the Housemate. "I just wanted to let you know, I'm here with the lovely—"

"NO," bellowed the Housemate. "I will not have THAT WOMAN in my house."

Ostensibly, the Housemate dislikes me because of my job. He hasn't always hated me. In fact, I have another theory altogether: he is annoyed because I am one of a very few women he could never, ever have. Not even if he paid for it.

For the Housemate is young, attractive, smart, and wealthy. Has no trouble with women at all and knows it. He has come on to me at least ten times in one year with no luck whatsoever. I could never go off in secret with the Boy's ersatz best friend. And his girlfriend E really does not deserve one more secret affair happening under her nose. Funny how and when morals decide to jump in, eh? A cheater, I can take. But a liar I have no time for.

"Listen, she's leaving quite early in the morning, and you won't have to—"

"I said *no*, didn't I?"

The Housemate can do this; he owns the house. The conversation continued in this tedious vein for the better part of ten minutes. Less than charmed, I went to the car and waited. When the Boy returned, we nipped to the chip shop for a snack and, certain the Housemate must surely be gone, snuck back after an hour. But my temper and libido suffered from the episode somewhat. Nothing a few cups of chocolate and an hour-long massage couldn't cure, of course.

"What are we going to do, kitty?" he said, half asleep. "What are we going to do?"

"Come up to London and move in with me," I blurted. It's time I moved to a more sociable area of the city anyway, one in which the crack addicts may yet stagger by the door but at least don't collapse just inside.

"Money's an issue," he said.

"You can live off me while you look for a better job up there, then," I said. "I can afford it easily." Oh, cringe, shouldn't have said that, don't remind him!

"This is all rather out of left field," he said.

"You would be able to fly to see your family instead of drive," I said. His family are very close to him in feeling, but not geography. Living in London would put him much closer to the major airports.

"True."

"And you'd have nicer furniture." My flat is furnished in the slightly naff flowery vein favored by landlords of the aspirant class. "You don't have to decide. I won't take offense if you say no. But it's an offer, anyway." Ah, negotiating the terms of modern cohabitation. Who said romance was dead?

It would solve one problem—that of the belligerent Housemate. Though perhaps faced with the day-to-day of my comings and goings, the Boy would soon go off the idea. But I sure could use a friendly face and a foot rub with the beating these stiletto-clad feet take on a daily basis.

mardi, le 16 décembre

Most transactions in the business are paid in cash. I find myself at the bank rather often and tend to use the same one every day. Cashiers are naturally curious people who would have to be brain-dead not to wonder why I come in with rolls of notes several times a week and deposit into two accounts, one of which is not mine.

One day I presented the deposit details on the back of a slip the Boy had been sketching on. He studied art, at some long-forgotten time in the past, and still tends to doodle and scratch at odd pieces of paper. The cashier turned it over, looked at the drawing, and looked at me. "This is good. Did you do this?" she asked. "Yes, well, I'm a . . . cartoonist," I lied. The cashier nodded, accepted this. Which is how the people at the bank came to believe that I draw for a living. Whether they took the next logical leap of questioning why any legitimate artist would demand payment in cash is unknown to me.

One advantage of this job is not being limited to the lunch hour for running errands. Therefore, I tend to go shopping in midafternoon. "Live close to here?" the grocer by the tube station asked one day as I picked out apples and kiwifruit.

"Just around the corner," I said. "I work as a nanny." Which is blatantly unbelievable, as I never have children visibly in tow and, unless the Boy is staying over, am only buying for one. Still, he now occasionally asks how the kids are doing.

I tend to bump into neighbors very seldom, except in the evening, at which time they see me dolled up in a dress or suit, full makeup, and freshly washed hair, meeting a cab. "Going out?" they ask.

"Best friend's engagement party," I say. Or, "Meeting people from work for drinks." They nod and wish me well. I slip out the door and wonder what story I'm going to tell the taxi driver.

mercredi, le 17 décembre

Met the As for lunch today. They don't always hunt in a pack, but when they do, no eating establishment is safe.

A1, A2, A3, and A4 were already waiting at a Thai restaurant. I was unexpectedly the last to arrive—at least three of them are tardy by nature. We exchanged kisses and settled at a corner table.

I count the time I've spent enjoying sex from the first time I slept with A1, a number of years ago. I remember the afternoon clearly. The man's large frame blocked the light from the single window of his flat. I smiled up at him, we were naked, entwined in each other's limbs. He reached down, put his hand round one of my ankles, and moved my leg until it crossed my body. He bore down on my doubled body and entered me.

"What are you doing?" I squeaked.

"I want to feel the fullness of your arse against my body," he said. Though it was not my first time—far from it—it might as well have been. Here was a man, finally, who knew what he wanted and, better still, knew what to do to get it.

A1 and I dated for several years. It was not an easy relationship except for the sex. Once our clothes were off, so were all bets. I knew I could ask him for anything and he could ask the same. For the most part, we always said yes to whatever the other wanted, but took no offense if the suggestion was rejected. He was the first man to tell me I was pretty whom I believed, the first person out-side of a gym shower I could walk in front of unclothed. And I adored him physically: A1 is tall but not too tall, muscular, hairy. His dark straight hair and gravelly voice were deliciously anachronistic. He was the sort of man who should have been around in the fifties as a captain of industry.

We would have unbelievable rows. The passion I felt for him was something I didn't know how to handle. It felt too intense and slippery for me, liquid mercury pouring out of my hands. We made it up in the bedroom, of course. Or on his kitchen table. Or his desk at work, after his boss had gone. In an elevator. In a university post office.

And we did it every way we could imagine, from the exotic (double penetration, restraints, golden showers) to the embarrassingly prosaic—missionary while he watched a football match on telly. I've done more and dirtier with other people since then, but never felt such a sense of stretching my own boundaries.

He was the first person to take a paddle to my behind; in return, I administered a doubled leather belt to his bottom while he bent over a sofa, holding his genitals away from the strikes. His impressively varied collection of pornography was the first hardcore I'd ever seen, and we acquired new magazines and sorted them into categories with glee. The things he did like—watersports, anal, women with frogspawnish come dripping off their faces—took their place; even things he didn't like such as bestiality and lesbian sex had their place, because he was a collector. The explicit permission to just look at someone's body, as opposed to a surreptitious glance in the gym or a furtive peek before the covers came up and the lights went out, was delightful.

I started seeing A2 several years after A1 and I split. He was a sensitive lover. Not gentle as such, but strong and slow. He seemed to me to make no unnecessary movements, and I was enthralled by his long, measured steps. Sometimes, with his pale skin and fair hair, he still looked like a teenager. Or even younger—an overgrown boy. From the beginning of our affair to the end, no body and no touch ever felt so right every time as his did. No fingers and no tongue ever came so close to being what I imagined the perfect lover was like. His body was spare but muscular. Tall but not excessively so. Not an ounce wasted.

He had a washing machine at home; I didn't. I went round one day with laundry and found a pair of my own knickers in the otherwise empty drum. "What are these doing in here?" I asked.

"I missed you when you went home last weekend, so I wore them," he said.

I examined the elastic. His hips were so narrow it didn't seem to have torn the underwear. "Maybe we should get you some for you," I kidded.

"Maybe we should," he said, not joking.

I had his key. After waking and breakfasting (poached eggs on toast if hungry, cappuccino and a slice of challah if not), I would cycle to A2's house. He usually rose late and was showering when I arrived. The bedroom door would be open and I went to the bureau drawer containing almost two dozen pairs of knickers. Choosing one, I would leave it in the drawer of the bedside stand and return to the front room. He would come out and dress. No comment on the knickers, which were for later.

We spent most of each day together. He worked from home; I had odd hours in a bookshop nearby. While I was working, he'd take a break from his, bringing me takeaway cups of coffee and tea. We read the literary supplements; I gave him bound proofs of upcoming books from the back room. My workmates were a mad, absinthe-drinking middle-aged woman and the often-absent, never-happy boss. Almost every week I ended up covering half of their hours but didn't mind. There were books and plenty of them. And it was exciting the few times an author of note came in the shop. I noticed, though, that most of them breezed in the door and went to check for their titles on the shelves before coming back to the front to greet me.

After work A2 would be waiting at home. No words, just through the door and straight to his sofa. He sat, arms thrown over the back, as I opened his jeans with my teeth. Always a harder trick to pull off than I remembered. Then the first flash of silk or lace, and his hard cock distorting the fabric. I put my face in his crotch and smelled the odor of a day's worth of sweat, piss, and pre-come through the knickers. I nibbled him, licked the underwear until it stuck to him.

A2 loved to pull at me, turn me over on his hands. He stripped me bare but kept the girly pants on. When he entered me—almost always anally—it was with the knickers pushed to one side, constricting the base of his penis, clinging to his balls.

After a few months the knickers weren't enough. I bought a summer dress, short, brightly colored. He tried it on. I laughed and fucked him in the dress and was only slightly depressed that A2 had thinner hips and better legs than mine.

"Let's go to the sales," he said one weekend. I didn't have to ask if the purchases were going to be for him or for me. Soon several short, pretty dresses joined the knickers in the drawer.

I knew there was another woman. He'd told me before we ever slept together. I probably fooled myself into believing it was almost over, for she lived hours away, and from what I knew had always treated him badly. But one week he went to see friends in the city where she lived. While I tried for a few days to ignore the itching weight of his key in my pocket, in the end I could not resist. I tore his house apart looking for evidence of her: e-mail, pictures. There was one in particular that broke my heart: her gorgeous face cracked in a smile and pink satin pajamas open to the waist. I found her name, her number, and rang her. There was no answer. I left a message on the answerphone: this is a friend of A2's, I just wanted to talk to you—don't worry, it's not an emergency.

She rang back. "Hello," she said, sounding tired.

It was hard to keep from screaming. The pulse in my neck was throbbing. "Do you know who I am?" I asked.

"I've heard your name," she said. I told her about me and A2. She was very quiet. "Thank you," she said at the end. The day after he came back, I used his key to go in but he wasn't in the shower.

He was waiting for me. I'd upset her, he said. What right did I have to do that?

There was no answer. I was shaking with anger. What right does anyone have to feel jealousy?

One of the teachers at school gave a talk to the girls in our year about his marriage. Love is a decision, he declared to a room of hormonally charged teenagers. We scoffed. Love isn't a decision; the films and songs tell us otherwise. It's a force, it's a virtue, we were at the charmed age when you can suck off your brother's best friend in your bedroom and still believe in a one true love.

Then I fell for someone who hurt me. Gradually I came around to the teacher's point of view. You have to open the door before someone can come in. That was no guarantee of control once they got there, of course, but it was something that was comprehensible, if not entirely logical.

In control, that's what I thought. But first-time jealousy tore me to pieces the same way first love had. We argued and fucked, and fucked and argued, then we argued more and fucked less.

And when we did have sex, it had changed. Once he used to put knickers on and bend over the edge of his sofa. Laughing, I would apply a riding crop to his behind. After a few minutes we'd run to his bathroom where he'd excitedly pull down the panties and look in the mirror. If I hadn't yet imprinted the pattern of the fabric on his skin, we'd go back and try again.

After, I just whipped him and whipped him until his skin was raw and spotted with blood. Until he told me to stop.

The times we shared a bed, A2 slept with his arms tangled around me. I kick and struggle against sheets and blankets in the night; he held me in. I rub my legs together like a cricket; he warmed my cold feet between his. Whenever his hand rested on my belly, I would wake, wondering not only at his stillness—he was only slightly less animated asleep than awake—but also at his lack of self-consciousness. The body is so unarmored: our species' success is dependent on what is inside our skin, not a thousand spikes mounted on it. I might have hurt him any time he was asleep. If he turned over, exposed his spine, I might have attacked him right then.

And once: I woke before the alarm to find my curtains open on a perfectly gray morning. Hearing a sigh, thinking him awake, I turned toward A2. He still lingered in the twilight of sleep and his long arms were at strange angles under the displaced pillow.

"Why are you tucking your hands in like that?" I asked, for his elbows jutted out but his palms were jammed beneath the bedding.

"So you don't snap them off," he murmured, and went into deeper sleep. The first starling of the morning started in a tree outside.

He broke things off with his other lover but I never quite believed it and we drifted apart, sleeping together less and less frequently until one day he was seeing someone else and so was I. We were each happy for the other.

Now, A1 squeezed my knee and affected a dirty-old-man cackle. A2 winked over his menu. A3 glowered in the corner—as is his custom—and A4 grinned brightly into middle distance.

"So what are you lads up to today?" I asked.

"Nothing very much," said A1. His measured words were like those of a schoolteacher.

"Nothing much at all," said A2.

A4 smiled toward me. "Wasting as much of your time as possible."

"Don't you fellows have jobs to go to?" They don't all live in London, but business brings them through on a semiregular basis.

"Theoretically, yes," grumbled A3. He's the ginger one. Dour northerner. And I mean that admiringly.

"Rubbish," said A2, turning toward me. "And your good self? Things to do, people to see?"

"Not until later," I said. The waitress came by to take our orders. A2 ordered the special for everyone. None of us knew what it was. Didn't matter. A3 seemed reluctant to give up his menu. A2 asked after the Boy.

"I've asked him to come up here and move in with me," I said.

"Mistake," said A1.

"Big mistake," A2 said. A3 mumbled unintelligibly. A4 continued smiling for no good reason. That's why I like him best. My phone buzzed in my pocket. It was the manager of the agency. She asked if I could be in Marylebone for four.

"Four the time or four the number?" She meant the time. I checked my watch. Very doable. The As pretended not to eavesdrop.

Most people raise an eyebrow when they find that my closest friends are mostly men, and for the most part, men I've slept with. Strange, I think. Whom else are you going to sleep with besides the people you know? Strangers?

Don't answer that.

jeudi, le 18 décembre

N and I had a minor falling-out at the gym. Nothing serious, such as whose glutes are benefiting more from adding lunges to the workout, but a parting of ways on the subject of restricting access to public services and benefits. He: in favor, at which point I believe the words "paranoid refugee hater" may have traversed my mind, if not escaped my lips.

We managed to keep from strangling each other and repaired to mine for risotto. Conversation stayed on safer subjects, namely shoes, rugby, and who in the *Footballers' Wives* cast sports the best cleavage. I'm sure we'll work out this schism in the end—both the cleavage debate and the ID card thing. That said, disagreements never resolve themselves as quickly once you can't fuck each other anymore.

vendredi, le 19 décembre

The manager is a doll, but easily confused. Case in point: I was sitting in the back of a cab while the driver tried to find the Royal Kensington Hotel—which, incidentally, doesn't exist.

I was a quarter of an hour late. We finally decided she must have meant the Royal Garden Hotel, Kensington. The driver waited outside while I checked the name and room number at reception. It was indeed correct. I gave the cabbie the thumbs-up and he drove off.

The client was freshly showered and wearing a white toweling robe. We walked through to the suite's front room, where another woman sat drinking wine, already topless. She was a small blonde cutie from Israel.

I took off her skirt and shoes and undid the ribbon ties on her black silk knickers with my teeth. I had been told she was his girlfriend, but something about it didn't quite jibe. He seemed to know her no better than I did. If she was a working girl, she definitely wasn't from my agency. Instincts can be wrong, though, and in threesomes with someone's girlfriend the best course of action is to lavish attention on the woman. It was no hardship—she smelled of baby powder and tasted of warm honey.

We moved on to the bedroom. He went at me from behind while she kneeled down to work at me with her tongue, fingers, and a mini-vibe. I found his exceptionally smooth body fascinating—someone's been spending plenty of time down the waxing salon, I thought—an effect compromised by his rough, untrimmed beard. The whiskers tickled and scratched as he lapped at my girl-parts.

"I don't know what you had in mind," I said as my time started drawing to a close, "but I think it would be great if you came all over both our faces."

The Israeli girl licked her lips and winked at me. A pro. Had to be, had to be.

Afterward I produced a small bottle of apricot oil and she gave both me and the client the most luscious massages. If I hadn't enjoyed it so much, I would have been jealous of her skill. I gathered my clothes from the rooms while she pummeled and kneaded his back.

The client went to collect my coat. I gave the girl a kiss and nodded at the bottle of massage oil in her tiny hand. "Keep it— you'll make better use of it than I will." He came back and put a possessive arm around her, and my mind switched over again. Escort? Girlfriend? I couldn't be sure. The tip he slipped me was equal to the fee.

samedi, le 20 décembre

I am heading home to see friends and family, as is my custom. The Boy has gone on to spend a few weeks with his parents, as is his custom. I think some things should be sacrosanct from the intrusion of couplehood, and watching your family get drunk and pass out in the toilet is one of them.

Train travel is a most exciting wonder of the modern age. Having invented no shortage of faster, cheaper, and more comfortable ways to travel, we insist on perpetuating an outdated, and dare I say it, wildly inconvenient method of transport. What other modes of carriage could possibly expect you to make your own way to the start and terminating stations, wait until the company's convenience to commence your journey, sit so long without even a free warm soda, and set up seats and tables so that you are inadvertently rubbing thighs with every pervert between King's Cross and Yorkshire? I love it, you know I do.

Having made this trip so often, I know—seconds before the conductor's voice breaks over the loudspeaker—when we are one minute from my stop. I know which carriage will put me closest to the exit and could conduct a tour of the station blindfolded. Even when no one is waiting for me, and I know there will be a twenty-minute queue for a taxi when I get there, the effect of stepping onto the platform at home is vivid delight. And the glow of being on my own ground lasts indefinitely, or until I pull into my parents' drive. Whichever comes first.

dimanche, le 21 décembre

Daddy and I went for a walk just after sunset. He claimed his legs were cramping from so much sitting around, but I suspect it was to get away from my mother, who has gone into celebratory overdrive. She's an equal-opportunity party animal, juggling five or six seasonal holidays at a go. The last we checked she was trying to whip up familial enthusiasm for an Eid firework party. Having only a vague notion of what Eid is, who celebrates it, or what shoes would be appropriate to standing in a back garden and craning my neck at multicolored gunpowder, I decided in favor of the walking option.

There was a nip in the air, just enough to set the cheeks and ears tingling. We walked past a cottage with smoke from the chimney—"Coal," Daddy said, authoritatively. We had a wood-burning stove when I was small, that we used to cook the family meals on as well. When it went and the new electric cooker and fake fire came in, I was very sad.

We returned to a dark house and a worried-looking man pushing his car back off of ours. He did the little foot-to-foot dance of trying to look innocent, which is especially tough when your front bumper is entangled in someone's station wagon.

Daddy did a low whistle. "Ooh, the woman's not going to be happy," he said to the strange man, as if the threat of my mother's displeasure alone could convince a perfect stranger not to do a runner. He circled round the scene of the accident—not much, just needed to lift the other car off the bumper, spot of scraped paint. Even I could see it wasn't serious. But the stranger had clearly had a bit of Christmas cheer and was panicking.

"Don't know, now," Daddy said, sucking his teeth. "Could be a lot of damage." The man pleaded for leniency. The usual story—points on his license, poor insurance, wife at home about to give birth to a multiheaded Hydra and only his being home on time could save her.

"Tell you what," my father said, stroking his chin. "Let's have about two hundred off you and call it even."

"I only have one-twenty on me."

"One-twenty and that bottle of whisky in your front seat."

A curt nod and the man handed over the goods. My father crouched low and, with a coordinated effort, they disentangled the bumpers. The man got in his sedan and drove off slowly, mumbling gratitude. We waved him round the corner.

"Well, that was potentially exciting," Daddy said, unlocking the front door. He handed me half of the notes. "Let's not tell your mother, shall we?"

lundi, le 22 décembre

The first prostitute I ever met was a friend of my father's. It was about this time of year. I was still a student.

He is not a pimp, I swear. My father is in the habit of taking on impossible projects. He'd probably qualify for sainthood if he was, you know, a dead Catholic. These altruistic efforts have ranged from resurrecting a doomed restaurant to rehabilitating a series of doomed women. It's a tendency that has led to no small amount of frostiness on my mother's part, but she has had some few decades to accustom herself to his softheartedness by now.

She could tell when he was embarking on yet another failed cause before he even opened his mouth. "There's only one reason you'd be coming in with flowers," she barked from the kitchen. "And it's not our anniversary." Maybe she's the one whose name should be put forward to the Vatican, actually.

It was winter of the year, several Yuletides ago now. The holiday cheer was largely lost on me due to a recent breakup as well as not being Christian. The vulgarities of the holiday are sometimes charming, or occasionally grating, but that year they were unbearable. All I could see were so many people gaining joy from an event imbued with only minimal importance by most of the world, as represented by endless yards of tatty tinsel and unwanted gifts. One afternoon, standing in a queue at the bank, I saw my reflection distorted in a cheap red tree bauble, and it occurred to me how temporary and meaningless all of it—the holiday, the bank, the world in general—was. I felt incapable of even anger at being alone. Defeated. So I did what any spoiled eldest child would do and went home for a few weeks to sulk properly.

As a restorative jaunt my father suggested I go with him to visit one of his "friends." She, I was told, had just been released from prison on fraud charges related to her drug habit. Having regained custody of her children, she was working as a cleaner in a hotel and trying to stay off the game. Charming. I smiled tightly and we drove off to meet the woman.

We sat in the car in silence for a quarter of an hour. "I know you know your mum doesn't approve," he said suddenly, by way of the obvious.

I said nothing and looked out the window, where people poured out of the shops into the night.

"She's really a lovely person," he said of the friend. "Her children are absolutely charming."

My father is the most ineffectual liar. In her depressing kitchen she regaled us with the story of a septic infection in her thumbnail that culminated in a week off work. Her two sons were as I imagined: the elder, about fifteen, eyed my figure under three layers of heavy clothing, while his younger sibling could not be shifted from the telly.

I could not stop thinking of my last boyfriend, who had left me suddenly among accusations of my snobbishness and utter lack of sympathy for other people. Well, as Philip Larkin put it, useful to get that learnt.

The other adults and the teenaged son left the room to look at his bicycle, a rusting heap retrieved from a Dumpster, which lay crumpled outside the door. My father is if nothing else rather handy and promised to look into its health. I knew the effort was more likely to result in a cash gift to the young man rather than any resurrection of the bike and was left, scowling, to watch the younger son attack the remote control.

As soon as the room was empty, he turned to me. "Would you like to see my bird?" he asked.

Good gracious. Is this some sort of euphemism? "Okay," I said.

We went to the window, and he opened it. Outside was a large holly bush. He clicked his tongue and waited. I waited. There was only the sound of motor scooters and festive drunks emerging from a pub.

He clicked his tongue again and whistled. A small bluetit beeped back and flew out of the bush to land on his shoulder. When he opened his hand, palm-up, it settled there.

Turning back in the window, he told me to put out my own hand. I did. He showed me how to play a game with it—I snatched my hand away so the tit would fall, only to catch it again as it opened its wings. "That's how I taught it to fly," he said.

"You taught it to fly?"

"A cat killed its mum, so we brought the nest in," he said. "We got crickets and fed them with a tweezer." There had been six in the nest, but only one survived. He showed me another trick, where with the tit on his shoulder he would look to the right, then left, then right again—and it would peep in each ear as he presented it.

The others came back in, the older son flushed with the satisfaction of having parted my father from some portion of his wallet. The bird flew out and the younger boy closed the window. Their mother was chattering gamely about some other minor recent illness, owing, she was certain, to the quality of food within Her Majesty's prisons. "You get hardly nothing, starving all the time, but you still get fat." We stayed for another cup of tea and a chocolate bourbon, then my father and I went home in silence.

mardi, le 23 décembre

Long coat . . . check.

Dark sunglasses . . . check.

One hour's alibi to the parents . . . check. I'm out the door and free.

I was on time for the rendezvous. He was late. I sipped a coffee and pretended to read the paper. He slid in the door unnoticed, sat across from me. I nodded hello and pushed the package across the table.

A4 lifted the lid discreetly and looked in the box. "You sure these are the goods?" he asked.

"None finer," I said. "Guaranteed results." He exhaled, his shoulders unclenching. "If you don't mind my asking, do you really need so much product to get through a week with your family?"

"They'd kill me otherwise." He opened the box again and sniffed deeply. "Soon as they start to smell blood in the water, I can throw these chocolate truffles their way. That buys me at least a few hours."

"Secret recipe," I fibbed. Actually I'd found it on the Internet. Butter, chocolate, cream, and rum. So simple even I couldn't cock it up.

A4 and I dated for some years, we even lived together for a time. We didn't have, as they say, a pot to piss in, but it was a comfortable domestic arrangement and we had a lot of common interests. Namely, complaining about the rest of the world. It lasted until I moved away in the first of several unsuccessful attempts to gain useful employment. I was upset, recently, to find that he thought the post-student house we'd shared was "a hovel." I always remembered it fondly.

"You're a lifesaver," A4 said. He's the one my father still asks after, as if we're still an item. He's the one I have the most pictures of. There is one of him in the mountains in a silver frame on my bookshelves. He's looking up at the camera, at me, a hand out to steady himself, and smiling. Sweet creature. Smiles often.

"You'll pay me back another time."

mercredi, le 24 décembre

I miss living in the North. The stories are all true. People really are friendlier up here. The chips really are better. Everything really is cheaper. The women really do go out in midwinter wearing less.

I miss getting pissed for less than a fiver.

jeudi, le 25 décembre

Right, I have been waiting absolutely weeks to say this.

Happy Christmas, ho ho ho!

(It made me laugh anyway. It's Hanukkah, and I am eating white chocolate gelt at the moment, which is cooler than cool. And no sign of a gift from the Boy, which is somewhat less than cool.)

vendredi, le 26 décembre

My first diary was a seventh-birthday gift. Fortunately, most of the intervening volumes have been lost. This morning, bored to death, I set about cleaning out a desk and found some old ones from a few years back. They were written in softcover exercise books with flowers drawn on the covers. They date from the time N and I met.

We met a few years ago and hit it off immediately. "Hit it off" being a coy way of saying "grabbed a room in the first hotel we could find." A couple of days later, when we came up for air, he mentioned his female friend J and the possibility of a threesome. He'd had threesomes with her several times before and vouched for her beauty and overwhelming sexuality.

We were sitting in his car, looking at the river near Hammersmith. "Sure," I said. I hadn't been with many women, but considering all the ground he and I had covered in a weekend, it seemed impossible to refuse. He rang her to arrange a meeting, and this is how the diary entry continued:

We met J at her place and went for brunch. Food was nice, talked about sex and underwater archaeology.

Back at hers I made hot cocoa for N and me. When he went out of the room, she kissed me and asked how many women I'd been with. Lied and said eight or nine.

We drank the cocoa in the front room and N said he might have a nap. J took me to her bedroom, which held a big white bed and pillowcases that spelled "La Nuit" in a serif font.

We kissed and touched. J seemed tiny until I took off my shoes—in fact we are the same height. Her bum looked so good in the cream striped trousers, but even better naked. The night before, N had said I had the best arse he'd ever seen, but J's, I think, is better. Her neck, skin, and hair all smelled so nice I was suddenly aware of my own sweat. "Did N do that?" she asked of the deep scratches on my shoulder. I showed her the dark bruises on my thighs and the faint marks from his cock on my face. She told me to lie down and blindfolded me and tied my hands.

She dragged a soft, multistranded whip across me. "Do you know what this is?" "Yes." "Do you want it?" She saved the hardest lashes for my breasts and fucked me with a double-headed dildo. When I pressed my face in her crotch, she untied me and took the mask off. I licked her through the knickers and then took them off—J was shaven down below.

It was easy to get her off with my fingers. After which I noticed N watching from the open door. Asked how long he'd been there. "Since the mask went on," he said. "I could smell the two of you before I even got to the door."

At this point J's boyfriend turned up and the diary gets a little vague. To make a long story short, he had a problem with N—namely, he didn't want N to touch J. Out of frustration N blurted that if that was so, J's man couldn't touch me either. Instead, N tried unsuccessfully to fist me. I was so distracted I couldn't come. J sucked her partner off, we all showered seperately, exchanged numbers, and N and I left. He dropped me at King's Cross.

He asked if I needed anything before the journey. Something meaningful to live for, I quipped. Food and sex, he said immediately, and I laughed. I've reminded him of this flash of philosophy several times since, but he never remembers saying it. Walking through the station, I felt lighter than air, dazed. Happy.

"Well," he said just before the train doors closed, "I guess four in a bed is too many."

I remember masturbating on the ride north. It wasn't easy; the carriage was crowded and people kept sitting next to me. I didn't want to do it in the toilet. But I had hours to do it in and unbuttoned my trousers as slowly as needed for perfect silence. It happened with an Asian girl sitting next to me, turned talking to her friend a few rows back. I had a coat thrown over my lap and pretended to be asleep. Afterward I rang N to let him know. It was somewhere around Grantham, I believe.

samedi, le 27 décembre

I have never been the sort of girl to make New Year's resolutions. Such things are bound to lead to teetotaler parties, ill-advised marriages, or worse. Once I resolved to use floss and mouthwash before brushing every day for an entire year. This was before I realized (some 1.4 milliseconds later) that maintaining such a level of dental hygiene was not only unlikely to last an entire week, but also massively unattractive. Would you want to wake up to a full-on Broadway musical starring your beloved's tonsils every morning? I think not.

Another year, I planned to keep a handwritten diary without giving up out of boredom or forgetfulness. Miraculously, I made it to the six-month mark, spurred on by simultaneous reading of the diaries of those vastly superior journalists Kenneth Tynan and Pepys. By comparison my own suffered from a lack of tales of having my wig deloused or all-night drinking sessions with Tennessee Williams. Nevertheless, even the most reluctant leopard may exchange her stole, and I have given some thought to what good deeds and resolutions I could enact in the next twelve months.

It is hereby resolved that I will never buy an own-brand bottle of lube again. Never.

I believe there is some chance of keeping this one.

dimanche, le 28 décembre

Ah, the bosom of home. So comforting. So convivial.

So stiflingly the same as it is every year. I'm off down south again, before Mum notices the dent in the side of the car.

lundi, le 29 décembre

(Phone rings) Me: "Hello?"

Manager (for it is she): "Darling, are you asleep?"

"Um, no?"

"Oh riiiight. You just sound so relaxed. I think to myself, I am so relaxed, but you are always much more relaxed than me. Do you read a lot?"

"Um, yes?"

"That would be why then. People who read are so relaxed. Anyway, I have a booking for you right away. I don't know what it is all of a sudden, but everyone has gone mad for you." They say that madames are known to play favorites with the girls, promoting some more heavily than others according to personal whim, but I have not yet noticed this. The business seems to have up weeks where I'm turning down offers and down weeks when I wonder if there'll be anyone at all. But the manager always seems uniformly businesslike.

"Um, good?"

"Verrrrrry good, darling. I will text you the details. Enjoy your book."

I had to take a different minicab from usual. The new driver did not endear himself—first he started going east, then seemed to be making a very elaborate loop that took in most of Islington. I was on the phone to A4 and only paying scant attention to the road. Twenty minutes later, when we turned back onto a road three blocks south of my house, I exploded. "I could have walked here faster!"

"Yes, well, traffic, this time of night," he said.

I looked right, then left. There were no cars in either direction. "I can't believe this." At this rate, I reckoned I'd be ten minutes late and rang to let the agency know.

South of Hyde Park, he turned into a mile-long queue of traffic even I would have known to avoid. "Excuse me, do you know where you're going?"

"Of course."

Ha. "I'm running late for a meeting." You know, the sort you go to in the middle of the night wearing lace-top holdups and matching bra and knickers under a flimsy dress.

"You know a better way to get there?" he sniffed.

"No, but it's not my job to."

"The traffic, this time of night, there's nothing I can do about it."

"Nonsense. You could have taken any of a dozen other routes. You drive me around my own neighborhood for twenty minutes? And turn straight into gridlock? Come on, I wasn't born yesterday."

He checked his mirror to confirm this was, indeed, true. "Like I say, there's nothing I can do."

"An apology would be nice." No reply. We sat in silence for ten minutes while the traffic crawled along. I fumed, and boiled, and generally stewed. "Can you just let me out?"

"Sure, lady, whatever." I got out of the taxi without paying and stepped into solid traffic. We had just passed a minicab stand at the top of Noth End Road; I headed straight for it. The second driver had me at the appointment in five minutes for the bargain price of four quid, so I tipped another six.

Luckily the client was very understanding and offered me a drink. I love English archetypes: public schoolboy, thirties, managing director of his father's company. The sort of person who says "chin chin" before a drink. Fan of Boris Johnson. I stripped down to underwear at the bottom of the stairs and he watched me slowly walk up.

I paused at the top of the steps, turned and looked over my shoulder. "So what do you want to do?"

"I want to make love to you."

"Like the full-on Barry White kind?"

"Oh yes." We wrestled in the bedsheets for the better part of an hour. His hair was soft and thick and smelled slightly metallic. "What can I do to make you come?"

"It's very complicated. We'd be here all night." I don't come with clients. Some people don't kiss, which I think is rubbish. It's just lips after all. But orgasms I save for someone else. This isn't difficult—I've never reached orgasm too easily.

"That sounds ideal."

"Yes, but do you have a drill press and six goats? Also, the planets are not in the correct alignment."

"Fair dues. I'll know for next time." He slipped me his card on the way out, said he wants to meet for a drink sometime. "The ball is in your court," he said as I tripped down his steps to the waiting taxi. In the staccato beams of the streetlights through the car windows, I peeked at the card. Pink and green, engraved, fashionable font, and would have been tempted if I was single, though I can't imagine how a couple that met in such a situation would explain it to their friends.

"I do not like his type," the manager said when I rang her on the way home. "Surely he will write a report." There are websites dedicated to punters reviewing the charms of various escorts, and even what you might think was a successful encounter does not guarantee a positive review. If only we could turn round and review them right back.

"Mmm." The cabbie circled a random block in Kensington for the third time. They must think I don't notice.

"So what was he like?"

"Perfect gentleman, actually." A disbelieving snort down the other end of the phone. "Had him wrapped round my little finger." Very quickly I got into the habit of saying that whether it was true or not. I don't want her to worry and I don't want to fall out of favor.

mardi, le 30 décembre

"There is a client, he wants to pee on you," the manager said. I swear if someone ever got hold of transcripts of my phone calls, they'd probably think I was a—oh wait, I am.

"He wants to what?" I asked, knowing very well what she said.

"Pee. On you. Don't worry, darling, not in your clothes. You will be in a bath."

"A bath of what? Urine?"

"No, just a normal bath."

I sighed weakly. "You know I don't do degradation." Not at work, at any rate. I know it sounds odd, but even when W was treating me worst, I knew it was because he cared. I'd be reluctant to let a stranger do anything similar.

"Oh, no, not like that at all, darling," she said. "He doesn't want you to be degraded. He wants to pee on a girl who enjoys it."

Eventually I agreed, but only with a significant markup in the usual fee.

The client was rather nice and seemed exceedingly shy. We talked for a little while and had a drink—spirits for me and a large beer for him. The better to fill the bladder with, I suppose. When it came time to do the deed, I stripped him from the waist down, got all my clothes off, and knelt in an empty bathtub.

He looked at me, looked at the wall above me, and sighed. Nothing happened for a couple of minutes. I was starting to get cold. "Is everything okay?" I asked.

"It's not going to happen. I'm too turned on," he said. He looked down again. "If I look at you, I'll get hard. If I look away, I'll think of what's going to happen, and get hard."

"Try thinking of something that doesn't turn you on."

"Such as?"

"Your mother shopping for underwear for you. With you in

tow. Aged thirty-five." He started to laugh. I felt the first trickle hit my neck, roll down my breasts.

Afterward I showered while he watched me. He started to make vague shy-guy noises as I dried my hair and dressed. "Are you okay?" I asked.

"I think I have some more," he said, blushing, gesturing toward his knob. "You don't have to say yes, but I don't suppose I could put it in a glass and——"

"Er, no thank you," I said. "Health and safety and all that."

"Some people drink it for their health," he offered.

"Yes, and some people think an all-meat diet is good for you." I put my coat on and kissed him on the cheek. "Perhaps another time, when I've had more warning."

mercredi, le 31 décembre

In London alone for New Year's Eve.

The Boy was supposed to visit—at least that's what I was told. Last night he rang after midnight to say he couldn't come up, in fact he had gone skiing, perhaps I could fly out and join him instead?

With less than twelve hours' notice. On December 31.

I hadn't even known he was on holiday. Why couldn't he get here? Because it would be too expensive to change his ticket, of course. I'm amazed that someone who professes so little ready cash can throw a pile together to hit the European slopes—but not to see in the new year with his girl. Nevertheless I scoured the Web to see if by some miracle I could be waking up in France. British Airlines were booking no flights before January 2. It was even too last-minute for Lastminute.com.

So I regretfully declined. He didn't seem that bothered, to be honest. Suspicious? Of course. His travel companion on this little jaunt is none other than the housemate who hates me.

Went into town for lunch, a haircut, and to wander round the Victoria and Albert Museum. I spied with my little eye . . .

. . . that everyone who got on the tube at King's Cross got off at Knightsbridge, leaving the crowded carriages virtually empty . . .

. . . a man walking two dogs—one huge rottweiler, one tiny pug. They were both burly, black-coated, and the rott took one step to every three of the pug's . . .

. . . an adolescent girl tucking into salmon and cream cheese on a bagel, with chips . . .

. . . three men walking together in matching black knitted caps . . .

. . . and three girls coming the other way in mismatching pink knitted scarves . . .

. . . on Exhibition Road just outside the Natural History Museum, leaves from this autumn have been mashed by thousands of tires to leave an orange-gold pattern in the street.

Janvier

Belle's A–Z of London Sex Work

H–J

H is for Hobbyist

A hobbyist is a man who is a habitual user of escort services. These range from the experienced and infinitely charming high tipper to the boorish tightwad who compares you unfavorably to every other prostitute he's been with. Be sure to treat every hobbyist as if he is the former. They will most likely write an Internet report on you.

I is for Invisibility

Don't stand in the lobby of a hotel on the way out talking to your manager on the phone about the customer and what her cut of the take is. I've seen people do it; it's horrid. What are you waiting for, hordes of adoring fans? Get out, get a cab, go home. Be discreet.

J is for Jealousy

When a regular customer—especially one you like or who tips well—moves on to another girl or otherwise inexplicably drops you, take it in your stride. They're not paying for sex because they want a relationship, silly. There will be others. There always are.

J is also for Jet Set

Very few girls will travel outside a hundred mile radius on a regular basis. A repeat client may well offer to take you around the world on his yacht, but don't be disappointed if it never exactly materializes. Even when they're paying for the sex, men are apt to inflate their income and connections to impress and amuse you. All I can offer is, don't count your frequent-flier miles before they hatch.

jeudi, le 1ᵉʳ janvier

N and I met in town last night to raise a drink and indulge in mutual holidaytide misanthropy. I hate going out on New Year's, but being alone is infinitely worse. N's preferred tipple these days is Bailey's on ice, which is virtually pudding in a glass. As I lifted my glass, a man we knew pushed past, spilling half my drink on my jeans.

"What's her problem?" I sniffed.

"Nothing a fortnight in a Turkish brothel wouldn't fix," N said. Thus inspired, we spent the rest of the evening compiling a list of people whose attitudes (we thought) would be much improved by such a holiday.

In need of a fortnight in a Turkish brothel (rough draft):

Naomi Campbell
Penelope Keith
Princess Anne
Cherie Blair
Pamela Anderson, though she may actually enjoy it
Blair's Babes
(E)liz(abeth) Hurley
Paris Hilton
Myleene Klass
Any Jagger ex or offspring
Condoleezza Rice
Jenna Bush

Jessica Simpson
actually, any blonde for whom the descriptors "It Girl" and
   "famous father" apply

vendredi, le 2 janvier

Regarding orgasms at work:

I don't. I don't equate number of orgasms with the level of enjoyment of sex, nor good sex with the ability to produce an orgasm. At the age of nineteen, if I remember the person and the conversation correctly, I realized that sex was about the quality of your enjoyment and that doesn't always mean coming.

On the other hand, I also remember that conversation largely consisting of comparing experiences with dropping acid. Nevertheless, the realization that sex is just an end in itself stayed with me.

Let's be honest, this is a customer service position, not a self-fulfillment odyssey. They're paying for their orgasm, not mine. Plenty of the men—more than you might think—never even come at all. They never imply it's a failure on my part. Sometimes they're just after human contact, a warm body, an erotic embrace. Most times, come to think of it.

The inability of punters to produce an orgasm in me is no way a comment on their shortcomings. As far as their part of the bargain goes, they're doing a great job, and I enjoy sex for more than the merely physical tingle. Being desired is fun. Dressing up is fun. No pressure to experience physical release for fear of damaging someone's ego, or give someone an orgasm for fear of never hearing from them again, is hella wicked.

Sometimes a race is a good day out—regardless of where you finished.

samedi, le 3 janvier

Text from the Boy:

Are you okay? Feeling sad because I'm afraid you don't want to talk to me.

I wonder if I'm abnormal sometimes. A little cold for love, slightly lacking in sentiment. As soon as someone's interest flags, my own feelings start to go that way too. As Clive Owen said in the film *Croupier*, hold on tightly—let go lightly.

I don't give people enough chances.

Maybe I know it's not right anyway. All romance is narcissism, A1 told me once. This was the same person who also told me women over thirty should never wear their hair long, so he's probably an unreliable source, but still. I'm doing us both a favor by not responding.

There are other things that have happened, things I never wanted to think or write about because I was afraid of being rash, in case everything straightened itself out. It might still. I could ring, or send a text, but they seem such poor approximations of communication. If I can't sort out what's in this head, how can I put it into intelligible sentences?

If I wait too long, the decision won't be mine to make anyway.

I decide to go out and spend all my money on underwear, then throw them about the room to decide my fate like a satiny, lace-gusseted I Ching. Let the gods of Beau Bra decide.

I bought a set in chocolate-colored lace, with pink satin ties at the sides of the knickers and between the cups of the bra. I don't think I got these for either work or Boyfriend. The carriage coming back was crowded with bargain hunters and tourists. I tried to guess what each shiny paper bag contained. A package of handkerchiefs? Comic books? Perfume? There was a mass exodus into the north of the city, people rushing off at each stop. Someone who can't wait to get home and won't even take off her coat before tearing through tissue paper. A man who was pulling the wrapping off a new CD already, dropping ribbons of plastic on the floor.

Tonight I am going out with friends to an annual dinner. The men will be stuffed into their dinner jackets, which have grown mysteriously smaller since last year, and grumble about the skimpy main course. The women will swish from table to table in jersey and diamante, hair smooth like petals.

The tube lurches closer to my stop. The song on my headphones is buoyant—the sort of pop confection on a thousand best-of-2003 lists. When I look up, I see how close the yellow handrail is to the ceiling light and brush the cover with my fingertips. A pram rocks on the unsteady journey, knocking over a mother's shopping bags. I can't help smiling. Further down the carriage, a bald man stares.

dimanche, le 4 janvier

N jeweled my arm for the formal event last night—purely platonically, you understand. Am still angry at the Boy and taking the hard line for now that "all men are twats, unless they're paying, in which case they're twats who are paying." N understands perfectly and accepts his appointment as "twat" with grace. This probably means he's trying to get me into bed.

We showered and dressed at mine, and I tied his bow tie before we left. He was planning to wear a ready-tied, but I insisted on the real thing. I will not be seen in public with a man whose tie falls into any of the following categories: clip-on, spinning, or metallic. There is a time and a place for comedy eveningwear. I believe it passed when Charles Chaplin shrugged off his mortal coil.

Throats dry, we stopped for a pre-revelry drink at a bar that was cunningly hidden under another bar. Several dozen other celebrants were there as well, and N introduced me around. A chirpy, raven-haired Nigella-alike planted herself to my left.

"Why, hello there," she twanged. "My name's T——." Her dress was doing a reasonable job of keeping her breasts restrained, but I didn't reckon on its chances for surviving the night.

I gave N a "do you know this woman?" look. He shot me a "no, do you think she'll sleep with me?" look.

She put her perfectly manicured hand on my knee. "I just love your accent!" she enthused. "Where are you from?"

"Yorkshire," I said. "And your good self?"

"Michigan."

Charming. But the crowd grew restless, and we moved on to the venue. Unfortunately, T—— and her date were sitting three tables from us. Dining at a table of mostly couples, I found myself seated next to the wife of a mutual acquaintance. She drunkenly looked me and N over. When he turned to talk to someone, she said, "So how long have you two been back together, then?"

"Er, ah, we're just seeing what happens. Only friends, you know."

"Of course you are." She gave me a sly wink to indicate that she didn't believe a word of it. This indictment might have carried more of a sting if she didn't simultaneously spill red wine down her dress.

The speeches were the highlight of the evening. A multiply medaled Paralympian with a seemingly endless supply of sex jokes, followed by a sport personality, followed by a paunchy silver-haired man. The quality of the speakers was such that even I, a rank amateur at anything smacking of nonsexual exertion, could pretend to be interested for twenty minutes.

Then it all broke down for the disco. I danced, I drank, I danced some more. Out of the corner of my eye, I noticed N on the sidelines bending T——'s ear. Good lad, I thought. After she went off to dance with her date, I sought him out.

"You sly dog. So did you get her number?"

"Actually, she was more interested in you."

"Really?" I looked back at the dance floor, where she was being spun round and round by three men. Probably an experiment in centrifugal force and its effect on fabric strain. So far as I could see, the dress was still refusing to budge—whether due to magic or double-sided tape, I don't know.

"Yeah, I think I ruined your chances though."

"How's that?"

"I said you'd only do it with her if I came along."

"You complete twat!" I punched his shoulder, probably hurting my fist more than anything else.

He kissed the top of my head. "Just saving you from yourself, dear."

lundi, le 5 janvier

SEX: A SPOTTER'S GUIDE

- *Sex Shop:* not normally known to sell sex as such. Lexical equivalent of calling a specialist vegetarian grocer a butcher.
- *Hot Sex:* reproduces, as nearly as possible, the visual effect of pornography. See also: Phone-In Sex.
- *Good Sex:* in which you get everything you want.
- *Bad Sex:* in which someone else gets everything he wants.
- *Sex Kitten:* a woman of reasonable charm, though often reliant on cantilevering lingerie.

- *Sexual:* usually related to the mating rituals of animal species or the burgeoning hormonal urges of youth. Word never used in an actual sexual episode without a lot of giggling. Exception that proves the rule, various Marvin Gaye songs.
- *Sex Education:* the interface between a banana and a condom. Not generally known to impart useful information.
- *Sex Bomb:* a weapon of mass destruction.

mardi, le 6 janvier

I rang the bell of the building; no answer from the speaker—he buzzed me straight up. He opened the door of the flat and disappeared into the kitchen for a drink. Inside, it was clean, almost sterile. Smoky glass mirrors everywhere—I was overwhelmed with the feeling of being in a restaurant. Rather incredible digs for someone the manager said was a student. Postgraduate scholarships probably extend far enough for a few pissups each term, but I doubt they cover having a lady of the night in for a session.

He: "Don't be so nervous."

Me (startled): "I am relaxed. So what is it you study?"

"I'll tell you later."

He told me his name. "Really?" I said. It's an odd, old-fashioned moniker. "My boyfriend is also called that." Ex, I scolded myself. Stop thinking about him in the present tense. We discussed the client's desire to move—to North London, which apparently has "the highest density of psychotherapists in the world." Knowing a few people round that way, I understand why perfectly.

He: "You're an odd one, I can't quite figure you out."

Me: "I'm fairly straightforward."

"An open book, right?"

"Something like that."

(later)

Me: "What is it you do again?"

He: "Psychoanalysis."

Which made us comrades, if not exactly colleagues. The conversation strayed to evolutionary biology and the role of pheromones in attraction. How well you like someone's smell is, apparently, related to the likelihood of producing children together with as few congenital defects as possible. Not the usual overture to incite romance, but it works well enough on me. He liked the sex intense, sensual, tongue-centric. I liked the mirrors. He held me open and took me anally, slithering in and out. After he came, I went to clean up and noticed a copy of Richard Dawkins's latest book in the bathroom.

Me (dressing): "I enjoyed that. And, you smell nice."

He: "Excellent, that means we can have children."

We both laughed. "Not quite yet." I dressed and left.

There were still shops open and I wanted to spend the money in my bag. Heels clattering, I walked through an underground subway. At the end of one tiled passage were boxes—homeless people. I am never sure whether to hold their gaze or not; swing wide of where they're sat or not. What is it about them that makes us so uncomfortable? Do the homeless have some kind of sympathetic magic that might rub off, and we will be rendered penniless if we dare get too close?

The men were young, talking. I caught the gaze of one. Broad Northern accents. I was aware of both the sound of my shoes echoing toward them and the weight of the money on my person. A kind person would just heave the notes in their direction, wouldn't she, I thought.

Rubbish, another part of my mind chimed in. They'd only use it on drugs.

Ooh, get you, high and mighty. Who just had sex for money.

Yes, well. At least I have a job. I'm not selling out. I'm not getting paid for something I wouldn't do for free anyway.

They might just be backpackers. Who would appreciate the cash.

They might just be rapists.

The corridor turned sharp right just past their makeshift camp. The two young men—quite good-looking, actually—looked up as I came near. "Out late?" one asked.

I smiled. Could tell them the truth. Won't. "Party," I said.

"Cool," the bearded one said. They went back to their conversation. Neither slowing nor swerving, I continued on out of sight.

mercredi, le 7 janvier

He: "White wine, I presume."

Me: "Why, how very thoughtful." (he presents a glass, we toast and sip) "Rather drier than usual."

"Thought I'd give it a try."

As a regular becomes more regular, rules slip a tiny bit. They're not supposed to be under the influence during an appointment—and neither are we—though a little alcohol isn't expressly forbidden. Having seen this particular man several times, I know that he must indulge in a spliff before he sees me. I can smell it, and am surprised it doesn't affect his performance.

Last night I arrived a few minutes early—Monday nights, light traffic—and caught him in the act.

Another habit he indulges in are inhalants during my visits. Now, I realize these aren't illegal (at least, I don't think they are), and am not opposed to drug-taking as such. Live and let live, victimless crime, and all that. I only rarely take anything stronger than a stiff drink—though those who knew me at uni would probably attest to the contrary.

Last night on his bedroom floor, I was sitting astride him. He, eyes closed, reached for the familiar small brown bottle and took a direct sniff. And then he offered it to me. What's the harm? I thought, and sniffed, and did so again when he picked it up ten minutes later.

And what a rush it was. I felt my scalp, face, and ears pounding, like when you blush but more so. Every sound seemed intensified, a little tinny. My fingertips felt like paws, a foot wide.

Thank goodness it only lasted a minute or so.

The inhalant, that is. The sex was rather longer.

jeudi, le 8 janvier

There are several things this job makes difficult to take seriously.

First: public transport. Perhaps in normal jobs, coming in twenty minutes late is excused with the "Northern Line, grumble, you know, bah" routine. But when a neglected husband has sixty minutes between lunch hour and his next meeting, and he took a Viagra and seriously has the horn, you cannot be late. The taxis and I are old friends now, darling.

Second: people giving you the eye on public transport. Maybe they think I'll follow them off to a hidden love nest? Or they'll follow me off and it will be love at first crowded, southbound-delays sight? No chance.

Third: one-night stands. Like the Army, I have fun and get paid to do it. Sometimes it's not as fun but I always get paid. I clock more oral sex in a week from customers than in my entire time at uni.

Fourth: boyfriend troubles. I don't want to be single and a prostitute. I don't want to be without him in my life. We called a truce. Yes, really.

Fifth: fashion. Flat boots, short hair, cropped trousers, ra-ra skirts? I'd never get work again.

vendredi, le 9 janvier

It was the Boy's birthday, so he came up to visit. Things were nice—he was clean and polite and clearly on best behavior. For most of the night, things were easy, relaxed, even. I leaned more and more heavily on his arm and he responded with an arm around me. Thank goodness, I thought. Just a blip. Nothing to fret over.

We decided to leave our friends in Wimbledon early (the better to strain the bed, my dear) with the flimsiest of excuses, only to run into epic stoppages on the tube. After being stuck at Earl's Court for an hour, Himself nodding off on my shoulder, a change of route was announced for our train. So we leapt off at Gloucester Road to make a transfer. Alas, the Piccadilly line was also toast.

I made an executive decision and dragged us outside to flag down a black cab. "How much is this going to cost us?" the Boy asked.

"Don't worry, I'll cover it," I said. Noticed him leaning in to quiz the driver himself. "Oh, come on, you silly," I scolded, bundling him into the cab.

I directed the driver first to an appropriate bank to withdraw cash. The Boy was sulking when I got back in the car. "The meter went back on while we were waiting," he grumbled. "Probably added at least a pound to the fare."

I wasn't too bothered. "He was waiting a couple of minutes," I said. Also, having grabbed a black cab instead of a minicab, I was fairly certain that—whatever the fare—he wouldn't try to drive us all over hither and yon. I live out in the relative sticks and forty-pound round-trips into town are not unheard of. In the course of work, naturally, it's an expense the client covers. Considering the time and the trip, if we got in for around twenty I'd be grateful.

The Boy pouted, withdrew his hand from mine and sulked out the window.

A bit later, we were about two miles from home. "I think we should get out here, we're close enough," the Boy said. The meter had just ticked over twenty quid, but I was in heels and uninterested in spending half an hour in the cold when we could be in bed making sweet lurrrve.

I looked at him sharply. "If you want to get out and walk, I won't stop you." I had no intention of going anywhere. This was his birthday, my treat, and what's money compared to being home in each other's arms?

The light turned green. The driver nervously checked his mirror. "Um, are you getting out here mate?" he asked.

"No." The Boy crossed his arms and sunk lower in the seat.

We were at mine inside five minutes, safe and sound. Mortified at the scene, I tipped the driver three pounds. We walked up the steps. I unlocked the door and stepped inside. "Well," I said.

"Well."

"Are you going to apologize? Because I am livid."

"I can't believe you let him fleece you like that."

"I can't believe you acted like that. It's only money."

"It's a lot of money."

"It's my money to spend, and I want to spend it on getting us home together. It's no more than a round at the pub would have cost."

Cue a nightlong argument in which, ironically, the whore bears the standard for Money Is Meaningless, while her boyfriend recounts favors done and expenses incurred by him throughout the past year. If he truly wants to change careers, perhaps accounting would suit. It ended rather abruptly with me writing a check for something approaching my hourly fee and shoving it into his hand. "Will that do?" I asked. "Does that make you happier?"

After a strained morning he wandered off to chat up the neighbor and palpate her shinier, better techno toys. There is no worse sound than the greedy giggles of a redhead displaying a PDA in juxtaposition with her cleavage.

I spent the better part of an hour scanning train schedules.

samedi, le 10 janvier

We were exhausted from arguing all night. He had a train to make at London Bridge. I was meeting friends and we left the house at the same time. At the tube station, we sat with an empty seat between us. He pored over a map of London pointlessly.

A Northern Line tube arrived. The carriages near our end were empty. I jogged up and hopped on. The doors remained ajar a few moments. I sat and looked around—he hadn't followed me on. I looked to both ends of the carriage. Popped my head out the door. The Boy wasn't there. The doors closed.

I sat down again, put my head on the large bag in my lap, sighed. A couple of stops passed. People crowded in, some groups, talking. I got off to change at Euston and momentarily thought about going back. No, I figured, he'd be long gone. But I stood on the platform, waited through a few arriving trains, just in case. After ten minutes I gave up. Sat down across from a young Asian man, a girl wearing a headscarf and headphones, and a bored-looking blonde with her shopping.

Just before London Bridge a face popped in front of mine. I jumped. It was him. I was surprised, didn't know what to say. This was obviously the wrong reaction.

"Oh, never mind," he said, going to stand by the door.

"Where did you come from?" I asked.

"What do you mean? I've been here all along."

"On this train? On this carriage?"

"Yes." He sniffed, held the handrail, looked out the window as the train slowed into the tube station. "Thanks for screaming. Now everyone thinks I'm a mugger or something."

"I didn't scream. You just startled me. Are you sure you were on this train? You can't have been."

"I was standing right next to you the whole way."

"No, I looked around. I waited at Euston. You can't have been."

He stepped off the train, onto the platform. A stream of people parted to flow around his bulk. "If you want to talk to me, get off and talk to me."

I sat down again. "I can't. If you want to talk to me, get on."

"No, you get off."

The doors started to close. I said his name, strained, my voice sharp and high. "Don't be stupid. Come on."

The doors closed, we pulled away. Last time I saw the Boy, he was waving.

I sighed. The train was almost empty. The blonde woman with the bags leaned across. "He was lying to you," she said. "He got on the tube at Bank."

dimanche, le 11 janvier

Anal sex is the new black.

Hands up if you remember when big-name porn stars didn't go there, when no one said it out loud, when the only people who presumably made regular trips up the poop chute were gay men and prostate examiners. A man who suggested his wife grab her ankles and take it like a choirboy was probably courting divorce, or at the very least burnt suppers for a month.

As with the mass amateurization of everything, though, anal has gone mainstream in a big way. Girls who used to ask whether you can go down on a boy and still be "technically" a virgin now wonder whether opening the back door still leaves you theoretically pure.

Hurrah, I say, because anal's wonderful. Then again I had the benefit of being introduced to the practice gently and considerately over a matter of weeks, by a man whose desire for me to be able to take him inspired the necessary patience to persevere. He started with massaging and stimulating the anus, then moved on to inserting his own well-lubed fingers. It wasn't long before small vibes were introduced. When we finally got to the main event, I was begging him to do it.

And other folks must be catching on too, because simply everyone does it these days. By the time it was mentioned on *Sex and the City*, all my friends shrugged. "So what?" they wanted to know. "We've been doing that for yonks."

I fully anticipate by next year Charlotte Church will have a glittery T-shirt that reads "My Barbie takes it up the ass." Maybe I should make one and send it to her.

Yes, anal. The new black. Out there is not so out there anymore. Last night N and I were perusing a top-shelf mag he picked up for me, one page of which featured a woman of grandmother age being fisted in both holes. And she was smiling. And, I wasn't even fazed. Few things shock me, really. But there is one that always gets to me—every time.

I know anal sex is the new black, because my bloody mother just rang to talk about it.

But as long as I had her on the phone, I thought I could break the news about the Boy. To her credit, she didn't say a thing until I was finished. "Poor little creature," she said, and it was just at that moment I felt the first tears dropping. Yes. Poor, poor me. What luck I have such a sympathetic mother.

Who then made me wait on the line as she turned to tell the whole story to my father, verbatim.

They agreed I should go home for a couple of days. I was powerless to argue.

lundi, le 12 janvier

My head fell further toward the surface of the table. I didn't want the steaming mug of tea in my hands. I didn't want breakfast. My mother sighed. She obviously wanted to say something. "I suppose at least each failed relationship raises my standards for the next one," I grumbled.

"Honey, don't you worry that someday your standards will get so high no one will satisfy them?"

If I had the energy to lift my forehead off the rim of the mug, I would have given her the evil eye to end all evil eyes. "I don't even know why it happened," I groaned. "I mean, I know why it happened, but not globally why."

Father rattled his paper and looked concerned. "Don't worry, sweetheart," he said. "He was probably seeing some other girl and just looking for a reason to end it."

"Oh, that helps very much, ta."

Come to think of it, maybe he was. Oh, there were a few times, a few texts, a few phone calls that seemed odd at the time. And one big thing, several months back. "You never surprise me," he used to say. He said it often. Usually when we were in the throes of a gentle argument, when my attitude rubbed up against his ego and the first word someone said wrong threatened to tip everything into oblivion. "You never surprise me," he'd say, and anticipating the coming list of Things I Have Done Wrong in the Last Year, I would go to another room and disconnect: closed door, television, toilet, whatever it takes. I already knew the list off by heart. It ranged from a brief period in which I went back to an ex, to less concrete items like whether or not I introduced him to other people as my boyfriend or as just a friend. Headphones on. One hour of silence would make him apologize.

I was in an expansive mood one morning in December. The sun was just coming up and, for reasons I cannot quite put a finger on, I woke with the birds. Never surprise you? We'll see. I walked down to the Kentish Town train station and waited for a train on the southbound platform.

A taxi dropped me at his doorstep at the other end. The air was damp and smelled salty. It was still before nine in the morning. The back door is usually unlocked and I didn't want to wake his housemate. I crept up the stairs and put a hand on the handle of his door.

Turned. No luck. Turned harder—Regency house, sometimes the weather makes the fixtures stick—no. Locked. I tapped on the door. Already my heart was sinking.

There was a noise of whispering inside. The creaking bed. "Hello?" came a whisper from the other side of the door. His voice.

"It's me," I said.

"Oh." More muffled talking.

"Um, can you let me in?"

"Wait in the back garden. I'll meet you there."

Heart sinking? It was obliterated. My stomach took up residence somewhere in the middle of my throat. "What's going on?" I squeaked.

"Can you go outside?" he said, only slightly louder. There was more noise from inside the room.

"No," I said, raising my voice. "Let me in." He came outside— very quickly. Shut the door behind him firmly. I lunged for the door. He held me off easily.

"For goodness' sake—don't embarrass me," he said. His eyes

pleaded with me. No way, I thought. There's someone in there. But there was no getting past him. He started to walk down the stairs, taking me, struggling, with him.

"What the hell is going on?" I shrieked. I could hear the other bedroom doors in the house opening, and his housemates came out to see what was happening. He bullied me into the kitchen. There was a girl in there, yes, he said. Friend of his housemate. In the spare foldaway bed? No, in his bed. Who was she? I screamed. Don't embarrass me, he kept saying. Don't embarrass me. She was a medic, he said. An army officer. A friend of a friend, but nothing happened. Like fuck it didn't, no one shares a bed and look— you're not wearing anything under that dressing gown, are you? I dove at his crotch. It was true, he wasn't.

"Trust me," he pleaded. "Go to the cafe at the end of the road. We'll talk about it later?"

"Trust you? Trust you? Can I trust you?"

His face fell. He made accusations. He played the Whore Card.

The phrase "losing your rag" has always seemed imprecise. I didn't know what it meant, exactly. One of those sayings that defies explanation and only makes sense in context.

This was the context. I lost my rag.

"You have never found me in bed with someone else. You never will. This is the price I pay for honesty?" I am digging my own grave, I thought. No one values the truth over perceived fidelity. I fuck other people for a living, and yes, I tell him as much as he wants to know, but, oh. Oh. Oh. My heart has always been in the right place, I think. My head stopped using words to communicate.

I left. I went to the shore and waited for the shops to open, bought a bag of coconut-covered marshmallows. The water was high and the wind against the tide made white horses on the sea. My phone rang and rang—the Boy. I turned it off. He left messages. Nothing happened, he swore up and down. It was a plot by his housemate, the one who hates me. The medic (blonde, thin, I waited long enough in the bushes over the road to see her come out. But not pretty. Not pretty) was very drunk, she fell asleep in his bed in her underwear, he was too tired to set up the spare bed for himself or go down and sleep on the sofa. Whatever. I didn't ring back. I caught a train home and took three appointments that day. After, smelling of sweat and latex, I listened to Charles Mingus and drank port until the wee hours. We made it up through texts, over a few days.

Still sat at my parents' breakfast table, the mug of tea cold in my grip. Daddy refolded the paper and left it at my elbow. Go home, go to work, get over it, I said to myself.

mercredi, le 14 janvier

I ran some errands shortly before an appointment and walked to the hotel from the bank in full-on makeup, suit, and heels. As I passed the park a man stopped.

"My God, you're beautiful. Are you a model?"

Cripes, has that line ever actually worked? "No, I work near here." Think fast—what's near here? "Over in Royal Albert Hall." I couldn't have picked a more unlikely place, could I?

He: "You like it there?"

Me: "It's pretty nice. The people I work with are interesting."

"Plenty of prima donnas, right?"

"Yes." (looking obviously at watch) "Well, I'm off to meet a friend for lunch, have to run."

"Are those real stockings?"

"Of course!"

"You're just too gorgeous. I wish I could take you out."

"Well, you never know. See you around."

"Bye."

jeudi, le 15 janvier

The self-fisting is getting remarkably easier with practice. For those who would rather watch than to touch—and there are plenty of those—this is proving very popular. However, I don't think any amount of practice would enable anal fisting, although someone did want to see how many fingers I could get up the back passage whilst he fucked me. I could feel the swollen head of his cock clearly through the narrow wall of tissue separating the two orifices, and wiggled the tips of my fingers to tickle his shaft. He came quickly, stayed hard, fucked again, repeat.

He: (falling back on bed after the third go in one hour) "I used to be better at this, really."

Me: (pulling up stockings) "How do you mean?"

"The old man's had it. I'd be surprised if it gets up again any time in the next month."

"I wouldn't know, being a woman, but I think he's done admirably." (patting the now-wizened bit of flesh) "Good job, you. Have a well-deserved rest."

"You really like what you do, don't you?"

"I think it would be hard to take if I didn't. My imagination is not quite sufficient to detach my mind from double penetration."

vendredi, le 16 janvier

N and I drank cups of tea at mine and listened to the radio. "Alright then," he said. "You're abandoned on an island in the South Pacific, which five records would you take?"

"A lot of rock, a lot of blues." I thought a moment. "Probably at least three blues albums."

"On a desert island by yourself? Isn't that a bit depressing?"

"I'm already alone on a desert island. Except this isn't a desert, and it's cold and wet."

"Remember you do have the odd man Friday," he said, patting my feet. We fell asleep together on the sofa listening to Robert Johnson.

samedi, le 17 janvier

These are a few of my favorite things (that punters never ask for):

- For me to come for real. Why should they? With someone I've just met, who doesn't know the unspoken road map to my body, it'll take something like a geological age with his tongue propelled by more drive than an industrial bandsaw. Of course I fake it, when asked at all.
- Glass marbles. Infinitely better than the rubbery love-bead variety. Cheaper than a glass dildo. Scales up well according to size and relaxation of orifice. The sound they make when they come out is as delicious as the temperature change going in.
- Food sex. I have never, ever been paid to lick chocolate sauce off someone or have it licked off me. In private, though, I like to think myself an excellent and carefully maintained plate (N.B.: does not include insertion of vegetables, which you don't eat afterward anyway).
- To turn up in my regular clothes. Random-person sex is cool. Random-person sex with someone who looks random is even better. Also I'm very lazy.
- Bathing him afterward. I love soaping a man's body, the slightly submissive attitude of kneeling to run my hands down the pillar of his legs, gently lifting each foot in turn to wash it. I adore drying a man, too: imagining what I

would want dried first (face and hair), what needs gentle patting (armpits and genitals) and what might get forgotten (back of knees, between the shoulder blades). Plenty want to wash me, though, so perhaps they are acting on the same desire.

- Rimming. Given a thorough wash with hot soapy water beforehand, I will do this. It feels like trying to push yourself into pursed lips. It's a challenge, and the tiniest flicker of your tongue goes further there than anywhere else. It's cunnilingus on the miniature scale. As with the last one though, they do it to me all the time. I shouldn't complain, really.
- To imitate an animal. For some reason I imagined they would. They don't.
- To imitate characters from *The Simpsons*. It has nothing to do with sex, but I'm pretty good at it—especially Milhouse and Comic Book Guy. Who knows, maybe I'll meet a man with a Patty and Selma fetish, and then my ship will have truly come in.

But for tonight, I have a date. A real date with someone who uses my real name and rings me on my real number. Okay, he may be a hologram, but I cannot know for certain yet.

dimanche, le 18 janvier

I haven't had a proper first date in ages. He's an acquaintance of N's, which gave us a conversational springboard, but I was quickly growing addicted to his looks, his voice, and his sense of humor. It surprised me to feel just as awkward and off-kilter flirting with someone as it always had before. Did I get a bit nervous having to leave a message on his answerphone? Check. Did I deliberate over what I was going to wear on our date? Check. Obsessing over the details, including Googling his name every few hours? Too right I did. Did my heart speed up just a tiny bit on seeing a text or e-mail from him? You betcha.

So we went out—the details are meaningless—and talked around and around each other, and around the topic of how mutually attracted we were. I kept looking at his hands when I thought he wouldn't notice. He must have been looking at mine, because all of a sudden, on the train, we were holding hands (dear God, we were holding hands) and he was exploring the spaces between my fingers with his lips (just shiver) and I put my head on his shoulder (yes, it fit perfectly) and he smelled my hair (oh, yes, please).

Then we went and fucked it up by having fucking.

Maybe it was the glass or three of wine. The music, which was just at the right bpm to make my head spin. But then I so did what I should not have done—I went straight from cuddling and kissing into Whore Mode.

And this poor thing, he got the works. The little squeals. The wrist restraints. The full-on, sweat-soaked, bed-rattling, neighbor-waking, deep-throating, dirty-talking, facial-cumshot, use-me-baby-till-you-use-me-up works. He fell asleep straight after but I couldn't close my eyes because I knew what had just happened. I had utterly hot, but completely soulless sex with someone who—up to that point—I actually wanted to see more of.

There's that line about the likelihood of buying the cow when the milk's on sale, you know the one I mean?

So we woke early and dressed. He escorted me to the station and I caught the first train home. I couldn't look at him and felt like an utter idiot. Note to self, never have sex on a first date.

lundi, le 19 janvier

Last night I dreamt about the Boy.

It was in a restaurant-cum-bar-cum-tunnel-to-the-underworld kind of place, located in a crumbling religious monument and with a playground out the back (can't explain; dreams are just that way) and I was having a drink with a girl from the gym with great tits. Great Tits and I were having a conversation in which I was outlining the end of the affair, and she asked his name.

I said his first name. She said his second, loudly. "Ah, you know each other?" I was about to ask, when I turned around and saw GT was addressing him directly. He was there. Sitting with his new girlfriend, a well-known porn star.

Cue major discomfort as Great Tits and the Boy went through greeting procedures. I smiled at the porn star, who was inexplicably naked. Then the Boy and I were walking outside, on a grassy upward-sloping tunnel to the playground, and I stopped and lay down, and he lay down behind me. He said he missed me, he missed fucking me. I felt him grow harder and slide up between my thighs.

"You can't," I said. And he pushed the first inch inside.

At this point the porn star (who, it should be pointed out for the extremely dim, is NOT dating my ex in real life, this is just a dream), still inexplicably naked, positions herself on her back in front of me. I dive in. She tells me she doesn't like direct clitoral stimulation. I rub her through the hood and tongue her inner lips. The Boy mounts me from behind.

I woke up half-wrapped in a bedsheet. I didn't come. I can't stop thinking about his hands, his hands. The way his hair felt. The smell of the skin on his back in summer.

mardi, le 20 janvier

They say when it rains, it pours, but is there a saying for the complete opposite? Perhaps "When it's dry, it's arid"?

The most recent bookings have all been time-wasters and mind-changers. There is always a certain amount of this at work—like the man who wanted to book an overnight but didn't ring the manager when he got to the hotel. So while I knew first name, time, and location, I wasn't about to turn up and go round all the floors knocking at each door.

Can you imagine? "Room service? No? I'll try next door then. . . ."

He did contact the agency a few days later to apologize. Seems he simply didn't write our number down and couldn't ring again. Of course.

Other times the cancellation comes from my end—I get nervous if someone changes time and location more than once. Too many overly specific requests also tend to put me on guard. Dressing up is fine. Dressing up like your septuagenarian grandmother and being asked to bring my own mortuary foam is not. A finely tuned Creep Radar is a necessary part of the business. This is, after all, an occupation that ranks somewhere between nuclear core inspector and rugby prop for job safety. Except I'm issued neither a foil suit nor a pair of spiked boots for protection.

I have also learned never to trust a booking made more than three days ahead, as these people almost never call back to verify the appointment details. At first I imagined my work diary filling up weeks ahead. But the most reliable calls come six to twelve hours in advance, even from regulars. The longer someone has to think about it, it seems, the heavier guilt weighs on them. Or maybe they decide to do it themselves. A copy of *Penthouse* isn't exactly going to give you a blowjob and a backrub, but then again, it's more likely to be found hanging around your local off-license and can be had for under a fiver.

Lame excuses, cancellations, aggressive patients, dubious over-the-counter remedies. Now I know how a doctor feels.

At least the four As have descended on Jour Towers for a few days. Quote of the night:

A2: "So what are we doing tomorrow?"

A1: "Well, we'll have to get that bottle of whisky first thing in the morning, definitely."

You couldn't buy a better bunch of chaps, I swear.

mercredi, le 21 janvier

N is approaching the one-year anniversary of a breakup. I am of the belief that it usually takes as long as the relationship itself for the pangs to subside, which means he should have been over this one, oh, about nine months ago. His ex was a bit of flighty girl. Frankly I never thought they'd make it. I was right, but this isn't the sort of thing you go telling your friends straight after the fact. Example:

"I sent her a Christmas card and a birthday card and she hasn't so much as texted me."

I'm thinking: Well, of course not, silly boy. She's probably married to an oil tycoon and has a litter of children by now. I'm saying: "How dare she. That is so profoundly unfair."

N has a charming ability to think the world of his exes. Naturally, I'm not complaining. "Pedestal-worthy" is a modifier more of my acquaintances should use. In the wake of his ex's refusal to contact him, N is seeking out every other immortal beloved to have crossed his path—*muy High Fidelity*. It started last month with His First.

They exchanged phone calls for a few weeks. He was sweet

about it. Talking to her seemed to bring a lot of memories to the fore—how they met and courted, secretly, over several years. Why she never wanted to marry or have children. The last time he saw her in person, the sad, strained final farewell. Like everyone else, I love a good passion. I love a good story even more.

Then N arranged to meet His First in person, and his reminiscences went from the rosy-hued to the frankly sexual. He's never had a woman since with bigger breasts. She taught him everything a man ever need know about going down on a woman. How she reacted to the taste of come. And so on.

"God, if she'll let me, I'd love to have her again. Just once, just for old time's."

I'm thinking: There isn't a single ex I would take back. I'm at least 95 percent sure of that. Usually. Depending on which way the wind's blowing. I'm saying: "Darling, great idea. I bet it's even better than before."

"You mean they're even better than before," he said, making a groping gesture in midair with his hands.

"Of course. Of course that's what I meant."

He looked at me and smiled. "So if I manage to get her in bed, and she's up for it, would you do a threesome with us?"

I'm thinking: Not a chance, hon. She'll never say yes, and even if she did, I wouldn't. I'm saying: "Go for it, sweetie. The more the merrier!"

N put his arm around my shoulders. "You're the best woman ever, you know that?" Happily he will continue to believe so for the time being—I am reliably informed that His First didn't let him get any more intimate than an awkward hug at the end. He can go on thinking I'm a sexual saint and it'll never be put to the test.

jeudi, le 22 janvier

"Darling, can you make a booking for this afternoon?"

I was varnishing my toenails and feeling slightly cranky. "No, I'm afraid it's my time of the month." I suspect she either doesn't pay very close attention to our cycles or is too polite to call me on an obvious lie.

Except in this case it wasn't a lie. It was a lie when I used it about, oh, two weeks ago.

"This maaaaan, he is very rich," she said. "He keeps asking only for you."

"Can't do it," I snapped, wondering where on earth I'd managed to leave the ibuprofen, and other incrementally more important things. Like not smudging the nail varnish as it dried, and reading the paper. "I don't think he'd want blood on the sheets."

"It's a hotel call."

"The hotel management. Whomever," I said.

"Darling, what I tell the other girls is, just use a bit of sponge."

A bit of sponge? "A bit of sponge?" What was this, some demented nineties contraception allusion, or the start of a slippery slope involving fulfilling Greek diving-suit fantasies?

"You just cut off a corner of a clean sponge, darling, and put it up your—"

"Yes, okay, I think I see where that's going." I shuddered. Having once—years ago—inadvertently forgotten a tampon during sex, I was not keen to repeat the experience. The thought of someone banging away at my cervical door as I grew ever more worried about the chances of retrieving a scrap of synthetic foam and, by extension, the inverse chances of ending up in the emergency room sounded distinctly untempting.

And barring that, what if he was hoping for a deep dive of the digits into my finger-licking nether regions?

"It should last the hour. When the other girls are on their time, I never book them for longer than an hour. You will be fine, darling."

She was right, of course, though perhaps explaining the missing bit of washing-up implement to whomever next walks through my kitchen will be awkward. As for retrieval, truth be told, the client never even came close to troubling the sponge.

vendredi, le 23 janvier

To my great surprise, the man I went on a first date with rang back. He hadn't taken my guilty conscience as a hint at all—in fact, he'd been hiking in the North and simply not been able to ring. So much for my surgical brush-off, then. But just hearing his voice did make me smile. Perhaps it is worth pursuing after all.

He invited me out to a play. Unfortunately, I do like to keep evenings free for work, and haven't been terribly in the black of late. Must be that pesky habit of spending all my money on underwear. I politely declined, but said we must get together later in the week.

"You can brush me off, I won't take offense," he said.

"Oh no, I'm not at all," I backpedaled. "I really would like to see you soon." It's not every man who offers to take you on the town after knowing he can score with you regardless. Most would take first-date sex as an excuse to crack open a can of beer and watch Grand Prix on all forthcoming dates.

But First Date, I suspected, was nicer than that. Much nicer. "You promise?" I could hear the smile in his voice.

"Guarantee," I said, smiling back.

samedi, le 24 janvier

It is the Chinese New Year celebrations. This is not something I would usually know, except today on leaving an appointment the client gave me two gold-foil-wrapped fortune cookies. I didn't think fortune cookies were particularly traditional, but enjoy the thought that perhaps a randomly chosen slip of paper in a cookie holds the key to one's future. It's no less likely to be true than looking in the back of the *Metro*, anyway.

The first fortune read:

You will receive a cheerful call next week.

which amuses me no end. Was that meant to be the next week after the fortune was printed, the week after the cookie was opened, or just "next week" in general? A pedant could thus claim that if said cheerful call does not materialize between now and the 29th, it was in fact meant to mean next week.

The second fortune read:

You will appear on television in the next year.

which is at once more frightening (bloody hell, I certainly hope not) and yet subject to the same restrictions as the first fortune. If I don't appear on TV in the Year of the Monkey, then clearly it will be during the Year of the Cock.

For completely unrelated reasons, I am now looking forward to the Year of the Cock.

dimanche, le 25 janvier

An odd side effect of this job is the sensitivity to personal smell.

I don't usually shower straight after the appointments. There's one regular client who bathes me at his house with a sponge and almond soap, but I tend to wait with others and shower at home.

So I may be walking out to a cab, or going up the stairs of my flat, and catch a whiff. Not of sex, not specifically—just someone's scent. The smell of their skin or hair or hand cream that rubbed off on my skin and clothes. Sometimes it's mixed with my own smell as well, and I know as soon as I can I will undress and sniff the creases of my clothing.

Will I remember these men if I smell them again? They say scent is the most powerfully memory-associated of all the senses. And that it is also the most neglected. It is so ephemeral. You become quickly tired of strong odors, but can't get enough of the tease, the slightest waft of an almost-remembered association.

The Boy smelled strong but not unpleasant. He used to sweat incredible amounts. After a long session in the bedroom he would lift himself up, sweat dripping down his back and chest. The smell was light, the taste salty; sometimes I would lick him dry. Even a bit of heavy petting will cause droplets to come out on his back. One touch and his palms go damp. He swore high and low that I was the only woman to have had this power over him. I joked that he must be part dog: a panting animal.

Crossing the street I smelled a cologne that must have been the same as the psychoanalyst used. I remember touching the smooth green bottle in his bathroom. One morning I put on a pair of shoes that inexplicably reminded me of a client from earlier in the week. Did I think at the time "This man smells of leather/old sneakers/sweaty socks"? No. But there was a deep note of similarity, and by lunchtime, I had to take them off because I couldn't stop thinking about work.

But these were both recent, and no test of long-term memory.

Sometimes a man will walk by who smells of A1. We've been friends so long our intimacy seems like an epoch ago. He smelled of hot sand. I am always tempted to follow these people wherever they are going. To catch their elbows before they disappear into the crowd at a tube station, or scribble a note to slip into their pockets. I want to know what scent they use. To ask what right they have to smell like what, for me, will always be sex itself.

lundi, le 26 janvier

N has a friend, Angel, who is also a working girl. I see her around occasionally—we share some of the same haunts.

I've always admired her figure but never really wanted it. All womanly curves have been banished in favor of narrow thighs and a perfect arse. She's a sculpted triumph of engineering, all legs and long hair, and toned to within an ounce of her life. It wouldn't be the worst thing in the world to wake up one day in her Versace-clad body. It possibly would be the worst thing in the world to actually try to achieve that shape.

I was out and about a few nights ago and nipped to the ladies' to reapply lipstick. Unhappily, it was one of these ultramodern places with a troughlike sink where the water splashes everywhere and a too-narrow mirror lit obliquely from below reflects the space between your collarbone and chin. Flattering to exactly no one.

Having ascertained that the toilet was designed by someone who hated women, I turned round to see Angel crouched on the floor, sobbing. I almost didn't stop. She hadn't seen me yet. But something about the fragile bow of her heaving shoulders made it impossible to walk away. "Are you okay?" I whispered, kneeling beside her.

It all came out in fits and starts—first man trouble, then family problems, then a recent surgery gone wrong, then the reason for the surgery. It turned out Angel was the victim of a notorious attack several years ago. It was the anniversary of the incident.

"That was you?" I whispered. She nodded. "I'm so, so sorry."

She showed me the cuts from the reconstructive surgery she'd been undergoing, just at her hairline. I hugged her gently. I told her about my last few years, losing family and futures, how sometimes you feel like a cork tossed around on an ocean. How being told to buck up and stiff-upper-lip it often makes things worse. Yes, the world really is an unfair place. Yes, these things are sent to try us. No, you don't have to smile all the time, every day. How it wasn't her fault.

I stayed in there almost an hour while people walked in, walked out, stepped over and around us. Then Angel stood up, straightened her clothes, ran a brush through her hair. And while I didn't expect this was the start of something beautiful between us, I thought perhaps there had been a connection made. Not mates watching telly on a Friday night and scarfing chocolate. But maybe a gentle, unspoken acknowledgment. A subtle nod across a room. A sorority of two.

So I saw her again last night. Another club, another toilet. I said hello. And she utterly blanked me. I ran straight to N, wounded by the snub. "Yeah," he said. "I would have a lot of time for her, but she can go from needy to brittle in about ten seconds, and you never know which one you're going to get."

mardi, le 27 janvier

Rang the manager to discuss upcoming work schedules. She was giggling too much to talk, which is distinctly not in keeping with her Eastern-European-glacial-über-babe facade.

"Er, are you okay?" Maybe I caught her at a bad time, or in the throes of gleefully administering cracks of the whip to laggard customers, or something.

"Darling, have you heard The Darkness?"

"Yes?"

"Oh, they just crack me up. They are so funny."

"Mmm. Well, in their way, I suppose." Perhaps I am excessively judgmental in believing that anyone who looks like the bastard child of Robert Plant and Steve Perry via Austin Powers's dentist has no business as a rock god. "Is it okay if I have Monday and Wednesday nights off until further notice?"

"Of course, darling. Take as much as you need." She then broke into a warbling rendition of "Get Your Hands off My Woman," which was marred by the fact that her falsetto was singularly incapable of approaching the stratospheric heights of the original. I sincerely hope she wasn't prancing around in a pair of lace-up white PVC trousers at the time. Then again, there would probably be unheard-of prices for such a performance (if indeed it hasn't already become a regular feature of the Spearmint Rhino oeuvre).

Someone asked recently what services I would be unwilling to provide, and I was unable to think of anything good. Now "imitating stick-insect Freddie Mercuries from Lowestoft" has become the first entry on the list.

mercredi, le 28 janvier

Last night I had friends over, not so much a celebration as an excuse to clear the pantry of bottles that have been hanging around since time out of mind. Rang a few people, sent a few e-mails, all very last-minute. Happily, chez Jour is just large enough to accommodate the dozen or so who saw fit to turn up without anyone having to go out on the roof. And I'd hate to do that to a body in this weather, really I would.

At one point, discussing the painting of the Italian Renaissance and the Low Countries, the conversation segued elegantly to the revelation that there is an exhibition at the Royal Academy of pictures of women with come on them. If true, I am so there.

By 3 a.m. I was left with two rather drunken but helpful guests who collected bowls and glasses, loaded the dishwasher, and shooed out the neighbor's cat. But they were clearly not in any condition to drive. Sleeping arrangements had to be sorted. Unfortunately, the two remainders were N and First Date, the fellow I disastrously slept with last week.

We hung on to the last shreds of conversation until it was far too late to do anything else. N was clearly not going anywhere in a hurry, and neither was First Date—I expect he wanted to get me alone again. It was well past my accustomed bedtime and I hoped one or the other of them would give up and go home, but they did not. "Well," I said. "The bed sleeps two and there are three of us—so it's the sofa for some unlucky soul, I believe."

They looked at each other. They looked at me. Neither volunteered for the sofa. Neither volunteered for the bed.

"Seeing as the two of you are both tall, why don't you boys take the bed? I'm the only one short enough to sleep here easily." Again, no response. "Don't all volunteer at once, guys."

Another minute of silence passed while I tried to decipher the eyebrow semaphore that passed between them. "I'll have the sofa," First Date offered. We took turns changing in the bathroom and I brought out a quilt and two blankets before turning in. First Date spread out the blankets.

"It's going to be cold tonight," I said. "Won't you use the quilt?"

He shrugged. "Leave it out, just in case."

N and I went up to the bedroom. N shut the door. "Don't do that," I whispered. "He'll think we're having sex." I pulled it ajar.

"Why do you care? Besides, he's probably already asleep."

I didn't know why I cared. It just seemed a bad idea to close the door completely.

A few hours later I woke, mouth dry from too much alcohol. Walked down to the kitchen for a glass of water. First Date was curled tightly on the couch. He'd put on the quilt and looked very cold indeed. I went back up to the bedroom, took out the sheepskin, and wrapped it around his feet. He didn't wake.

jeudi, le 29 janvier

People are either more trusting than I expect them to be or I appear more trustworthy than I am. Recently I successfully strong-armed the landlady into a spot of redecoration at my place. With the excuse that most of the kitchen fittings need replacing anyway, I have made the case for a full-on Chintz Removal which will hopefully culminate in a pagan ritual in which all Colefax and Fowler prints are gleefully thrown onto a crackling blaze.

In the meantime, I will be experiencing minor household disturbance. Not unbelievable, mind, just inconvenient. I was talking to one of the As about the impending redesign recently.

"Well, if they get their pants together at work, I'll be at a conference the next fortnight. Do you want the keys to mine?"

"Surely, darling, but aren't you afraid I'll spill something on the carpet?" A is notoriously fussy about his home and has been known to reserve only a single shelf for his girlfriend's belongings. Even if she lives there.

"I trust you," he said, sipping a whisky and soda. "I know you know how to iron the sections of the paper just as I like them."

Ah, if only he were kidding.

Another case in point: a recent customer booked me for the better part of an evening at his own home. Having exhausted most of a bottle of gin, the springs of his bed, and all reasonable conversation, he slipped away for a quick shower.

Such interludes make me nervous. It's not as if I plan to rob the place, but I am a compulsive confessor—even to things I haven't done. At school if the entire form was being reprimanded for the action of a single student, I am sure I felt the guilt most of all. Especially if I wasn't involved.

Most customers are wary of us anyway—when in their own home instead of a hotel, they more often put off the bathing ritual or suggest a joint shower, so as not to leave me alone. I'm not offended.

But this client, he threw on a dressing gown and scampered off to the bath. I sat on the couch. Considered pawing through his CD collection, but decided that would be rude. I carefully examined the watercolors on the wall. And with nothing more to do, no calls to make or return, nothing to read, I did what any reasonable person would do.

He emerged from the bathroom to find me busily washing up.

Perhaps I am more trustworthy than I thought.

vendredi, le 30 janvier

Snow yesterday afternoon—near UCL, students dashed out of the Union and Archaeology to gather up handfuls of snow and throw them at each other. Clusters of girls walked by in twos and threes, huddling under umbrellas. Though it had gone dark, the light was calm, diffuse: a warm glow of streetlights reflecting off the puffy duvet-sized flakes coming down.

I went to meet A2, who hasn't had a date any time this geological era. He recently hooked up with someone at a conference, though, a girl from Manchester. It seems a long way to go for sex. He assures me it isn't just about the sex. A2 is a great chap, but an extremely poor liar.

We installed ourselves in a gastropub-cum-bar to watch the buses outside pile up in the icy street. It was one of these places with a high ratio of leather seating to bar space, where they turn up the music automatically at 7 p.m. regardless of how many customers are inside. We were practically shouting over the background noise to hear each other.

"So what do you think of latex?" A2 bellowed.

"Latex?" I asked, unsure if I misheard. "A good idea, generally." Unhappily, I am discovering a recent sensitivity to the stuff, having come away from a blowjob at work with swollen, tingling lips. Hardly a scientific experiment, though. It could just as easily have been the spermicide on the Durex.

"No, I mean like—" he mimed putting on a rubber glove. "Latex. The feel of it, you know, for—"

"You're talking about rubber sex already?"

"She's a hell of a girl," he mused. "So, have you ever done it?"

The squeaky squeaky? "Not full coverage, no. You mean with the catheter and head mask and everything? No." Ugh. *Up your urethra* is probably the least arousing phrase I can imagine, ever.

"I so want to go there."

"Careful, you'll scare her off."

"It was her idea. So—tips?"

"Lots of baby powder, I should think. I don't even want to think about what this would smell like."

"Mmm, I do."

Where do people come up with this stuff? And wouldn't it get rather sweaty in there? "Freak. You said this was—and I quote—not just a sex thing."

"Takes one to know one."

"Who, me?" I put a hand to my chest in mock surprise. "I would absolutely never. I'm as pure as the you-know-what," I said, nodding toward the snow outside.

"Sure you wouldn't. You having another?" A2 yelled over a god-awful cover song by an unmentionable boy band.

"Something hot, if they have it. With plenty of alcohol. Only way to banish this music. And the mental image of you humping a blow-up doll."

samedi, le 31 janvier

In weather like this, one must admit defeat, ignore the "never too thin" mantra altogether and give in to a new paradigm. This can best be summarized as the tights-fishnets-socks under trousers, "please don't let me have to use a public toilet juggling all this getup" design for life. It is perhaps a small price to pay for living in a winter wonderland of slush.

And in such days as these, only a cad would casually throw out a line like "You've gained some on the hips." Which is why I had to kill N and bury the corpse under a layer of permafrost on Hampstead Heath. No jury would convict.

Février

K is for Killer Moves

Or, the thing a girl is known for. For some it's the look, others the intimacy, others a peculiar talent. Anal and light domination come up fairly frequently with me, but they're not the killer moves. It's the oral. I've been complimented on oral technique often enough to ask a man before I start on him whether he wants to come in my mouth or not, and if so, how long should I make it last? Many of them do not believe the timing of their orgasm is in my hands (or lips, as it were). Of course it is, silly things. That's why they're the men.

L is for Lousy Kissers

There are a lot of these in the world. It's not your duty to reform them, though a gentle suggestion, well timed, can be the best thing a man gets out of the encounter. Other times you have to know when to hold your tongue. Especially when he cannot hold his.

M is for Music

I blame the conventions of overbearing cinema soundtracks for the crap that is supposed to accompany a session of hedonistic lovemaking. Music is a matter of taste, and it's usually obvious whether a man has put something on because he wants to hear it and it turns him on or because he thinks it's what ought to be done. Doing the deed to the syrupy strains of Luther Vandross is a misguided attempt to set the mood. Someone who pounds your arsehole to the beat of Stravinsky's *Rite of Spring*, on the other hand, is clearly passionate about the music.

N is for Noise

The alternative to music. He wants feedback; give it to him. But for goodness' sake don't lay on the porn screeches in a cheap imitation of passionate frenzy unless he clearly requests it. They're paying for sex, not stupid.

dimanche, le 1er février

First Date and I agreed to meet to see a play. No big-budget West End production, this: he suggested we go to a show put on by some of his friends at a pub. It was something by one of my favorite Renaissance playwrights, and I was dubious of the adaptation. "You'll be amazed what they've done with it," he assured me. "A real two-hander."

I giggled. I think perhaps the phrase means something different to luvvies than it does to call girls.

The night after the party, when he slept in the sitting room and N in my bed, all three of us rose early and had a cup of coffee in the kitchen. I walked them out to the street, waved N off in his car, and walked First Date round the corner to his. I was scared I might be in for a touch of the coldness I'd shown him, but no, he lit a kiss on my mouth before driving away. I thought perhaps another chance was deserved. It did rather show up my abilities as a hostess to force the poor lad to stay over on my sofa.

Went across town by tube to meet him. He was already in the pub, having a drink with a friend whom he introduced me to. This friend's claim to fame was having been the child star face of some commercials, and as he looked at least fifty it was no surprise I didn't recognize the product—much less the adverts. We talked briefly about computers instead. I think they're horrible little beastly things, with no great use besides facilitating the production and distribution of porn. Much like men, really. And not so bad for it.

The two-hander was in an upstairs room. It was clear from the start that I was not going to like it much, but First Date's long muscular thigh was pressed against mine, and he laughed in the right places, and aside from the overacting going on twelve feet ahead of us, it was nice to be in a dark room together.

The audience filed downstairs afterward for drinks. I saw the lead actor some few minutes later and joined the crowd in paying him lavish, undeserved compliments.

"What did you really think?" said one of First Date's friends, looking at me with a canny smile, when the actor had walked away.

"Bloodless," I said. "Without passion."

"Example?"

"I can do better than that," I said. Turning to First Date, I quoted a line from the play, a line given by the lead actor. I pawed his shirt as if he were Helen of Troy—the pinnacle of feminine beauty. And he played it well, moving off my advances archly.

We both turned toward the friend. "Point made," he said. First Date and I emptied our glasses and left.

He offered me a lift. It wasn't really on his way, I knew, but I accepted.

We talked about everything and nothing. I outlined how things had ended with the Boy. He told me about his recent ex-girlfriend. My mind wandered to A2, and I found myself saying, "I suppose it was a revelation to learn that just because someone loves you, you don't have to love them back. And you can't tell that person their loving you is wrong."

There was a pause. "That's good," he said, zipping round Hyde Park Corner. "Because I love you."

Ack, no, please. I felt trapped by my own words. "Thank you," I said. And I knew right at that moment I didn't feel the same. Not yet. Maybe never. We went back to mine, had sex, slept. He woke early—habit of an honestly employed person, I suppose. We had a quiet breakfast and he went home.

lundi, le 2 février

Client: "May I take your picture?"

Me: (spotting the palm-sized video recorder nearby) "No."

"Please? I won't include your face."

Hmph. Thanks. "No, I'm sorry—it's not our policy to allow photographs or recordings."

"I just want to see you spreading those lips while my dick goes inside."

"Good, we can do that. We'll use a mirror. But no pictures."

"Other girls do it."

"I'm not other girls."

(pouting somewhat) "Other girls from the same agency do it."

Is that supposed to swing my vote? Mister, I don't care if you have snaps of my mother going down on your dog. "Terribly sorry, no."

"Not even a photo? It'll be mostly me anyway."

"No." This was getting tedious and, more to the point, taking up quite a lot of our time. I smiled sweetly, stood right against him, and played with the top button of his shirt. "Shall we?"

So we did, though he peppered the talk during our session with comments like "Wow, that's amazing, wish I could get a picture of that," and "You really should be in porn, you know?" (There was the time N and I toyed with the idea of funding a sabbatical in Poland by working in Eastern European skin flicks, but that's another story for another day.)

He just didn't let up. To the point where bucking enthusiastically and making all the right moves was becoming difficult because I couldn't escape the feeling of being watched. At the end of the hour I was so spooked I couldn't help scanning the room for hidden cameras. At least it was a hotel room and not a private house, but when he went to use the toilet I still opened all the drawers and looked under the bed.

It's a good idea to stay suspicious, in my experience. It hasn't served me badly yet. No one has ever taken advantage and I want to ensure it never does happen. That's part of why I work through an agency.

I know my place in sex work is a privileged one, as far as having sex with strangers goes. Many—though not all—prostitutes are addicts, in damaging relationships, abused by clients, or all of the above. It is probably a measure of my naïveté that I do not ask the few other WGs I meet if they are happy in their work. Honestly, I did not even notice that streetwalkers existed until well into my teenage years. Sometimes it's hard to tell a girl heading for a club from one who's, er, not.

Once at university I came home from a night out. I lived in a block of flats near the center of the city, and the taxi dropped me at the end of the road. As I walked up to the door, keys in hand, a man spoke.

"You looking for work, love?"

It took a second to realize what he was asking. "Oh. No." I wasn't wearing anything terribly suggestive, just—correction. I was a student, and students coming home from clubs invariably look half-dressed. It was an honest mistake.

But I didn't scream or run or sneer. "Are you sure?" he asked.

From time to time there were streetwalkers in the area. One weekend I went out early to buy a paper and saw a woman staggering across a main road through the city. She was dressed as for a night out, but it was broad daylight; she looked too young to be a student, too underfed. Another time, sitting with friends in the local, we saw a woman come in to make change from a 20-pound note. The barmen exchanged looks; they clearly knew her.

"I'm sure," I said, and refrained from adding, *but thank you anyway.*

mardi, le 3 février

The redesigning at home is going well, although I cannot be inspired to write much about soft furnishings. Suffice to say that the previous look (Laura Ashley meets Peter Max in Tahiti, where they decide to go on an acid trip together) is being updated to something vaguely within this century.

A most interesting object was delivered yesterday. The landlady had the furniture made some few years ago by a firm that kept the details on record, and they have been kind enough to supply attractive new cushion covers for the overstuffed monstrosity (I mean the sofa, not the landlady). The new covers were brought up just after lunch, along with detailed instructions on how to put them on and a tool to aid in application.

This tool, it must be said, looks exactly like a paddle.

A very classy paddle indeed. Of the same glowing hardwood as the frame of the sofa itself, with a smooth rounded handle mimicking the turned legs of the furniture. A tapering, broad, flat side, apparently for stuffing the cushions in their new skins.

But it doesn't look anything like an upholstery aid to me. It is, quite frankly, a well-made and extremely horny paddle. It has a leather thong threaded through the handle, for goodness' sake. And it matches the furniture.

I looked at the paddle, then at the deliveryman. "Do you want this returned when I'm done?"

"What? No, just keep it or chuck it away. We don't need it back."

"Thank you." A more welcome and unexpected gift I haven't had in ages. It's as if Valentine's Day has come early.

mercredi, le 4 février

Client: (setting the dresser mirror on the floor) "I want to watch you watching yourself masturbate."

Well, this makes a change. "What with?"

"Your hands first. Then a vibe."

"And then you . . . ?"

"No, I just want to watch."

He provided a chair and I sat. Wriggled out of my knickers and drew the skirt of my dress around my hips. There it all was, on display, as I'd rarely seen. Yes, I usually do a spot check after waxing and before going out, but this was different. And hand mirrors feature strongly in both work and sex at home, but this was just me, alone, inviolate. Belle from a fly on the wall. And being the self-obsessed creature I am, I was possibly as fascinated as he.

I watched my lips grow fuller, redder, wetter. Much darker than I imagined, almost purple, as I've seen the head of a penis do so many times. The aperture itself widened and gasped. I could hear its gentle smacks like a mouth opening and closing as my hand rubbed faster and my hips moved less gently.

The effect was of watching myself on television. I suppose it must have been for him as well—he paid far more attention to the reflection than to me in the chair. I wondered why bother with the expense of paying someone to masturbate when there was no interaction, then realized. He wanted to be the director.

But as I approached the point of no return I would slow down and readjust my position—ostensibly to give him a better look or varied position, but really to keep myself from coming.

It was remarkably difficult to keep from setting off the hair trigger for most of the hour. He sat on a bed, then knelt on the ground, coming closer and closer to the mirror, occasionally making requests regarding the speed and action of the vibe or the location of my free hand—but didn't touch. When he came, it hit the glass, sliding thickly over my reflected image onto the carpet.

jeudi, le 5 février

I came in soggy and grumpy, having been caught in a sudden burst of rain in Ladbroke Grove and without my umbrella. I'd been out to meet a man for a date, and let us just say it hadn't gone well. There were three missed calls, all from the manager's mobile. I rang her back. "Hello, sorry I missed you earlier."

"Not to worry, darling." The manager, for once, was not listening to horrible hair-rock. "You had a booking."

"I went to meet someone for lunch and forgot my phone. Anything interesting?"

"This very nice man. He always asks for you."

"Ah." This has happened about once a week since I started working. "The French one?"

"He is such a lovely gentleman."

"Yes, and he always gives less than an hour lead-time on a booking. I can't get out so quickly." My house is too far out of Zone 1 for that. "I presume you gave him to one of the other girls?"

"Yes. But he always asks for you, darling."

"Tell him to give me more notice next time, okay?"

"Mmm." There was another voice in the background and the manager went oddly quiet, then whispered, "Sorry, have to go! Nice talking to you, goodbye!" She has a boyfriend who doesn't know what she does for a living. It seems odd to me—but then it's her job that is illegal in the UK, not mine.

Text from First Date soon after: *Torture Garden. What think you?*

Well, if he's trying to keep my interest, he's certainly doing well. I am so there with bells on. Clamped to my nipples, of course.

vendredi, le 6 février

Walking through a tiled corridor to the District Line at Monument yesterday. A busker was there, playing Dylanesque riffs on a guitar and making up lyrics about the people walking past.

and I said, my friend, there will be a woman / and she will walk by you / and you will know her by her white suit and pink shoes / there will be a beautiful woman

I couldn't help but smile, looking down at my shoes. Dusty pink peep-toed courts. Very forties or seventies, depending on how you work them.

and my friend, you will know her / you will know this woman by her smile

I kept walking, but laughing the whole way, and looked back to grin at him before turning the corner.

samedi, le 7 février

N came round after the gym to help with the cushions. By "help" I mean "sit on them whilst I boil the kettle," which is helpful in its way, I suppose. Someone has to make the first stain on the upholstery.

(By which I mean nothing ruder than spilled tea. You sick creatures.)

N's eyes lit on the cushion-squeezer-cum-paddle immediately. When I came back with the steaming mugs, he was already doing a few test whacks on his thigh.

"New piece of kit?" he asked.

"Came with the sofa," I explained.

"Class."

One of N's other exes, the one who broke his heart, has started turning up at the gym intermittently. I notice it's never a time he's likely to be there. Sometimes I linger in the locker area, listening in case she talks to anyone. Knowing her current situation would carry a high premium indeed. And if she knows who I am, she hasn't acknowledged it. I'm not certain whether to tell him yet or not. We were only halfway through the tea before the conversation turned, as it inevitably does, to her.

"I don't know whether to just call her," he said. "If she's seeing someone new, I'll feel rubbish; if she isn't, I'll wonder what the point of us breaking up was."

"You know, when someone decides it's over there's nothing you can do."

"I know. I just thought, finally I have everything sorted, finally I—holy fuck."

"What's wrong?"

"Look out your window."

I did. A residential street, cars parked on the opposite side. Some house lights on, some off. Almost-invisible droplets of rain blown sideways, showing up as a shower of orange under the streetlight. "Yes?"

"It's his car. It's your ex's car."

I squinted. The eyes are not quite what they should be these days, but I don't drive and have readjusted my notion of "normal newspaper reading distance" to approximately two centimeters from my nose. But yes, it looked awfully like the Boy's car—Fiat, V reg, half a block down.

An inadvertent shiver. It was cold by the window and I pulled the drapes. "Lot of cars like that around."

"Wasn't there when I parked," N said. "None of your neighbors have one."

I turned back toward the sofa, unfolded my arms, picked up the cup of tea and sat down. "Mmm. I don't think so. I don't know."

When N left an hour later, the car was gone, anyway.

dimanche, le 8 février

So: it is the mid-eighties. Sometimes in the summer my mother leaves me with a Jewish youth group on weekdays. Usually we hang around a community center, playing board games or being forced into strange sports no one knows the rules of, like korfball. Sometimes we take trips.

One time we go to the beach in two minibuses. It's not a warm day, but the beach is a treat (we are told), so we mustn't waste the day (we are also told). A teacher at school once brought back a bleached starfish from her holidays abroad, so I spend the day walking barefoot up and down the shore looking for one. Of course there are none. Some other girls are sitting cross-legged in shallow water, pretending to shampoo their hair with sand. They ask me to join them but I don't. It looks too cold.

We are brushed down obsessively by the leaders before being allowed back in the buses. But there is still sand in everything when we come back, so the adults order the girls into one room and the boys into another to change out of their swimsuits and shake out their towels. Between the two rooms is a cloakroom-cum-corridor, and the boys don't realize, but two older girls go to watch them change.

I didn't get to look. Not from want of trying: the older girls were tall enough to block the view, and wouldn't let anyone else near. They described what they saw (inaccurately, I later realize). For years after, I believe the male member has a spiraling ridge going down it, the physical equivalent of the verb "to screw." When someone's older sister has a boyfriend, she is "being screwed."

There is a popular song all the older girls like, and they argue about who loves the singer most, whose name would sound best with his. His protestations of asexuality are meaningless to them. No, not meaningless: they make him harder to win. He is as separate from the boys around us as a person can be. He is beautiful, antique, otherworldly, and from Manchester—and if we know anything, it's that Manchester is far cooler than where we are.

In my first flat after university, I am unpacking dishes in the kitchen when the song comes on the radio. It is the first time I have heard it without a chorus of twelve-year-olds singing along.

That summer of the youth group was also the summer my parents' friends start to call me "the little Alice." As in, through the looking glass. "Where is the little Alice?" they ask, and I run from wherever I am, happy to impress. I am brought out at gatherings to impress with feats of memorization. They keep me in the room, a bit of a parlor game, come watch this ur-adult. I know they're patronizing me by speaking this way, but at the same time I am pleased because I can talk back to them in their own language. One friend of the family refuses to dine at our table if not seated next to me. He asks what I think about politics, and I am surprised to learn I have an opinion. However uninformed. It really hasn't changed much since, either. Then he asks me to recite poetry, going over it line by line. I recite it back verbatim. "Someday you might even absorb all this," he says, laughing.

So I am in the kitchen, alone, listening to this song as an adult, not as Little Alice. The lyrics are quite sad, actually. Without realizing it, I have begun to cry.

mardi, le 10 février

Fuck: A Spotter's Guide

- *Good Fuck:* makes a lot of noise, alerting neighbors to actual sexual activity on the premises. Leaves nothing behind and does not phone immediately after. In short, should probably be charging for services rendered.
- *Bad Fuck:* counts ceiling tiles, then demands betrothal.
- *Fuckable:* not so much conventionally attractive as exuding animal qualities. Unless, of course, that animal is an otter.
- *Fuckwit:* not likely to engage in actual fucking anytime soon.
- *Fucking Hell:* is populated by women of the tanned arid blonde variety who would rather talk about their diets, spirituality, and tiny dogs than engage in sex. See also: Chelsea, Tantalus.
- *Fucked Over:* no longer the recipient of regular fucks.

mercredi, le 11 février

In the last week, I have been set up on three more dates. This might mean my friends are concerned about my emotional well-being, or afraid of what might happen if I am single for too long, or both. And I don't want to get attached to First Date too quickly; while he's a nice person and we get on well, the more I think about him, the more I find his intentions a little . . . intense.

None of the intended gents, however, were quite what I had in mind for a love match.

Bachelor #1 was a lovely bloke—tall, strange dark eyes, devastating Welsh accent. If there's anything that drives me batty, it's the mellifluous tones of men from the Valleys. Superficial, I know, but we all have our weaknesses.

Alas, the fellow must not have been clued on the details of my working life. Halfway through the starter, he related an elaborate anecdote which essentially came down to ridiculing his best friend for "dating a whore's sister." Ah. Well. Pity.

The meal was nice, though.

Bachelor #2 met me at a pub already drunk. Another fine figure of manhood, but having distinct problems negotiating the relationship between his body and the force of gravity. Inside of half an hour he was clinging to the bar for support, having discovered I am unsuitably small to support fifteen-odd stone of wavering man-weight.

A couple of hours later we were in the queue for a club. In spite of the rain and general yuckness, they were operating a one-in, one-out door policy when the place itself was clearly nowhere near full. Bachelor #2 took umbrage with this indignity and decided to address the bouncers on the matter. They, quite reasonably, chucked the lad out on his ear. I peeled him off the pavement, got him back to his in a taxi, located a bag of peas in his freezer, and slapped it on his swelling cheek before making my excuses. Being already unconscious, I doubt he noticed.

Bachelor #3 was the sort of person for whom the mantra "Better to keep quiet and be thought dim than open your mouth and remove all doubt" was created. After a solid hour of my bright chatter (being personally unafraid of whether people think me dim or not), he finally came out with a few winners:

"I can't say I'm a fan of [the subject I studied at uni]."

Wiping out an entire academic discipline with a single sentence. That's fine, that's okay, I'm not precious about such things. So off again the conversation went, this time to music, a subject about which he was somewhat more animated.

"I'll listen to anything, except country and western."

What, a life without Dolly? Without Patsy? The Flying Burrito Brothers? Admittedly, the current crop of Nashville output is appallingly samey, but to write off the likes of Wilco and Lambchop altogether?

To paraphrase the country-and-western diva, I waxed my legs for this?

jeudi, le 12 février

In a taxi, sort of drowsing off in the back. I'd had the sort of day where you wake up already tired and it never quite comes together from there. My phone started ringing.

"Darling, I hope you're okay." It was the manager. I'd forgotten to alert her on leaving the last client.

"Sorry, yes, I'm fine." The taxi sped north, the streets were quiet. "Everything was fine, he was very nice."

"You always say they're 'very nice.' You sound so happy."

"Happy? I suppose so. I'm not unhappy." I mean, the man was somewhat trollish, but she's not interested in knowing.

"That's because you haven't experienced any aggression in the job yet."

I laughed. Compared to real relationships, these men are absolute pussycats, and easily pleased pussycats at that. Even sleepy and disconnected, nothing I couldn't handle—so far. "I suppose it just shows how well you take care of me," I said.

Arrived home soon after and went to bed. I had my phone under my pillow just in case, as I was expecting another call. It rang around midnight.

"Darling, are you still up? Can you do another appointment?"

"Mrrrrrf arrrrrm mmmmmmmph fhmmmmmmm."

"Okay, you get some sleep. Stay happy, darling."

vendredi, le 13 février

Usually I hold fairly positive opinions on clients—being as they are the water that floats my soap, and usually pleasant enough in a ships-passing-in-night kind of way. If someone waxes fanatical on the charms of his school nurse circa 1978, for instance, or insists on making me read out the newspaper in a fnar-fnar porny voice while he imagines he is having Fiona Bruce up the backside, I just steel myself and get on with it. But some things are beyond the pale. Some things chill me to the bone.

When the client referred to yesterday's hotel visit as "afternoon delight," for instance. For the love of Harvey N, man, have you no taste whatsoever?

samedi, le 14 février

But of course, the manager is wrong. I am not all that happy. 'Tis the blessed season of togetherness, where we honor the anniversary of the beheading of a Christian saint by exchanging overpriced tat.

The crass and obvious fakery of the Valentine holiday is powerful enough to get even me down. It's not simply the fact of being alone, though I am not technically alone—in London, you really never are—I have friends aplenty and work enough. No, it's more the smug mutual pampering couples get to experience.

I don't begrudge anyone their good time. I've been known to smile at couples canoodling on the tube or drunkenly fumbling on a park bench whilst pregnant women and little old ladies are forced to stand. If you have an other, significant or somewhat less than, I wholeheartedly encourage you to lavish one another with lurrrrve on that day.

What gets my goat is the shameless cashing-in by manicurists, hairstylists, and purveyors of raunchy lingerie. I make an effort to keep myself baby smooth and silkily attired at all points in the year, and what's my reward? Nothing. Book a spoil-yourself spa weekend for two in February, though, and it's discounts ahoy.

Ahem. I think I deserve a little better here. Sure, Valentine's may be the lifestyle economy's equivalent of Christmas, but how about lending some sugar to the peeps who keep you afloat the rest of the year?

I brought up the subject with the woman lately charged with waxing my bush. She wasn't impressed by the logic.

dimanche, le 15 février

Having very little else to do of a weekend, I went to visit N's mum. She's an excellent woman, robust of mind and body, and lately widowed. It seemed appropriate to spend Valentine's Day with someone whose attitude toward men runs approximately, "Don't worry dear—by the time you find a good one they just up and die on you anyway."

She has been thinking of selling the family house now that all her children are grown and she is alone.

"It must seem quite empty now," I said carefully. One never knows just how far and how quickly your foot can enter your mouth when conversing with the elderly.

"Not at all," she said. "I have the little ghosts, you see."

"Of course you do," I said. Dappy old bird. I thought nothing more of it.

Later we went for a walk round her block. It's in a neglected village north of London that has never been fashionable, where there is still a local butcher (and not selling organic free-range cilantro-and-Tamworth-pork sausage to the gourmands-come-lately, either), where the pubs are still locals and not jockeying for the attention of Michelin and Egon Ronay restaurant reviews, and the residents drive normal-sized cars and not Land Rover behemoths, or more shocking still, use public transport.

In short—the sticks. And quite lovely for it.

We wittered around in the corner shop and bought a paper and sandwiches. I insisted we get two cupcakes from the bakery with pink icing and a little plastic heart pressed in the tops. We went further, down to a cemetery. The weather wasn't great, a bit gray and blowy, but there was a touch of blue making its way through the sky. N's mum sat heavily on a stone bench next to a memorial.

"Go on, read it."

I did. A family—the father, mother, and four girls—their names and dates of birth inscribed in the curly lettering of the early Victorian. "Do you notice anything?" she said.

"They all died on the same day. Some sort of accident?"

"A fire," she said. "In the house where I live now." A white-haired lady walking a terrier paused nearby. She waved at N's mum while her doggie soiled the eternal memory of some decorated officer. "They were asleep the whole time."

"You're having me on," I said. But I couldn't help imagining a bed of little girls, their blankets and pajamas catching fire. A fate we have eliminated, presumably, with central heating and flame-proof furniture. The sort of thing that only happens now when a near-bankrupt father goes off the rails and does his whole family in.

"When you wake up tomorrow, come down to the kitchen and see if it doesn't smell of smoke."

"How do I know that's not just you burning the toast?" I said with a smile.

"It's not," she said. "It's four little ghosts, who never even woke up." We walked home and read the paper and ate our sandwiches. I texted N to say I was having a nice time with his mother and secretly wondered whether I'd be able to sleep the night. Every crack of a twig and whip of wind outside sounded like a growing flame; every few minutes I sat up in bed, convinced the air smelt of fire.

Woke to a smoke-free kitchen and text:

Enjoy the weekend. Don't let her start telling ghost stories. N

lundi, le 16 février

A knock on the door this morning as I was drying my hair. It was one of the builders, holding a single pink rose.

"Er, um," he said, charmingly.

"Is that for me?" I asked. The builders were meant to be finished by now, but there have been problems with the new dishwasher that they are either loath to describe to a delicate constitution such as mine or are incapable of putting into words. Their morning requirement of tea and their vague assurances that it will all be finished soon are becoming permanent features of my home life. If one decided to cement our union, I'm not sure I would be able to discourage him, except by engineering a tea shortage. "How very sweet."

"It's not from me," he insisted. "I mean, I mean . . . it's not from me, someone said to give it to you."

"Lovely. And is there a note?"

"Didn't see one."

"Whom did you say this was from again?"

"Dunno." He thought a moment, scratching his chin with the tube of plastic wrapped round the rosebud. "Some bloke?"

"And what did he look like?"

"Average size?"

It's good to know their general vagueness is not just an act to secure tea privileges. I suspected plumping for more detail, such as whether the suitor came on foot or by car, would be met with similarly useless information. "Well, thank you for delivering it," I said, taking charge of the flower. The builder turned and trundled off to his van. I noticed the plastic bore a sticker from the florist and fruiterer around the corner—so no clues there. Given the turnover of customers they must have this week, I can't imagine the staff would remember who purchased the rose, either.

I have queried all reasonable candidates but no one will claim responsibility for the gesture. It therefore follows that I must have a stalker, but as it is a good time of year for stalkers, I'll let it go for now. Who said romance was dead?

mardi, le 17 février

By 1992 I had been studying French for six years. I was never much good at it. We never read anything interesting at school. I had a Canadian friend, Françoise, who told me Marguerite Duras is "sexy." So I bought a copy of the shortest of her books I could find, because my French is rather poor and I had long stopped enjoying translating. The book was *L'Amant*.

Translations are a lot like pasta. At first, because you don't know anything, you'll buy whatever's on offer. Audiobook of Keith Harris reading Günter Grass? Sure. Comic-book version of *The Iliad*? Hit me. But the more of a taste you get for the originals, the more demanding you become. You try your hand at a simple translation, armed with only the basic kitchen essentials, and the result is not bad. Your friends are impressed. To be honest, so are you. You invest a little more time and effort, and the returns are positive. Finally you go all out on the pasta maker–dash–Oxford Classical Grammar and turn into a one-woman translation–dash–noodle machine. You buy the supplementary books, join the appreciation societies, and watch the right programs. Then you realize how time-consuming your interest is and, worse, how much of a bore your friends think you are, going on about 00 graded semolina/Hesse in the original German like it mattered. You let it slide. Those who don't either end up doing it professionally or soon find themselves the social equivalent of a hand grenade at any party.

But even when you give up on making your own pasta/translating from the original, you have just enough knowledge to ruin the thing you enjoyed in the first place. You'll never enjoy "just" a bowl of pasta. "Just" a nice book to read. Neither of them tastes very good when it's bland, cardboardy, off-the-shelf, sanitized-for-Western-Europe rubbish. So I bought *L'Amant* in French to see if I could read it. Also, it was the only version that did not advertise the film on the book cover. Nothing turns me off a paperback quite as quickly as the dreaded words "Now a Major Motion Picture."

So I start reading it. I don't like the book. It is not sexy. For a dozen or more pages, she writes about the heat in Asia, a silk dress, a hat. She is describing a girl who is like me—small for her age, burdened with a heavy mass of hair, delicate and odd. Françoise must have been lying. No one who is like me can be sexy. Perhaps in some passages I can see what is meant, though having to constantly refer to a French grammar to puzzle out the author's finely crafted lines breaks up the meaning too much.

Then I am surprised. By the end of the book—which I will not give away, because to relate what happens (though the ending itself is not a surprise) will diminish it—I am in tears. Something that did not happen to me broke my heart. That was how I knew I was capable of the feeling.

From time to time I read it again. Often when I am feeling alone. The end, it always comes in such a rush, always the same effect.

mercredi, le 18 février

It used to be simple to buy faintly embarrassing items and hide them in the rest of my purchases. Of course, this is not so much a clever ruse as a socially accepted fiction. No shop assistant is fooled by an extra-strength deodorant hiding amongst the or-anges—it's just not nice commenting on a single sore thumb in an otherwise unremarkable cascade of groceries. And we all have bi-ological functions.

On the other hand, put too many of these in at once, and you're cruising for jokes. A witness to my usual haul of cosmetic goods might suspect I'm buying for a minimum of six postoperative transsexuals. So there is one chemist I go to for normal things and another for everything else. Example:

Typical shopping at Chemist 1:

shampoo
toothpaste
bath salts
cucumber gel mask
loofah scrubber

which might, at worst, be expected to stimulate a solicitous, "Ooh, a facial mask? Treating yourself?" As opposed to

Today's shopping at Chemist 2:

tampons
vaginal pessary (for irritation)
condoms
sugarless breath mints

lubricant
individual postwaxing wipes
self-tanning liquid
razor blades
potassium citrate granules (for cystitis)

which was met with the vaguely disinterested "There are halitosis remedies on the far end of aisle 2, if you're interested."
Bitch.

jeudi, le 19 février

The builders have moved on to the vexing problem of my freezer. This is a surprise, not simply because I would not have ascribed to them the expertise in complex internal condensers, but because I had no idea there was anything wrong with the freezer at all.

"What's that noise?" one of them asked yesterday afternoon, distracted from his detailed study of a cracked floor tile (which I hasten to add he was the cause of—an unfortunate incident involving the installation of a new dishwasher while one of my more voluptuous neighbors elected to begin her daily jog).

"I don't know," I said, looking up from the paper. "The freezer, most likely." Its occasional whirry cricket-sound is something I have grown used to and find rather comforting.

He opened the freezer door. "For the love of—when was the last time you defrosted this?"

Defrosted? Don't they do that themselves if left long enough, as with the decade-old wellies at the back of the closet which I fully expect to have sealed any holes if and when I need them again? "Not sure I ever have done."

He surveyed the wasteland landscape of icicle-coated bread loaves and mummified bottles of vodka. "Do you realize the buildup in here keeps the vacuum sealing mechanism from working properly?"

Whazzat? "Pardon?"

"The door doesn't close. That sound is the freezer constantly trying to replace the cold air seeping out."

It would explain the draft in the kitchen, anyway. "I don't suppose this means I get a new freezer?"

"It doesn't."

"And I don't suppose defrosting freezers is part of your remit?"

"It isn't."

Pity the neglect of household appliances does not warrant getting new ones off the landlady. I really must look over the contract more carefully come time to renew. So while the builder looked on during his break, sipping tea and enjoying the many and varied delights of one of the country's finer tabloid dailies, I attacked the ice storm with hands swaddled in tea towels, vegetable knife at the ready, like some intrepid polar explorer or demented suburban cannibal—take your (ahem) pick. And the tile still hasn't been repaired, either.

vendredi, le 20 février

A2 of the latex love, so happy in his newfound fetish, is extremely concerned about my romantic well-being. I do my best not to comment that if the alternative to being single is smelling like an explosion in a rubber factory, I'll pass, thank you.

We met for a cup of coffee and to check out the talent in town. Or rather, he eyed the talent as I did my best to deflect the inevitable matchmaking.

"Over my left shoulder," A2 hissed, and I looked to see who lay beyond. "No, don't look straight at him. Just have a quick look."

What was this, junior school? Do You Want to Kiss Me—Tick

Yes or No. "You're starting to sound like my mother," I sniffed. "Anyway, too short."

"How do you know? He's sitting down."

"Oh, believe me, I know." Button-down blue cotton shirt, tucked into too-high trouser waist. "He probably has all the Patrick O'Brian novels too."

"You have to be kidding." A2 clearly cannot see the forest for the rubber trees. "You can't reject someone on taste—no, not even on taste, on your assumption of their taste."

"Can do, will do, done."

Some minutes later as we picked at a shared pain au chocolat, he spotted another likely suitor. "On your left. Tall. Reading."

I looked over. Sure enough, a long drink of water was unfurling his limbs under a table, holding a paperback copy of *Requiem for a Dream*.

"Not bad," I mused. Oh wait—no. "Eep, smoker, forget it."

"You're going to reject someone based on that? But you've dated smokers before."

"So over that," I said. "If someone's going to have an expensive, pointless hobby, I'd rather it was skiing. Or better still, buying me expensive, pointless things."

"If you carry on like this, you'll die alone."

This from the person who once told me, aged twenty-three, that he hadn't had sex in six months and was therefore taking himself permanently off the market. This from the person who perennially lusts after his first lover, whom he hasn't seen since they were both seventeen. With friends like this, who needs relatives?

I scoffed. "What, at this wizened old age I'm already past it? Besides, my talc-coated friend, we all die alone anyway."

samedi, le 21 février

There is a client, I've seen him twice now. Hard face, high cheek-bones, water-clear eyes, and eyelashes to envy. A cool person, handsome in a harsh way, gentle. Smart. We talk about books, he's an engineer of some sort and hates his job, and we talk about plays and films. I enthuse about Ben Kingsley in this or that role, about Anthony Sher. He half-smiles. No idea why he's single. Perhaps he just wants to be alone?

I walked out of a block of flats toward the river to find a taxi. On the way to the taxi-stand I passed the entrance of a tube station, where a legless man was soliciting donations. "Help the disabled, please help the disabled," he chanted.

A drop of sweat ran down the inside of my thigh, perhaps the only part of me that felt truly warm. When it reached the top of my stocking, I felt it soak in, dissipate. A moment later, the legless man's voice again. "Help the disabled, please help the disabled." His cadence was flat but sing-songy, in time with the beat of footsteps from people streaming around him. "Help the disabled, please help the disabled."

I stood in queue but there were no taxis for a few minutes. A short, round man with overflowing plastic bags came up to me. "Have you accepted Jesus as your Lord?" he asked. It sounded like reflex, devoid of meaning, as automatic as a "hello."

"Afraid not, Jewish," I said. Stock answer. More a cultural than a religious thing for me, but usually sufficient to drive the crazies off.

He nodded in sympathy, his eyes never rising above the level of my shoulder. "The Jews wanted a king, and God gave them a king, but he was manic-depressive, you see, and would go out and hide in bushes screaming at people."

"Not a very effective king, you might say," I said.

"I'm going to freeze standing on the bridge," he said, and gathered his shopping bags and walked away.

dimanche, le 22 février

Today, I have been given:

a pound coin change (from a two-pound coin; took bus)
a pair of white socks (from gym; left them)
a personal alarm (from friend; just . . . because)
a silver and amber bracelet (from a client)
five of those weirdly Day-Glo daisies (from a nonpaying
  admirer)
the bill from the builders (er, wasn't the owner supposed to
  handle this?)
strange looks from a taxi driver (he so knew)
a cold (see first item on the list)

So Ken Livingstone's much-vaunted improved public transport proves itself quite capable in the "public" criterion, if not so much the "transport." Ah well, good time to tuck up with some good books and demand pancakes from my nearest and dearest.

lundi, le 23 février

The mystery car is back; I don't want to look but can't look away; I'm not convinced it's not just paranoia; must remember to lock all the locks; the builders are giving me strange looks; am thinking of investing in a bubble wig and giant pair of Jackie O sunglasses and not just for the sake of rocking the vintage look.

Otherwise, a bit better today, thank you for asking.

mardi, le 24 février

he: "Um, you have a . . . I'm not sure . . ."

me: (looking over shoulder at man kneeling behind me) "Is everything okay, sweetie?"

"There's a . . . I don't quite know how to tell you this . . ."

I was suddenly quite worried—what? Razor bump? Spare thicket of missed hair? Week-old tampon? The stub of a tail? "Yes?"

"You have bruises on the backs of your thighs."

"Oh, that. Just means you're not the first to tread this road vigorously, dear. Is it okay? We can do it another way."

"Well, actually," he said, growing harder and somewhat more forceful. "You could tell me how they happened."

mercredi, le 25 février

A1 hit a milestone birthday. His partner made the arrangements and booked a table at an overrated Indian restaurant in Clerkenwell, which was acceptable, being as she has no taste.

I was looking forward to getting out in a large group. Work can be intense. It's like having a series of blind dates over and over again, struggling to keep your end of the arrangement effortless and light, all whilst knowing very little is going to come of it. Draining. The current spate of real first dates hasn't helped either. And while I enjoy hanging in cafes and coffee bars with a small group of friends, there is always the danger that by knowing too much about each other, all useful conversational skills will be lost. Only with people who've known you since puberty can you be entertained by

"Remember the . . ." (vague hand gesture)

"Yes, just like in the movie."

"Oh God! And the arm thing B used to do!"

(random *Star Wars* quote)

(reference to mid-nineties politics)

(satisfied silence, or fits of inexplicable giggles for half an hour).

It's not a fortress that admits new champions easily, and girl-friends of N and the As usually find themselves on the outside re-gardless of their charms and abilities. There was the one who was raised on a commune in South Africa, built her last house from the ground up, and had never been to a McDonald's (actually, a rather admirable trait). But she couldn't quote freely from *The Princess Bride*, and thus found herself in a constant state of puzzlement, es-pecially when A2 tried—and failed—to propose to her by ex-plaining that Life Is Pain.

We need to get out more. With other people. Normal people.

I arrived late, looking swish in a black silk shirt and tailored trousers. Hair pulled up, subtle pearl earrings. Okay, so I looked like a Goth personal assistant. No matter. The table was lively; the drinks were flowing; the conversation was achingly, happily, beau-tifully normal. I sat across from N, who'd brought his friend Angel, the other working girl whom I'd had a run-in with last month. But she'd seemingly come to her senses and appeared lovely and chipper.

Halfway through the meal, Angel begged use of my phone—her battery had gone—to send a text. And yes, I'm a trusting soul, and was busily flirting with the blue-eyed Adonis on my right, so didn't check to see what she'd sent or to whom.

So I was surprised when First Date turned up as the gifts were being opened. He smiled at me. I smiled back. He looked round the table and sat next to Angel. Interesting. I should have known they knew each other, but never would have figured them for a potential couple.

The Adonis smiled, introduced himself across the table. First Date shook his hand. "And you're here with . . . f?" Adonis inquired.

"Her," he said, nodding at me.

I laughed nervously. "Are you?"

"Didn't you just invite me?"

I glared at Angel, hard. "I suppose it might look like I had done," I said. "I'm not responsible for this—sorry for the confusion."

The tail end of the supper I spent lavishing my attention on the pale, shy girl next to me while Adonis and First Date—who, it turns out, had mutual acquaintances—chattered about university days. N begged off quickly, the Adonis made his excuses, everyone at the other end of the table was going to some random's house to continue drinking, and I was left with Angel and First Date. She went to collect her car, suggesting the three of us move on to a late bar she knew.

First Date and I stepped into the street as she dashed round the corner. "I'm sorry," he said.

"Water under the bridge," I said, though it clearly was not.

"I didn't know that text wasn't from you."

"I know."

"Am I . . . am I in the way?"

I turned to him, angry at the situation, angry at feeling manipulated, even if he wasn't the cause. Angry for feeling angry; why get mad at all? Most of all I was angry at his woundedness, his need to be needed by me. His voice had the timbre of . . .

"Because I love you."

Yeah, that thing.

I sighed, closed my eyes. We stood on the pavement for a long time in silence. I looked at my shoes, he looked at me. This wasn't what I wanted and this wasn't how I wanted to be. A man came by, asked for directions, we sent him off to the next block. The fear was coming over me, a black mist, the feeling of being trapped by well-meaning friends, by fate. "I'm getting a cab home," I said finally. "Alone. You go meet Angel at the bar or she'll think we've deserted her." Or gone home together, I thought.

jeudi, le 26 février

The next morning I woke to three missed calls and a text.

The first two calls were from numbers I didn't recognize. No voice mail. Not too unusual, but I smelt a rat. So I rang them back.

"Good morning. Did you by any chance ring my number last night?"

Both were confused, because they were clearly people who didn't know me—but, if the caller ID was an impartial judge, had tried to call. Turns out Angel had sent more than one text. And they had tried to reach her on my number.

Nice one. I am such an idiot. At least they weren't international calls.

The third missed call was from First Date, sometime in the wee hours. The text was from him too.

Are you still seeing N? If so, are you aware I didn't know?

Sigh. I rang him as well; he was already at his desk. "Hello, sorry to disturb you at work."

"That's okay." He sounded surprised.

"I read your text." He didn't answer. "I'm not seeing N. I haven't in ages. Who told you we were?" Still no answer. "That's okay, I really don't have to ask, do I?"

"It just seems like you two are still so close, and with you both being single . . ."

"That automatically means we're more than just friends?"

"Well, no, it doesn't." He paused. "But Angel was very surprised when she found out you and I were a thing, and she said, didn't I know about you and N?"

"Excuse me . . . us two . . . we're a thing?"

"Um."

"Okay, that aside—and someone you barely know is a more reliable source of information on my life than I am?"

"Well."

"This is bullshit."

"Hey, calm down. I love you. I care about you. I—"

Argh, those stupid words again. "I don't feel the same way. If you didn't know that, you do now. I'm not going to belittle your feelings and say you shouldn't feel them, but you know nothing about me. Either way, the things you feel entitle you to nothing." Argh, stop it, I know I'm yelling now and this is coming out all wrong. I want to make my point clear without him thinking I'm an arse.

No. Forget that. The sooner he understands this, the sooner he can go looking for someone he really loves. I don't want to talk to him. I don't want this. I'll be a jerk.

"It's all just a misunderstanding, I'm sure we can talk about this with her. . . ."

"Oh, just . . . quiet. I don't want to talk about this. I don't want to talk to her. Or you. I'm not really interested in this at all."

"But I—"

"Goodbye."

A pause. I could imagine his face, what I would and have done in the same situation. Bargain for time or accept it gracefully? To his credit, he chose the latter. "Goodbye. Good luck to you. I'll miss seeing you."

"Thank you." I hung up. And went to the computer to send that woman a blistering e-mail about the mystery numbers and her conversation with First Date. I felt a coward hiding behind the in-box, but I was not sure I could keep from raising my voice on the phone. Type, revise, send. And then I ate breakfast, and felt a bit sad, and a bit of a twat, and even the thought that none of this matters anyway didn't really cheer me.

vendredi, le 27 février

After a bit of time passes, it can be difficult to remember how, why, when you liked someone, and nice to revisit it from a safe distance. The boy who felt me up in a public swimming pool when I was fifteen. The relationship at school that ended because of his aversion to cunnilingus. A1, whose skill in manipulating my body was as funny as it was frightening. The first time with someone I still think of fondly, someone I fell quickly and hard for, and the thousand or so times we were together after that, and the last time with him too.

The few whom I could not get enough of. The way they smelled, felt, tasted. The number of times I was with the Boy and wished he would just shut up and fuck me already, because I had never come with anyone that way, ever. The times sex felt as much a spiritual calling as a biological need. And how those moments kept me going for weeks afterward, like pearls dotting the cord of our moribund relationship.

These are nice, these little sketches of people I have enjoyed. It passes the time on trains and in taxis.

samedi, le 28 février

Am spending some quality time with my family before they go abroad on holiday, catching up with the local gossip and generally causing trouble and getting in the way, as is the eldest daughter's prerogative.

So, my mother is going to a wedding next month. A commitment ceremony in which the two brides will be dressed in white and will exchange rings and live happily ever after. Old family friends. We couldn't be more pleased. Except that Mum can't find a date for the date. Because her usual squeeze, my father, has been deemed Not in the Right Spirit.

It's not that he disagrees with the notion of lesbians (what man really does, at least in theory?) or has some bizarre hang-ups about the sanctity of marriage (note to world leaders: in an age where the highest-selling female artist worldwide can drunkenly trip down the aisle in jeans and a garter only to have the transaction annulled twenty-four hours later, but committed life partners cannot call each other wife and wife, something is a little rotten in the state of Denmark). No, it's actually Dad's overenthusiasm for the blessed event that has led to him being stricken off the guest list.

Because he insists, completely seriously, on hiring strippers to come to the reception. My father is not the sort of man who makes jokes, and worse still, he has social antennae legendary for their insensitivity. We were lingering over bagels and he was relating the story to date. Mother rolled her eyes as if it was a genetically encoded reflex, which I suspect it is. "Male strippers or female strippers?" I asked with just a touch too much interest.

"Oh, honey, no," Mum groaned.

"Female strippers!" he cried. "Naked ladies everywhere!" Have I mentioned that my father is an embarrassing perv? Runs in the bloodline, I suppose.

"I'm not certain that's entirely appropriate for the wedding," I said. Mum nodded sagely, her enameled black bob bouncing.

"You're right," she agreed. She turned on Daddy. "You see? You see? NO ONE thinks it's a good idea—"

"Yes," I said. "No good at all. Now, a hen night with strippers, that would be cool. . . ."

"Don't encourage him!" Mum shot me the evils as he gleefully contemplated the possibilities.

dimanche, le 29 février

Yesterday Mum and I went shopping. We haven't been unleashed on a retail palace together in years, but believe me, the shopgirls will be telling the tale to their children and their children's children. We're loud, we're efficient, we're armed with serious credit and cannot be stopped as we tear a smoking trail from shoes to lingerie.

She's after the Palm Beach look (well, what matron at her age isn't?). Lily Pulitzer–esque prints, bright brights, silky, sweaters, white trousers. I'm genetically programmed to want the same, but live in a grimy city and you can't wear cream-colored wool where there's any chance of sitting in schmutz.

We hit the shoes first. Same size, same taste; she cleaned three shops out of strappy sandals in spring green and blue; I did the same, with versions in camel and black. Handbags, suits, knickers: all fell before the might of our campaign of terror. She must have bought at least three outfits to wear to the wedding, as well as enough holiday gear to clothe an army of Mum-clones. I had to forcibly restrain her from beaded, flower-printed twinsets while she advised me my ankles "look chubby" in vintage-style shoes.

Such is the power of unconditional love. Only a mother can shriek "VPL!" to her daughter at a volume loud enough to rock the foundations of the building and live to tell the tale. (And for the record, my panty line was, indeed, visible. I hate when she's right.)

She: "Honey, you looked so adorable in the green! Are you not getting that?"

Me: "I don't know, it makes me look too busty."

(thrusting her own ample chest to the fore) "There's no such thing as looking too busty. What, you want to look like an adolescent?" And she threw the garment back on my pile.

I quiver in the shadow of a superior intellect.

Mars

O is for Oil

Never acceptable as lube. If you don't know about the unfortunate interaction of oil with latex, I refer you to any and all HIV-related literature of the last two decades.

Aside from degrading barrier protection, it's a rubbish lubricant in general. A man once suggested (whipping out a tub of Vaseline as he did so) attempting to fist me with a petrolatum-based aid. Are you joking? That stuff traps heat and makes it feel like someone's deep-frying your labia.

It's not a bad idea to carry a small bottle of massage oil, though, for the odd massage. Men like that, and often tip after. More often than they do for the actual sex. Weird creatures.

P is for Plastic

Tits, not credit cards. Do men prefer perfection or the real thing? Are all the other girls in the agency that naturally buoyant, or is there surreptitious cantilevering at work? Should you save your profits for an upgrade? Even the most down-to-earth girl will start to wonder if her career wouldn't enjoy the boost pumping up the volume might bring. If you wouldn't do it in real life, though, I can't say I'd recommend doing it at all.

P is also (obviously) for Porn

There's a fair amount of snobbery from those who buy tastefully hot, hardbound picture books on Neolithic erotic cave paintings against those who appear in hard-core porn. Believe me, honey, the snobbery goes both ways. African tribal sculpture of a man with an erection does not a libertine make.

Basically, if there isn't the possibility of come staining something in the process of its creation, it's class-B porn. Sorry to burst your bubble. Jenna Jameson, massage parlor attendants, and the guy who mops the booth at the peep show work in sex. People who wear pink baby-doll tees and stand behind a counter selling organic recycled nonphallic vibrators don't. Saucy art-house films set in France during the 1960s student protests are not porn. Double fist penetration while blowing a dog is. Rule of thumb: the more likely couples are to view a sex product as a relationship-strengthening tool, the less hard-core it is.

lundi, le 1ᵉʳ mars

Am still up North, sleeping on a sofa of one of the As, looking for a good massage therapist locally and drinking too many tequila-based concoctions. There is this cat, whenever she sees me she makes for my lap and rattles her purrbox like a rusty motor. Extremely cozy and warm-fluffy at the mo, and vaguely toying with the notion of never going back to London.

Kidding! I'll be home in a day or two. Wearing my brand-new gossamer pastel blue underwear, to boot.

mardi, le 2 mars

It is probably the lot of everyone to fear old age. When you are young, it does not seem possible that someday you will be as ancient as your relatives, and similarly impossible that they were even, in their turn, young.

It's when you leave the first flush of youth that the fear starts to creep in. The eyes of old people on the street—people whom you did not even notice, not so long ago—seem to bore straight into you. You will be here soon, they seem to say.

Only recently I saw my own future. Or to be more precise, heard it.

I was at home. My mother and grandmother were talking in the kitchen, unaware that I, checking my e-mail in a room around the corner, could hear every word.

But I paid them no attention until my ears seized on one phrase. *Pubic hair.*

Specifically, my mother saying to her mother, "I feel old. Why, only the other day I noticed my pubic hair is now almost completely gray."

To which my grandmother replied, "You think that's bad? Wait until they start falling out."

I think I had better kill myself now, before it's too late.

mercredi, le 3 mars

Of the four As there's only one of them I haven't slept with. This would be A3. When we first met, there was immediate, overpowering chemistry. We snogged a bit but didn't go any further.

He lived in a neighboring city, and when he went home, I was lonely. You know the feeling where all the pent-up energy goes straight to your legs, and you just want to run and run until you jump off a cliff? I confided in A2 and told him what had happened. I'd fallen hard and had to see the man.

We devised a plan: I would turn up at A3's door at the weekend as a surprise and see what happened. Meanwhile I had four days to plan and fret. So I did what any girl would do.

I slept with A2. Confused yet?

No? How about this, then—I was seeing A4 at the time. We were on the outs, but still an item, just. Jumping ship was high on the agenda, and this looked like a good opportunity.

So, A4 is out of town on a conference, I'm sleeping with our mutual friend A2 and planning to throw myself at the feet of A3. When the weekend comes, I turn up at A3's door.

He had a girlfriend. I had no idea. Until she answered the door. Her confused smile said she had no idea what was going on, and I felt exactly as low as I was acting. I made like Paula Radcliffe on speed.

A4 and I split properly; A2 and I made a brief go of things and it didn't work out. But it's water under the bridge now: they're all friends with each other. Most people who meet us reckon A4 is my husband, A2 my brother, and A1 our uncle—not because he looks old, we assure him, he just oozes manly authority. But there is the slight lingering problem of A3. After all these years, he's still seeing that girl. And sometimes on a night out he gets a bit pissed and overly friendly with me.

Too little, darling. Years too late.

We were at a restaurant a few nights ago. A2 introduced me to a colleague of his. As if he had to point him out at all. I noticed the man as soon as he came in the door.

"Nice," I whispered to A2.

"I thought he was just your type," he said, smiling.

He was. Neatly dressed, fit body, hands I could imagine all over me. Smart, polite, gorgeous mouth. "So where's he from?"

"South coast, originally."

"Mmm. Where've you been hiding this one?"

"He lives in San Diego."

"Ugh. Why?"

A2 shrugged. "Job."

I frowned. I didn't want a repeat of First Date. A seven-thousand-mile long-distance affair is out of the question unless handsomely remunerated for travel expenses. I've crossed the ocean for a heart of gold before, only to find it not worth the effort. But in the interest of social lubrication I flirted with him and the other boys over the meal. Afterward A2 was feeling tired and went home, leaving Dr. California in the capable hands of me, A3, and A4.

We went on to a pub. A3 was obviously drunk. "I like your pig-tail," he said, stroking the bellpull of my hair. His fingers curled around the end and tugged. The skin on the back of my neck tingled. Don't get me wrong, I still fancy the pants off this man, but can't be doing with painful love polygons anymore.

"Thank you," I said, turning my head so it slipped out of his grasp.

Dr. California racked up a set of billiard balls. We four toured the table for a couple of hours, me on a team with Official Ex A4, he with Unofficial Crush A3. A couple of people I hadn't seen in years walked by; we exchanged updates and laughs. My eyes followed Dr. C's lithe form around the room—eyeing the table, setting up a shot, the confident swing of the arm below the elbow on the follow-through. Competence so turns me on.

A few times, passing off the cue, I slid my hand over his lower back. Hard as.

A3 glowered at me, growing more drunk and moody. Finally he mumbled something about the last train home. On his way out the door, he put his arms roughly around my waist. I kissed the end of his nose.

"Good night," I chirped.

He squeezed harder, drawing me up on my tiptoes, and planted a kiss full on my lips in front of everyone. He hadn't been that forward in years. I pushed my face past his mouth into the side of his neck. He breathed hot against my ear. "You be careful. Wouldn't want to damage that new lad," he said, and left.

We put the cues away. The three of us finished our drinks. A4 gathered coats and went to the door.

I put a hand on Dr. C's arm, holding him back until A4 had gone outside. I turned toward him, his bright open face. "May I kiss you?"

"Please," he said. We snogged in the open doorway, blocking the exit. "Where are you staying?" he asked. A2's sofa, I told him.

"I have a huge bed at the hotel," he said.

"Perfect."

A4 was outside and waved us off at the corner. About a block from the hotel, Dr. C turned to me. "You don't remember me, do you?"

"No?"

"We met three years ago. I thought you were sexy then, too."

"I'm sorry, I don't remember."

He smiled. We went through the hotel's dim brown lobby and up to the second floor. I nodded at an acquaintance on the way. Sometimes it occurs to me how small the world is. By morning, I thought, all my friends and family will know of this.

The door was barely closed when we started grabbing at each other's clothes. Dr. C was as fit in the altogether as he'd been dressed, and his hands as good as I'd imagined. I took his penis in my mouth. "Ahh, that's fantastic," he murmured. "American girls don't know what to do with a foreskin."

He felt right to me, he tasted and smelt amazing. The sex was good but not like at work. It was joyous, reveling in his body, feeling good for sharing mine. I couldn't stop touching him, nibbling him, wanting him. He felt like someone I'd been with forever. And he took me again and again with amazing intensity. Each time he came, the muscular spasms ripped straight through me like a sound wave, setting off my own alarms, starting an orgasm from the inside out.

We slept a couple of hours, woke up, shagged again. Listened to the morning news on the radio. The usual stories—bombs, death, foreign elections. There wasn't much conversation. I didn't know what to say. Thank you, that was luscious, you know we're not going to see each other again, don't you? I was going to London in a couple of hours; he'd be flying back to San Diego later in the day. And yet it was a comfortable silence, the kind I could imagine stretching indefinitely into couplehood.

I brushed my teeth. When I came out of the toilet, he was

dressed. He watched me put on my coat; I had to meet a train. "Do you need a taxi?" he asked.

How many times have I heard that question? "No thank you, I'll walk."

"It isn't far?"

"It isn't."

He stood up, came over. Put his hands on my hips and kissed me tenderly. I'm reading too much into it, aren't I? It was a kiss that promised more if I wanted it. An open-ended question that already knew the answer. "Safe trip," he said.

"Goodbye," I said, and left. California is thousands of miles away. I smiled. The morning was warmer and brighter than I had reason to expect it to be.

vendredi, le 5 mars

Back in London on a reasonable spring day—not murderously hot, but pleasant enough to sit outside reading the papers and think about possibly leaving the coat at home. Was out and about when I saw S, one of the Boy's friends. The last I knew of him, he was freshly dumped by his redheaded lass, who was making time with the Boy's housemate. I suppose technically S is my friend as well—not knowing one of us better than the other—but presumed that anyone who did not contact me within twenty-four hours of the breakup to offer a cup of brew and the advice that all men are bastards anyway, was probably on the Boy's side.

I smiled and waved. He crossed the road and kissed me on the cheek. "It's been ages," he said. "How are you?"

"In rude health, as ever," I said. "Not to mention rude everything else. How are the motorcycle lessons going?"

"Dreadfully well," he said. "I'm looking at a Ducati 996 T reg this afternoon." The surest sign of a convert—slipping impenetrable abbreviations into conversation. Bless his cotton socks.

"Smashing," I said. "Or rather, not, I hope." We laughed.

"Bite to eat?" We sat in a dismal oriental cafe and ate mystery meats in an obvious base of powdered soup. At least the tea was copious, hot, and free. S has been seeing a woman he met through whatever leather-clad underground circles motorbike enthusiasts move in. He had to run along and I was starting to suffer MSG-related indigestion, so we walked down to Bayswater tube station together.

"I hesitate to ask this, but—"

"I was wondering if you'd bring him up," S said.

We paused on the pavement. The postlunch crowds parted and flowed around us. "Mmm. I was just wondering, what did he say was the cause of the breakup?" Cringe-worthy, I know, but curiosity does get the better of one.

S flapped his hands helplessly. "Oh, the usual man things," he said. "So little time, not being close enough . . . I think he's quite immature, really."

"You're not obliged to say that to please me," I said with a smile.

"It's true. He has not had much experience with women."

"I'm tempted to say if he goes on like that, it's not likely to improve." Of course, I would say that, wouldn't I?

"That's what I told him," S sighed, and checked his watch obviously. I was probably keeping him, not to mention being a boring girl hell-bent on analyzing a failed relationship. Nothing makes a man make his next appointment faster. S pecked my cheek. "At any rate—a pleasure seeing you."

"Marvelous to see you. Best of luck with the motor."

(Knickers today, butterfly-printed with shocking pink lace round the leg openings.)

dimanche, le 7 mars

Am recovering from a fancy-dress party which included getting jiggy to the worst music of the last two decades while a rabbi threw himself on the floor and pretended to be swimming and a man dressed as a tree dirty-danced over him. Because apparently Jews are literally commanded to get pissed and make noise on Purim.

Makes Carnival look rather timid in comparison, no?

Spent most of the morning hungover and reading multiple copies of the *Big Issue*, one bought from every homeless vendor I saw on Friday, and nibbling the pastries a neighbor brought by first thing today.

May have to go back to bed now. Knickers today: none, who wears knickers to bed?

lundi, le 8 mars

Sometimes I feel so tired and wouldn't mind someone else stepping in for a bit to do the grunt work while I take off on restorative jaunts north. The selection process for such responsibilities, though, would have to be airtight.

One criterion would have to be intelligence. And abs to die for. I could do sit-ups from now until the singularity and still not have rippling muscles down there. Flat, yes. But not a six-pack. Not even a four-pack of dry cider. Wherefore all the masochistic gym punishment? I should turf this job out to a better-looking body double and stay in, writing and eating cookies.

People whom I wouldn't throw out of bed for pretending to be me:

Karolina Kurkova,
Karolina Kluft,
Theoretically, anyone named Karolina.
Anna Kournikova,
Anna Nicole Smith,
Many, though not all, Annas.
Lisa Lopes,
Lisa Simpson,
A reasonable fraction of the world's Lisas.
Liz Taylor,
Liz Hurley,
Her Majesty Liz II.

Please send a brief cover letter (one side of A4 only) describing why you should be me, plus contact details and references to the usual place. I shall have my imaginary personal assistant sort them and contact you for interviews.

Attach photo of self in best underwear. Style over substance, as ever.

mardi, le 9 mars

The client was a young man, probably not much older than me. When I entered the room, he was dressed casually, in a tight T-shirt and baggy trousers I could easily imagine any one of my friends in. Immediately I felt how overdressed I was by comparison, how high theater my suit and makeup were to his street clothes.

"Hello," I said, smiling, and confirmed his name. There is always the slight possibility I might have knocked on the wrong door. Would someone turn away an unbidden hooker? Probably only when called on to pay before the sex.

"Hello," he said. He had lovely, smooth brown skin and an American accent. The room was crowded with unpacked luggage and piles of books. Was he here on business? Yes, he said. Leaving tomorrow. He nodded toward the money in an envelope on the desk. I put it away without counting. I trust them.

Many clients are in London on business. Most book a girl for the beginning of their stay rather than the end, and if they like her, book her again during their stay. If they don't get on, there's still time to try another. That he had waited until his last day made me think he wasn't expecting to have to pay for a liaison on this trip, and booked a girl out of desperation or boredom.

"Red or white wine?" he asked, perusing the contents of the minibar. To be honest, I prefer spirits, but will only choose from what is explicitly offered. If they do not specify—as in "What would you like to drink?"—I either ask for whatever they're having themselves or a glass of water. My mouth tends to go dry early on, and the first lip contact should be moist, welcoming, but not quite sloppy.

He held the glass out to me, we raised a half-ironic toast—"to new friends"—and drank. I noticed the arm holding his glass was tattooed. A small dagger in black. It looked ominously alive.

"Nice," I said, reaching over to finger the inking. The first moment of contact can be hard to engineer. Men who kiss you at the door are easy to fall into physical intimacy with, but more often the client is nervous, and I make an excuse to reach across and make contact. Almost as if by accident, like the moment on a date when the other person's proximity is an implicit permission to grab and kiss.

He took my wineglass away and pushed me back on the bed. His forearms were stronger than his softening middle, suggesting a former athlete going to seed. I looked up at him, lips parted. His trousers were half down and he was wearing no underwear. It occurred to me, just that moment, that there was something reckless about the way he handled me, and all the protection in the world would not stop him if he wanted to harm me. I leaned forward and took his cock in my mouth.

As a girl who is advertised as providing "all services," I know many customers book me on the expectation of anal sex and am prepared for that. They typically let me suck them for a while first, move on to a brief encounter with vaginal sex, then either ask nervously about approaching the back door or accidentally-on-purpose start heading that way. This man did neither.

Pushing me back on the bed, he bent above me, moving my legs up above my head. He licked his fingers and worked three of them into my cunt. I reached forward to draw his hand out, and sucked the digits. I like to know what my own taste is, partly because I enjoy the flavor, partly to know what's going on down there.

I stopped him and rolled to the side, extracted a condom from my purse, and pumped a heavy drop of lubricant on my finger. While he unwrapped and applied protection, I lubed my pucker. He burrowed his fingers back in and, using his wrist to pivot me backward, aimed his cock toward my back entrance. The full length sank straight in. He'd clearly worked it out beforehand— just the right angle for his member.

He pumped this way for half an hour and literally pinned me to the bed—all I could do was moan and make encouraging noises. His hand furrowed inside me, rubbing the bottom of my vagina to feel his own cock through the muscle wall. I felt the first shuddering spasms and his come fill the condom.

He didn't want to be held. I went to the toilet and cleaned myself, came back and dressed. We discussed Iris Murdoch, and I left. There were no taxis outside, so I walked as far as Regent Street, where the lights of the shops and the cars blurred into illusion.

mercredi, le 10 mars

I saw cherry blossoms this morning, it must be spring. They have probably been out for weeks but the tree near my door has suddenly and amply sprung into blossom. And the days, they're growing longer too.

Today the builders left. The ginger one stood awkwardly in the kitchen as the landlady passed her eye over the white walls and clean pine cupboards. She didn't seem half as pleased as I was with the result, but didn't say anything, just signed off an invoice and left.

The other one, the tall one, nodded toward the table where he'd left the spare keys.

"Thank you. I've become very used to you, you know," I said as he reached the door.

"No, thank you," he said (in a South London accent I wouldn't dare replicate in speech, much less writing—suffice to say they found my way of saying "room," "house," and "year" as amusing as I found theirs). "You're quite a lady, you are."

I laughed fit to burst. Lady, indeed. Lady in a green velvet thong at that.

vendredi, le 12 mars

He: "It's my first time."

Me: "First time with an escort?"

"First time, full stop."

(much fumbling ensues)

He: "Do tell me what to do. That's why I wanted it to be a call girl. Girlfriends never say anything useful."

(after)

He: "Honestly, how was that?"

Me: "Enjoyable. You have nice hands. Musician?"

(he nods) "What do you think of me in general?"

"Nice. Clever. Fit. You're a fine catch for someone."

"If you had met me somewhere else, would you fancy me?"

"How old are you?"

"Nineteen."

"Not if I knew your age." (he frowns) I say he looks older than that. But I didn't sleep with nineteen-year-olds even when I was nineteen. (that doesn't seem to have helped; he's looking even more depressed) "I'd fancy you. I would. You're a dangerous sort." How so, he wonders.

Must be careful here. Say something truthful, but nice, and not obviously flattery. It's tempting. "I wouldn't want to be the first person to break your heart." (he frowns again) But he shouldn't fret. I'm sure there are plenty of women in the world who would.

samedi, le 13 mars

Pub Games for Whores, part 1 in a series of 1.

FRIENDS OR LESBIANS?

The rules are laughably simple: attach yourself to a female friend and—this is important—without resorting to kissing or dirty dancing, convince everyone within a reasonable radius that you are a couple. Why the ban on liplock? Because shaking it with the ladies in public is what straight girls do to pick up straight men.

This went so successfully once that I rebuffed a less-than-gentleman making advances on a friend. Threading my arm through hers, I asserted, loudly, "Back off, mate—the lady is with me. You want to take it outside or do I kick your sorry arse right here?" The sad specimen skulked away from the bar. Unfortunately, this chivalry did not result in a sexual reward from the woman in question.

Popular variant: Plant yourself in the corner of the room and speculate on whether the women you see talking to each other are friends or "friends." Many a happy hour at university was spent thus.

THE CRASHING BORE

Embrace the chattering classes for an evening. You're a freelancing consultant; your interests include South American red wines, Japanese culture, and season-two *Buffy* on DVD; your topics of discussion range through mortgages, high-protein diets, and why the congestion zone should not extend to Kensington and Chelsea. Enthusiastically recommend bars So Bar, Front Room, et al.

I saw the best minds of my generation smacked out on tapas and talking about parking restrictions in Zone 2.

I'LL HAVE WHAT SHE'S HAVING

Who hasn't wanted to fake orgasm in a public place? Make like a Bailey's advert and enjoy your drink more than a body ought to.

THE IMPLAUSIBLE OCCUPATION

When a man cracks on to you, make up a fake job to tell him when he (inevitably; men are conversationally predictable) asks what you do. Some tried-and-tested favorites include: aerial acrobat, mobile phone ringtone programmer, foot model, gamelan musician. See how long you can continue to make up specialized knowledge for your fake CV. Extra points if he actually holds that job. "Really? You're an epidemiologist? What a coincidence!"

SPEAKEE NO ENGRISH

Self-explanatory. Especially fun if you are not obviously ethnic.

ARE YOU TALKING TO ME?

"So I was running arms out of Serbia, right? And I was stopped by the UN troops at the border. Little did they know I was high on speedballs and had a sawn-off shotgun cocked and locked in my inside jacket. . . ." The Travis Bickle option. Be a scary bastard. Pepper conversation liberally with references to Kalashnikovs, John Woo films as lifestyle, and *Soldier of Fortune* magazine. Ninety-nine percent of men will run screaming from a sociopathic, possibly armed female. As for how you handle the other 1 percent . . . well, it might be fun. But be sure not to leave your back unguarded.

TOO MUCH INFORMATION

The more extreme the better. Discuss at length (and full volume) the specific details of your sex life. Rimming, bondage and domination, masturbatory fantasies involving Dick Cheney and a genetically engineered pig. It's all fair game. Highest points to the person who can make the most customers vacate the premises.

Most of my conversations are like this.

TICK TOCK, TICK TOCK

"Such a pleasure to meet you . . . because according to my basal temperature this morning, I'm ovulating for the next twenty-four hours. Do you live close by or shall I ring a taxi?"

The Back Foot

Accost a random gentleman. Surprise him with the revelation that you've slept together recently, and he never rang you back, and you are most upset. Loudly recount the ins and outs of your night of random passion. Judicious hints that he was failing in several key anatomical areas are effective additions to the routine.

Do be careful: if he's with a group of male friends, he scores the points, not you. Best catch him out with his partner or alone. And try not to get too carried away. Bunny boiling is an addictive sport.

What The?

Pick up a conversation with a complete stranger as if you've known each other for years, and they just wandered in to the discussion mid-sentence. Be certain to use a lot of familiar body language, such as casually touching their arm, asking after family, and so on.

N.B.: I met A1 this way.

The Truth

Tell someone you're a call girl. Then laugh. No one would believe it. "Oh, I'm just having you on. I'm really a nun."

dimanche, le 14 mars

The end of the affair was written from the beginning. He is a man who hires women for sex, I am the whore, and at some point his taste will move on.

I have grown accustomed to him, and while I do not love him I admit more than a few times to being just as interested in staying up all night talking as in the carnal transaction.

In the upstairs bathroom is a large tub with gold-colored taps and four drawings on the wall of a village in France. He says these are gifts from the artist. I have looked at those pictures so many times while bathing afterward that when the painters who whitewashed the walls put them back in the wrong order, I noticed before he did.

"So they are," he said, squinting at the pastels. "Well spotted."

He knows a great deal about me, this one. He knows my real name and what I studied, and often mentions—he works in a related area—that should I ever need employment in the future, well . . . and he slips his card in my pocket for the dozenth time.

It's like having a protective uncle. Who fucks you.

Sometimes we don't fuck as such. He doesn't like latex, but I'm not a risk-taker by nature. So he wanks on me. I stretch out on a bed or couch or sometimes the floor, head propped up with a pillow or two, as he straddles my torso below the breasts. While I play with my nipples and his balls he jerks his shaft over my face. Afterward, we'll find a mirror and analyze the result together— points awarded for consistency, accuracy, and volume. And because he enjoys washing me, he'll let it dry a little and dab most of the damage off with a damp washcloth.

The last few weeks have been difficult to organize. We never had a set meeting day and time, though it was usually a weekday, and usually after ten. I've been busy lately. So has he. If he doesn't reach me first, he'll take another girl from the agency.

I see I've missed his call and text back. This goes on for several weeks. I'm starting to miss the glass of bubbling Pol Roger he always pours when I come in.

When I went away, he rang three times. He's getting anxious. It's like the end of a relationship: the clinginess, the unfounded suspicion.

Then, the resolution. Just a text one morning:

I suppose we are fated to never meet again. Will miss you. X

I'll miss him, too.

lundi, le 15 mars

I'm not sure if it signifies a significant turn in my thinking, or for that matter my housekeeping skills, but I cannot be bothered to segregate the work knickers from the home knickers any longer. This doesn't mean I end up in a boring sporty thong on the job, but does sometimes result in going to the grocery store with an inch or so of lace frill and striped satin inadvertently poking out the top of my jeans. I am given to understand that in some cultures, this is a desirable trait. I shudder to think.

mardi, le 16 mars

N rang. "Not seen you around in a bit."

"No."

"Is everything alright?"

"Fine."

"Liar." He was correct, as usual. "What's going on?"

"I don't know. First real spring day, perhaps. I was out walking by the river in the sunshine, and it occurred to me that a year ago I was doing the same thing with someone I loved and thought I was going to marry."

"Must be in the water. I just thought about my ex today too." This is the one who chucked him suddenly, without so much as a fare-thee-well. "I'll come over if you like." I just sighed heavily. "I'll be there in ten minutes, then."

N knocked briefly and let himself in. I was sitting on the couch frowning. "Hey, gorgeous," he said, rubbing my hair. "Why don't we nip out for a bite to eat?" I wasn't hungry. But we went.

"So if you could meet your ex and whomever he's with now," N said over salad and a pint at some obnoxious gastropub, "what would she be like?" Fat, I guessed. "Mine, I'd like to see her with someone who's perfect—except he's impotent."

"No, not fat. Stupid."

"Someone who's perfect, but impotent and has a horrible set of in-laws."

"Stupid, and smells funny."

"Ooh, that's good. The ultimate physical insult. Impotent, bad in-laws, and tells her she can't have a job outside the home." He finished his pint and started on mine, which was barely depleted.

"Stupid, smells funny, and has terrible taste in music." I thought about claiming my drink back but it was clearly a lost cause—he downed at least half of it in one gulp. "Actually, scratch that, he'd never be interested in someone with bad taste in the first place. He would have vetted that straightaway."

N swallowed a mouthful of bitter. "Impotent and bald."

"Mine will be bald in five years' time. I believe that. I have to believe that."

"Impotent, bald, and cheats on her. Because she would know that I never would have done that to her."

"Stupid, smells funny, and terrible in bed."

"Terrible in bed. Now we've hit the heart of it," N smiled. "Bald, impotent, and won't fist her."

"Really? She was that into it?"

"Oh yes," he said. "I never told you about the fist and the cucumber? Simultaneously?"

"Worse still, you never took pictures, did you?"

"We always said if all else failed in her career, there was yet money to be made in film."

"Talent. No wonder you fell for her." I picked at the damp edge of a beer mat. "Stupid—and not just intellectually challenged, but unable to shut up as well—and sleeps with one of his brothers."

"Which one?"

"Doesn't matter. No, better yet—his father."

"She still has to smell funny, right?"

"Absolutely."

"Bald, impotent, won't fist her, and short."

"What's wrong with short?" I'm not terribly far from the Earth's crust myself and don't think this is a reflection on a person's value. And, I never get dizzy from standing up quickly. So there.

"Nothing, it's just that she was tall. I want her to have to look down and see that bald head as often as humanly possible." He put the empty glass back on my side of the table.

"Fair enough." I smiled. "You still miss her, don't you?"

"Too damn right. You're still in love with him, aren't you?"

"You know I am."

"I find it strange," he said. "Theoretically I'm over her, but if that's so, I should probably make an effort to date other women rather than avoid them altogether."

"Ah, I know that stage," I said. "I'm in more of a 'sabotaging perfectly good potential relationships' mode." Not to mention being afraid the Boy might make his reappearance just as I found someone worth hanging on to.

N patted his stomach. The pub was empty of all but a few staff and a couple who looked at their limp overpriced food in horror. "Shall we go?" N said. I nodded. "I've had enough alcohol—I could take you home and piss on you if that would make you feel better."

I pursed my lips and pretended to consider, changed the subject. Asked him, was it better to be brokenhearted or to not know what that felt like? Now he knew, he said, he'd never want to cause anyone to feel that way again. You never know, I said. You might break my heart. He wrapped his arms around me and started to tickle. I squirmed. "You rat bag," he said. "I can't break your heart—you don't love me."

"Stop that," I said. Stern, but still smiling. He knew I was serious. Got up, put his coat on, went to the door. I told him I was going straight to bed when I got home.

"After you tap this conversation into your little computer," he corrected. Said good night and left.

mercredi, le 17 mars

Ooh, these are one of my favorite pairs: ruched pink silk with antique lace and matching bra. Pity to just be wearing them under jeans and a sweater when I go to the shop for milk.

Once I attended a booking directly from a job interview. This was acceptable but not ideal; the clothing was almost right for an afternoon meeting, and the makeup certainly was, but it was a bit odd to be walking around with a CV tucked away next to a box of condoms. And a little worried that someone may have glanced in my bag and noticed them at the interview.

Would that help or harm the chances of employment? I wonder. And yes, I was offered the job, but didn't take it in the end—just more office admin rubbish that would end up nowhere in a year's time.

Another time I readied myself in a museum toilet. This was very early on, when I was convinced that the punting world would beat a path to my door, and went round with a light summery dress, strappy heels, latex bits, and change of knickers in a bag just in case. This was before I realized that I didn't have to work at breakneck pace to make my bills and expenses, and also that most punters would accept a meeting one or two hours later than requested if they really wanted me. If not, well, there are plenty of fish for hire in the sea.

I applied lipgloss and mascara as dozens of tourists trailed in and out of the toilets. If there is a uniform for tour groups, and I assume there must be, it is this: overlong shorts, white sneakers, voluminous T-shirts advertising the last place visited, visor, hair in pigtails, shoulder bag.

I can't begin to imagine what they thought I was dressing for.

jeudi, le 18 mars

The client stood, trousers off. I sat in a chair in front of him. My shirt (white, as requested) was half-unbuttoned. "I want to write my name in come all over you," he said.

I smirked. "You can't fool me, you nicked that line from *London Fields*."

He looked at me strangely. Oh no, I thought. Better watch my mouth. "Amis fan?" he said idly, pulling himself with one hand.

"He's not bad," I said, reaching into the shirt to pull my breasts free of the bra.

"*Time's Arrow* was pretty tricksy though." A glistening drop of pre-come lolled on the tip of his glans.

"Very high-concept. Good book for a long train journey." I pulled at my nipples to his appreciative nods.

It was hot and close in the room. The weather has not been so bad and I thought of asking him to turn the heating off. "I want to smell your sweat mixing with my spunk," he said, as if reading my thoughts.

Later, I met another client. A large hotel in Lancaster Gate. The room was small and highly decorated, which surely made it look even smaller. For the money they must be charging here, I thought it seemed a little cramped. End-of-hall room.

He was in shirtsleeves. Short sleeves under a blazer—I hate that, it jars like light socks with men's shoes.

"Your nipples are hard already," he said appreciatively (black lace balconette bra and matching boy-style briefs). The window was wide open.

I draped my arms over his shoulders and asked, "Are you not a little cold in here?"

"I'm fine."

"There are goose pimples all over your arms." I smiled and walked to the ground-floor window to pull the drapes.

"Good for the metabolism."

"Bet I can think of something better," I said.

vendredi, le 19 mars

Think I'll stay indoors today. N came back from Belgium with a veritable metric ton of porn to sift through, including the always-reliable Lady Anita F (Hotter Than Hell!!) title and another mag with a tasty bob-haired girl doing the waterstuff all over some poor boy who no doubt deserves it. Will let you know if anything interesting, er, goes down.

samedi, le 20 mars

One of the first few golden days when people start deciding to leave coats at home and fishbelly-pale arm skin makes an appearance. I went out to buy a paper and, inspired by the sunshine, couldn't stop walking.

After an hour of beating the pavement I came to an attractive shop window. It's a place I've noticed but only from a taxi, and after opening hours. I always liked the name of the shop. Very suggestive of my job, actually. On the locked door was a small sign that said "Please ring both bells." I rang and waited.

A man let me in and smiled. It was small inside, crowded with clothing, costume jewelry, and gold-leaf cherubs. I fingered the clothes on their close racks. Nice enough, in a fancy-dress sort of way, perhaps a bit Goth. And expensive. The sort of place that I often wonder how it stays in business. The products must be so limited in their appeal that you find yourself desperately hoping that the twelve or so people for whom this shop must be heaven on earth manage to wander down the road sometime soon.

The man disappeared in the back and the bell rang. It was a young teenage girl, his daughter. She was wearing a short dress and sweater, and pink wellies. She called him by his first name.

First-Name Father asked his offspring to wrap something. She sighed and stomped around a bit. Now, my parents are hardly paragons of conventionality, but they always made sure to send me away for a good few weeks when not in term. Best for all involved: they get a bit of parenting relief and you are not forced to roll your eyes and grumble about how unfair the world is more than, oh, twice a day at most. "Fine," she spat, and set about mummifying a brooch in hectares of black tissue. I recognized instantly the cadence of speech indicating an intersection of private school education, indulgent parents, and general overtones of Southernness. Nothing quite raises my hackles like a prepubescent who believes she is the greatest thing going and, in all probability, will someday be hailed as such.

The bell rang again and First-Name Father disappeared almost instantly. This time it was a tiny woman dressed head to toe in clothes from the shop. By which I mean she resembled a bruise-colored meringue. She and the girl started complaining loudly about the low temperature inside and the stroppy little cow disappeared to demand her sire do something about it. I was fairly impressed, actually—at that age I believe my spoken repertoire did not extend past "I don't know" and "Go away."

"Is someone helping you?" the woman asked me. I'm not terribly tall, but must have stood a full head above this miniature Morticia who, from the layers of black corsetry and full-skirtedness, looked distinctly like the New Romantics after an unfortunate accident in a wallpaper factory. About fifty years ago.

"I'm just browsing, thank you."

Morticia hung at my elbow while I politely fingered brocade coats and crinolined skirts. They might have been attractive as well, with about a stone less of velvet ribbon each. "Your window dressing is very nice," I said, hoping a spot of talking would drive her off. "I often come down this road on the way to work but have not been in before."

"Where do you work?" she asked.

Think fast, girl. "The V&A," I said.

"The what?"

"The Victoria and Albert." She didn't look less puzzled. How could she not know the costume museum? Odd for one so blatantly overdressed. "The V&A Museum."

"Oh, the *museum*," she said, as if humoring me. Cripes, lady, I thought. It's only round the corner.

"Are these—um—your designs?" I ventured.

"Yes," she said flatly, and turned her head to hurl abuse at her daughter. The shop was still disagreeably cold for them. I wondered if she wasn't anemic and almost suggested a restorative session of basking on a hot rock.

"Lovely," I rasped.

"Is there anything else I can do for you?" she asked, impatient. I had been looking at a delicate and not absurdly overjeweled pair of butterfly earrings, but opted against on principle. Morticia herded me toward the door.

"No, thank you," I said as she held the bolt of the lock open and whisked me back into the warm air. Traumatized by the experience, I promptly went and dropped sixty quid on bright glass earrings at a shop over the road.

dimanche, le 21 mars

I want so very little out of life, really. All a girl asks for is

- a haircut that looks the same regardless of wind speed or direction
- to be smiled back at, by people I smile at
- shoes that make you look taller, and look nice, and can be used for actual walking
- for only disabled people to park in disabled spots
- instant mastery of all things kitchen-related
- a bit of sunshine now and then
- a worldwide ban on polyphonic ringtones
- a worldwide ban on phones which give you no options save a polyphonic ringtone
- a cessation of all suffering, backdated to the beginning of time

lundi, le 22 mars

A4 and I met for lunch at a Polish restaurant. It had come highly recommended as an antidote to the self-conscious bitter-leaf trattorias and über-kosher bagel purveyors of North London. I always feel too skeptical for one and too secular for the other. Inside, the restaurant was dour, decorated in heavy seventies earth tones, bad repros of Polish historical battles, and a layer of grease that might well have been imported from the kitchens of my childhood. The food could have been straight from my mother's stove: beetroot borscht with cream and vegetables; fried potato latkes with applesauce and sour cream. The waitresses, too, were authentically heavy and dour in their tight-pulled blonde pigtails and gray aprons tied round rolling middles. When they acknowledged a customer at all, it was with the same language of grunts that I'd encountered in restaurants on trips to northeastern Europe. Everything—everything—was fried and came with a side of cabbage. I was smitten.

Our table sat next to the window. We looked out at the busy sidewalk and lunchtime traffic: businessmen munching chips, people crowding into queues at the bank and chemist, a cheap Chinese eatery overflowing with students. Inside the restaurant, though, it was a world apart, shielded from the modern noise outside with no more than the creaking strains of a mechanical dumbwaiter as background music.

We were amused to hear a woman at the next table struggling to make sense of the menu. This was not fare for the calorie- nor image-conscious (I myself had taken the precaution of skipping breakfast). Whilst waiting on her main course, she flagged down one of the slow-moving waitresses. "Do you do cappuccino?" she asked. A4 and I stifled snorting laughs. The pink-cheeked waitress furrowed her brow. "Cappuccino?" the woman asked again. She mimed steaming milk through a machine. "You know—schhh schh, schhh schh?" The waitress shook her head and walked away. A4 and I were almost crying from stifled laughter.

I went to look at the desserts in the case. An apple strudel, swathed in layers of pastry, dusted with sugar. Dense-looking tarts. As I returned to my seat a gentleman swiped at my midsection.

I looked down at the table. Four fellows in suits, middle-aged, having a business lunch. Did I know this man? I wondered. I couldn't place the face. Former client?

"Er, bring us a basket of bread, would you," he demanded.

I laughed, a short sharp bark. "Sorry—I don't work here," I said and walked off. How odd.

mardi, le 23 mars

I am a cheap date.

At several hundred an hour, this is a rich claim to be making. But it is the truth. Considering the economics of sex—in which a man is prepared to invest some time, and a bit of money toward gifts and entertainments, in order to coax a woman into bed—I am assured by clients that the cost of a call girl is on par with the price of picking up a woman on a business trip. And she's not likely to come round and cook your rabbit later.

But I don't mean at work, where the judgment of whether my services are worth the money would doubtless involve a level of math I am not capable of. I am a cheap date in real life.

On paper it sounds great. Woman arranges her own transportation, buys her own pint and perhaps a few for you, and should there be a resulting relationship, is not terribly fussed about receiving gifts, holidays abroad, or other trinkets of your affection aside from the affection itself. If you go away together, she'll contribute her share; if you fail to book a restaurant on one of several major milestones, she will smile and say she prefers staying in. She does not arbitrarily demand shiny things in pale-blue Tiffany boxes—if she sees something she likes, she'll buy it, and if you do make an extra effort, she will of course be grateful. But does not take it for granted.

I'm a high-maintenance plot, but hire my own groundskeepers, as it were.

It has taken some time to conclude this is not what men are attracted to. They enjoy the chase, don't they, the idea that a woman's value is reflected in the effort you spend to win a smile or a kiss. Even if she turns out to be rubbish in bed, by the time you have pried her iron-banded thighs apart with weekend breaks in Sardinia and a shiny carbon chip on a ring, you'll be so grateful to be there at all that it will not matter.

I reckon this means people would tend to be worse in bed than their ancestors, the need to win a mate with lingual talent being bred out of the population (N.B.: not scientifically proven). It might also mean that women with doe eyes, slightly turned-in toes, and a skill for simpering should predominate.

Film noir gave us a term for the low-maintenance cheap-date type of woman, as personified by Ingrid Bergman and the other cool blondes. They were, in the gruff parlance, Class Acts. A Class Act does not bombard you with whimpering phone calls to the effect of why are you out with your mates watching the footie when you could be choosing sisal floor mats with me? A Class Act does not take a split badly, or if she does, does so without so much as a peep. A Class Act is the silhouette disappearing into the night that you will no doubt remember—but will never talk to again.

A Class Act will spend a lot of time alone, drinking spirits. A Class Act will never emerge from a local church in a shower of petals. A Class Act will never be a mummy, yummy or otherwise.

A Class Act will never have a husband who visits prostitutes.

Forget I mentioned it.

mercredi, le 24 mars

Last night when I checked e-mail, Hotmail offered a link to "Dating Tips from the Animal Kingdom." Expecting the piece to delight and entertain was about as fruitful as reading the back of a shampoo bottle in search of fine literature, so I offer instead an alternative list of dating tips from the animal kingdom.

- Our good friends and coevolutionaries *Canis familiaris* (the domestic dog) show that when in doubt which hole to aim for, thrust wildly. You are bound to land in something good.
- Shrimps' hearts are in their heads. Men have neither hearts nor heads.
- The tongue of a giraffe (*Giraffa camelopardalis*) is half a meter in length, long enough to clean its own ears. If you can do the same, there may be a career option you had not yet considered. . . .
- Dolphins engage in group sex. If those squeaky gray-skinned fisheaters can do it, so can you.
- The females of the bonobo species (*Pan paniscus*), closely related to humans, are known to use sexual favors to gain status and food. A point to remember next time you're short of change at the corner shop.
- Some ribbon worms will eat themselves if they can't find food. Unfortunately, men unable to find sex are rarely so talented.
- The anal glands of cats, genus *Felis*, are used to mark their territory and identify themselves to other cats. Whether this explanation will convince the hotel not to charge you for excess laundering is questionable.
- The sailfish, the swordfish, and the mako shark can all swim at a speed of over fifty miles per hour. If you meet someone unpleasant at a club, it's unlikely you'll be able to escape as quickly.
- Lions have been known to mate over fifty times a day. This is probably the sole criterion to become King of the Jungle.
- A rhinoceros's horn is made of hair. Men who are lacking in

the horn department, on the other hand, are not advised to grow longer hair to compensate for the fact.

- Human birth control pills work on gorillas. If you have more success finding contraceptives and a female gorilla than a mate, something has gone horribly wrong.
- Time is limited and some opportunities may never repeat themselves. Take a tip from swallows of the genus *Hirundo*, who mate in midair, regardless of the number of people on the flight.

As an aside, whilst researching this list, I ran across a site devoted to dolphin dildos. By which I do not mean dildos shaped like dolphins. I mean dildos the size and shape of a dolphin's member. Eep.

jeudi, le 25 mars

N and I had breakfast at a greasy spoon (his: full fry-up and chips; hers: scrambled eggs on toast). He's not been sleeping well and it shows, but can't explain why. Maybe long hours at work, maybe family worries, maybe a belated sense that it should be spring but it is so cold and wet that the internal clock is still ticking over in winter time. Someone we know started a rumor last week that the clocks went forward before Mothering Sunday instead of this weekend, and it threw him off, and he's not had a night's rest since.

He's heard things, things about me. Stories are getting around. Nothing earth-shattering, just a comment or two from a person or two coming back round to him. Have I mentioned N appears to be the secret hub of all knowledge in London? You know a name—he knows someone who knows someone. Is something you heard true? He can get the goods. He's a dealer, and his drug is information.

There's envy involved, usually the engine behind the worst, most damaging rumors. Other things. I hate this Sturm und Drang. Someone I slept with who asked me to keep it secret—I didn't even write about it—turned around and told, oh, about half of the city. A few personal things. That I don't mind. It's the asking for privacy, then blatantly stripping it off, that I care about. Poor etiquette in a lover. "Maybe I should say something to him about it."

"Not a good idea," N advised. He pointed out that this man is young and a bit feckless, and I was more likely to give him a pat on the head and a coo of forgiveness than the slap he so clearly deserves. "The onus is on him now. He's the one who's going to feel uncomfortable when he sees either of us."

"Maybe I should start rumors of my own."

"Keep your own counsel. Better in the long run."

"I feel my evil antennae twitching . . ." I said, waggling forefingers in the air.

"Don't."

"Ah, bollocks, that reminds me . . ."

"What?"

"On his way out the door, he asked me if it was true I'd had a threesome with you and someone else."

"What did you say?"

"Yes."

He cringed. "Well, I don't care, and you obviously don't, and I don't think the other girl does either. But I wonder why he was interested? If I were him, I would have asked me and not you."

"Yes. Or asked if I'd ever been in a threesome, in case angling me into one was a possibility."

"Exactly. I wonder why he was so interested in a piece of trivia about my private life as he's getting out of your bed?" N scratched at his stubble. "One too many one-night stands," he said. "Be careful what you say about someone else's sex life," he advised.

I shrugged. I drank the very strong, very fresh coffee. He asked if I'd seen the car outside my house again. I have. He asked if I needed anything. I said I didn't.

"Get out if you can," he said.

"The business, the house, or the ex-boyfriend?" I asked.

"All three," he said. "I don't know what you're planning, but whatever it is, have a spare rabbit hole."

He pushed a crust of toast around the plate. The cafe that had been crowded when we sat down was almost empty of people. I bought a piece of carrot cake for later. He tipped the waitress and drove me home. His left hand rested on my knee the whole journey.

"Just be careful," he said. I waved him off and went upstairs.

(Knickers today: transparent black with cream lace edging and a peephole in the back. These are currently topping the league table of favorites.)

vendredi, le 26 mars

Am entertaining for the weekend and N is coming round to vacuum the flat. He volunteered. Wonder if I leave the washing up, will he volunteer for that as well?

I don't run into the neighbors often, usually only on the way out the door. So they either think I lead an unutterably glamorous life of nonstop parties and premieres, or they know everything. Or they just think I like to dress up. Anyway, very little noise ever comes from those quarters. Until last night when I came home at 2 a.m. and was kept awake another hour by the distinct sound of books being thrown, one by one, against a wall.

Odd.

Also, have noticed at the gym that my Achilles tendons seem stiff of late. Am told this is the result of habitual wearing of heels. I know that every season we are bombarded with the propaganda that flat shoes are cute and sexy too, but trying to talk me into low heels with a skirt is probably a conversion project along the lines of the settlement of the West Bank. Will simply have to stretch more.

samedi, le 27 mars

For all of the good advice I have received over the years, no one has ever opined on what may be the greatest challenge of my working life. How to deal with a non-standard-issue cock.

Penises can be strange for many reasons. They might have an unusual length-to-width ratio, or curve in a funny way, or remind you of your father's brother's penchant for turtleneck sweaters. In fact, if you sum up the ways in which a dong can be odd, there are probably more strange ones than unstrange ones. This gives the old man quite a scope for personality indeed.

For the most part the differences can be stacked in the "odd, but not distractingly so" or the "odd, but not medically abnormal" bins. And when a member confounds these classifications, I never know what to say.

Treat the matter lightly? As in a saucy purr of, "My, what unusual tackle you have." Show a modicum of medical interest and ask, "Have you ever been to a doctor about that?" Recoil in horror? Ask advice on how he would like it handled? Or would sir prefer I didn't comment at all?

I had the pleasure of meeting a customer with a most normal penis. Normal in every detectable way. It was his foreskin that was unusual. Instead of parting at the top, so the glans could nudge through, this gentleman's sheath opened at the side.

At the side. Of his penis. Halfway down the shaft. An aperture too small to wedge his cock through. Meaning that he was hooded at all times, even when aroused.

I smiled. Looked at it, looked at him. Didn't say anything. He didn't offer advice. Should I attend to the head (completely covered) or the opening (drooling with pre-come, but several inches back)? He was older than me, divorced, so obviously someone had come across this anomaly before. Was it uncomfortable when he was hard? I wondered. Would he have problems with certain positions? Would this affect the condom? Would it be insulting to ask?

I lavished attention on both the head and the opening, being careful not to curl my hand round the shaft too tightly. When we progressed to intercourse, I pinched the tip of the condom as I put it on to collect the semen, wondering if it mattered. He took me from behind, but didn't say if there was a reason above personal preference. He removed the condom himself afterward. I never did have a proper look at the result.

dimanche, le 28 mars

I had been set up yet again, this time with someone introduced merely as "your future husband," no pressure or anything.

lundi, le 29 mars

I have this friend, right, only she's not really a friend. More of an ally, or an acquaintance who won't quite go away. And I'm not usually an unkind person, promise, I'm not.

I met her via A3, who kind-of sort-of had a thing with her a few years ago. By which I mean that he fancied her until he found out how desperately awful she was, at which point there was no turning back. As Churchill said, when you're going through hell, keep going.

EOBAYH, we call her. Short for Each One Big As Your Head. This reference to her massive . . . tracts of land, being almost unpronounceable, has shortened itself to a two-hands-ballooning-from-chest gesture that signifies an overample bosom. Sample: "I ran into [hand gesture] the other day, apparently she's doing the low-carb diet."

"Yes? Is it working?" Because Hand Gesture's assets are all natural, there's a bottom to match the top. Not to mention a middle. And ankles you could safely moor Thames pleasure cruisers to.

(raised eyebrow in response, indicating that, if anything, she has grown more ample)

Hand Gesture probably has the highest ratio of failed diets and gym memberships to actual pounds lost of anyone I've met.

Don't get me wrong. It's not polite to ridicule someone's weight. A4, for instance, has been known to carry an extra pound or two and we never utter so much as a peep. But Hand Gesture has earned the right to be mocked by automatically declaring anyone smaller than her to have an eating disorder. Which by definition is the entire living population of the world save the scarier neighborhoods of Glasgow and a few bubbes in Miami. A conversation with Hand Gesture will most likely include a passage along the lines of, "I ran into Ruth the other day, yes? She just had a baby—right back to her original weight, eating disorder—and she was telling me about a new band her partner's in. . . ." and so on and so forth. Endlessly. She saw your mum the other day? Eating disorder. That blonde on *Teachers*? Eating disorder. New slimline Vanessa Feltz? Bulimic cow. Conversely, nibble so much as a rusk in front of her, and you're bingeing.

Anyway. Last week A3 was in town and rang to see if I wanted to meet for lunch. It was rather disorganized—he had two meetings beforehand, one in Bayswater and one in the City. But my daylight schedule is dead easy to rearrange, and we decided on 3 p.m. on Friday. Bought a sandwich an hour before, noodled around the shops for a bit, arrived at the restaurant. The staff looked a touch surly at having customers in the post-lunch hours, for which I felt not the tiniest tinge of guilt. A spotty student-type led me wordlessly to the table.

He sat me opposite Hand Gesture and her magnificently up-holstered chest. Damn, I hadn't known she would be there. Though if I had known, I probably wouldn't have bothered turn-ing up. She was the only other person there, scarfing through the complimentary bread and olives. So much for low-carb diets.

"Hello, darling," I said, feeling none of the goodwill I hoped I oozed. "A pleasant surprise to see you." I asked after her family and she brought me up to date on who was looking too skinny, who should eat something, and—while there was no physical ev-idence to confirm this—the stones that had been simply dropping off her lately through diet and exercise. She offered me a chunk of bread and, still rather full from the sandwich, I waved it away.

"You're certain?" she asked, eyes scanning my breasts, which are by no stretch of the imagination as big as my head, much less hers. "You're not one of these . . ."

I put on a pained look and fluttered a hand up to my chest. "Celiac disease, actually," I said, twitching the corners of my mouth and making as if to cry. "They diagnosed last month. My bowels are literally falling out of me, I can't digest gluten and have come out in a rash all over."

"My . . . no. Really?" she asked, mouth slack.

I leaned forward conspiratorially. "The worst part is the explo-sive diarrhea," I whispered, just as the rest of our party arrived and seated themselves. "You simply can't imagine how awful it's been. You're ever so lucky. It would be a blessing to have real thighs again."

Of course, this meant I had to nibble poached fish and a terrible salad for the rest of lunch, but it was worth an hour of neither words nor food passing her mouth. I'm not usually an unkind person, really I'm not.

mardi, le 30 mars

The client leaned over me, pulling at his member furiously. "I'm going to come on your face," he said. It was the sixth time in ten minutes he'd said it, growling, as if trying to convince himself.

That was all. "I'm going to come on your face." No instructions for me, though I played with my breasts and nipples, sucked my own fingers after touching myself, hoping that would help. All that I had known before the appointment were the details of the meeting and a request to wear a lot of makeup.

My effort didn't seem to help. He was looking at the wall, not at me. A few times his frantic hand slowed, and he dipped down to my lips. He was going soft and I sucked him hard again. He never looked down, not once. Then the masturbation would start again. And the mantra. "I'm going to come on your face." I writhed on the sheets and groaned. No reaction. I bent my head forward and licked his inner thigh. Again, no reaction.

Half an hour later, he still had not finished. I murmured and probed, wandering fingers, gentle questions. But it seemed he wanted nothing from me, save to be the canvas he painted. It made me feel the way unturned clay must, wanting to form into something, some fantasy, but not being allowed. His shoulders slumped and he fell, sweaty, into my chest, "I'm sorry, honey, it ain't gonna happen," he said, as if it had been my idea all along.

mercredi, le 31 mars

Funnily enough, the liaison with "my future husband" did not go to plan. I hold this up as a prime example of why my friends should not choose my dates, but A1 is undeterred and determined not only to make his mark as matchmaker, but to find the root of my problems with partners.

So he was idly surfing the Web while I hunted for any scrap of cake in his house. None was forthcoming, and I made a deal with the devil and concocted a cup of chocolate consisting of the heat-whitened end of a chocolate bar, most of a waxen bar of choc from an Army rat pack, and instant coffee. It swirled, oily and evil, in a white mug. "When and where were you born?" A1 asked.

"Why?"

"Natal chart." Online astrology is one of the sure signs of imminent societal collapse. Told him anyway. "Oh dear. Oh, oh dear."

"What's that?" I sipped the greasy faux-chocolate drink. Foul, yes, but not unsatisfying. Must find a better method of dealing with hormonal cycles though—for it is spring, when a young woman's fancy turns to bikinis.

"Mars is in Cancer." (Or whatever on earth he said. I'm not au fait with this particular brand of superstition.)

"Which means what exactly?"

"You're emotionally manipulative."

"Alert the press. I wonder who didn't already know that."

Avril

Belle's A-Z of London Sex Work

Q-S

Q is for Quality

Don't get lazy. It's perfectly acceptable for one's mind to wander on the job, but totting up your credit card receipts while some poor john bones you from behind will not go unnoticed. Feigning interest is the social lubricant of modern life and not too much to ask in one hour out of the day. Think of it as increasing the chances of a tip and repeat business.

Q is also for Quitting

Some people say once you've been paid for sex, you are never really out of the business. I'll report back in 2037 whether this is true.

R is for Relationships

This is not a film or a fairy tale. You will not end up marrying a rich, attractive single man you met on the job and live happily ever after. Do not date the clients, do not confuse the nature of the relationship. Enjoy the man if he's nice but never forget where the line is. Would you expect a personal trainer to follow a client home from the gym, or get together on weekends just to hang out? No. Out of the question.

S is for Sexy

Sexiness is not a square-yards-of-cloth to exposed-skin ratio. Sexy is not the inevitable result of being blonde, tan, and thin (though it seems to work for television hosts). Sexy is the result of being pulled together and comfortable in your skin. Holding your stomach in when your clothes are off is not fuckable. Slapping your ample behind and inviting him to ride the wobble is.

jeudi, le 1ᵉʳ avril

SHARK

Etymology: probably modified of German *Schurke*, "scoundrel."
Function: noun, intransitive verb

1: any of numerous marine elasmobranch fishes that have a
   fusiform body and lateral gill clefts and are rapacious
   predators
2: a crafty person who preys upon others through usury,
   extortion, or trickery
3: one who excels greatly in a particular field
4: the act of entrapment of a person, usually younger or less
   experienced

I've been eyeing up someone at the gym for the last few months.

This is not a habit, really. Gyms are for exercising, perhaps a bit
of socializing, but the widespread idea of workouts as meat markets is gruesome by any standard. On the upside, if you do meet
someone in an atmosphere of lycra-clad, endorphin-soaked mad-
ness, you can rest easy that he has seen you at your worst, covered
in sweat and hair undone, and found you attractive.

On the other hand, I wouldn't want to date anyone who regu-
larly saw me at my worst.

At the start of the year, though, one man in particular caught my eye. Shy smile, soft-looking hair, impressively muscled build. I made inquiries. Gleaned his name.

"Gay," barked N, who is not gay himself but claims to have the most finely attuned straight-man gaydar in the south of England. It's rubbish, but I dare not say. "Without doubt."

"I don't think so," I sighed, trying not to stare as the object of our conversation worked his way around the free weights.

"Ten-pence bet says he is."

Them's, as they say, fightin' words. "You're on."

"It would indeed be a pleasure," N said, rubbing his hands, "to see the master shark lose this one."

vendredi, le 2 avril

Conversations with clients are not exactly what one might call "normal," but still have their rigid conventions. It's nice to know where someone is from, a general outline of what he does. Most of the men are business travelers and not frequent consumers of sex services. A little idle chatter puts both parties at ease.

There's a fine line between curiosity and nosiness, though, and while meeting a working girl is a bit like going on a first date, some lines of interrogation are simply off limits. These include questions about one's parents, location of one's house (as I only do outcalls), vehicle registration number. . . .

On the other hand, the fact that you are unlikely to meet again means a customer can ask the sort of questions that would get anyone else a rapid introduction to the pavement. Context is everything.

Example 1: "Do you think you'll marry and have children?"

I like children well enough. I especially like when they go back to their parents.

Sometimes—sometimes—I am struck by the charm of a precocious *bébé* and think rearing young'uns a good idea. And if someone could take charge of children between the ages of eleven and sixteen, it would sweeten the deal immensely.

Clients are perhaps the only people I can answer this question honestly to. The ambivalence toward a future family, the uncertainty whether this world is a suitable place to chain oneself to another being or beings, frankly, troubles me. As many of them are married and have children, they appreciate this. Sometimes they offer advice.

Some adore their children and family life. Some are . . . well, they're out paying for sex, aren't they?

My parents are sometimes fool enough to ask after my future plans for babymaking and receive the stock answer of "I simply haven't met the right man." Any paramour who dares let this query pass his lips is on a one-way trip to speed dating and singleton hell.

Example 2: Questions about taste in films, books, and music.

Potential mates receive an honest answer. My taste in cultural minutiae might be dodgy, but it is my own, and anyone hoping to merge his material possessions with mine in a happy reenactment of *Homo erectus* setting up housekeeping in the Olduvai Gorge, will have to live with a collection of music that could best be described by the term "selective appeal."

In a client situation, I try to discern what his taste might be and stray not too far off the beaten mainstream. Trying to cover the finer points of free jazz whilst administering a soapy titwank is possibly straining the privileges of my position.

Example 3: "How many people have you been to bed with?"

No client has ever asked. Sometimes they ask how long I have been working, but whether they attempt to deduce the number of my past lovers based on the answer is unknown. Given that my working practices have been sometimes sporadic, it's unlikely they would reach an accurate total.

Non-clients always ask. If I think the man has a good sense of humor, I tell him a number that is roughly accurate. Or at least within the same order of magnitude. I don't know the real answer myself. For geeky men with extremely good senses of humor, I offer the total in scientific notation or hexadecimal.

If I think he does not have a good sense of humor, I try to change the subject or turn the question back on him.

Why does it matter? Quantity is no guarantee of quality. Frequency definitely isn't. But a low total is not indicative of personality either. A high number of ex-lovers could just as easily say "I'm good at hostessing, and the lack of stalkers implies my selective powers are decent" as it does the more common interpretation of "I'm a big wet girlslut with a drinking problem." Men—and women—who have been shocked by my answer were often heard to mumble, "But you look like such a *nice* girl!"

I am nice. Very nice indeed.

At the age of seventeen someone split with me because he was my third partner and this was an unacceptably high number to him. The next man, number 4, claimed the number of my previous lovers was unacceptably low. There's no pleasing some people.

The last time I had a lover with more former partners than me (that I knew of) was at the age of nineteen.

Example 4: "We only have a quarter of an hour. May I come in your mouth?"

In a normal situation, this might meet with a grimace at best and a restraint order at worst. At work, though, typical responses range from "Go on then!" to "Okay, but I would rather you came on my face."

dimanche, le 4 avril

A year or two ago it became apparent how neatly I've left the first flush of youth behind. The Maginot Line was, of all things, music. Watching videos after a prolonged absence from popular culture, I noticed to my horror that those who are not old enough to re-member Lionel Richie the first time around consider him some sort of Grand Pooh-Bah of soft rock. Lionel was everywhere, sporting mini-dreads, bling, and cred. Wrong, wrong, wrong! Did no one else have their early memories of music television inex-orably scarred by the sight of Mr. Richie crooning earnestly to his own clay head? Sometimes I fear for the younger generation, truly.

Which reminds me that my mother's birthday is looming and I really must remember to make her that Neil Sedaka Tzedakah box I'm always promising—or is it threatening?—to craft.

lundi, le 5 avril

WAX

Etymology: Middle English, from Old English *weax*; akin to Old High German *wahs*, Lithuanian *vaskas*
Function: transitive verb, intransitive verb, noun

1: a substance secreted by bees and used for constructing the honeycomb, composed of a mixture of esters, cerotic acid, and hydrocarbons
2: any of various substances resembling beeswax: any of numerous substances that differ from fats in being less greasy, harder, and more brittle and in containing

principally compounds of high molecular weight (as fatty acids, alcohols, and saturated hydrocarbons), or a solid substance of mineral origin consisting of hydrocarbons of high molecular weight

3: something likened to wax as soft, impressionable, or readily molded

4: to treat or rub with wax, usually for polishing or stiffening

5: the process of removing body hair in the most painful, yet somehow satisfying, way possible

6: to follow the object of your affection around the room in an attempt to get them to take notice of you

I stood by the paper towel dispenser, blotting sweat off my neck until the 10-Pence Bet came into view. He was setting up a bench-press-cum-torture-device. When he turned away to slide a weight off the rack, I slid in behind him.

"Work in sets with you?" Gym-speak for asking if you can alternate on the weights. Never regarded as an overt come-on: people who are waxing you are more likely to stand off to the side and watch.

It was a ludicrous request, of course. I couldn't have spotted the weight he could probably lift with his little toe. "You lifting?" he asked. Soft voice, nice.

"Maybe the bar plus twenty," I said. Damn, I actually sound like I know what I'm talking about.

He nodded. We went through three sets each. I stood on the opposite side of the bar as he pressed out his reps, watching the long-sleeved shirt strain at his chest. On my sets I tried hard to look cool and serious, not the giggling feeble creature I play when N's in the gym. We finished on the bench and moved off to other sides of the gym. Play it cool, girl, I thought. Don't follow him around the room. Don't wax.

Half an hour later I walked through to the aerobic area. He was on a rowing machine, had been for a few minutes—the sweat was just starting to trickle past his hairline. I sat on one a few seats away and strapped my feet in.

"Hard workout day for you then?" he asked.

I smiled. "Just cooling down." I rowed through five minutes, watching his reflection surreptitiously in the glass opposite us. His sweat was really starting to pour. He had taken off the long-sleeved top. I finished and walked out the door behind him, caught a glance of his back squeezing together at the end of each stroke. The droplets sliding down the crevice of his spine.

I was alone in the hall leading to the changing rooms. *Wait a few minutes*, I thought. *He'll come out and you can say something.*

Don't. He'll know you waited.

Coward.

Tart.

What would I say, anyway? "Oh, to be the person who gets to lick that sweat off you," then walk away? The door cracked. I didn't wait to see who it was. I ducked in the ladies' faster than a greased goose.

mardi, le 6 avril

N and I went out for Italian and beer. We sat outside waiting for the food. It was a mild evening, I was a little tired from a long session of working out frustrations in the gym, and the drink went straight to my head. We talked about the coming month, what he was doing with work, a bit about women he was interested in. I confessed that I'd been doing a little Internet snooping on the Boy.

We must be in sync—N, who has been so good about not obsessing on his own ex, revealed that he'd been doing the same. "So did you find anything?" I asked first. Nothing, he said. Maybe she was married. Maybe she moved. I thought it was too soon. She was an impulsive girl, a bit dappy, but settling down already would beggar belief even for her. He asked if I had found anything.

"A little," I said. "Enough." He's moved, he's probably single. Nothing earth-shattering. We sipped at our drinks. The food came. The first course was bigger than we expected, he finished mine off. The second course came, I just had a salad. I suppose I feel I've violated the Boy's privacy by looking, but couldn't stop myself.

"Mutual inability to let go," N said.

"Yes." We sat in silence a bit longer, chewing, waving off the ubiquitous fresh-ground-pepper boys with their porn-sized grinders.

"So, meet any nice girls with big tits lately?" he asked suddenly. I laughed so hard I almost choked on a mouthful of arugula.

mercredi, le 7 avril

CHILD

Etymology: from Old English *cild*, akin to Gothic *kilthei* (womb), Sanskrit *jathara* (belly).
Function: noun

1: a young person of either sex between infancy and youth
2: one strongly influenced by another or by a place or state of affairs
3: a product or result
4: anyone born in a year I had a double-digit birthday in

"Guess what," N smirked.
  "What." I was in no mood for guessing games.
  "I've been talking to your little friend," he said.

"Which little friend?" N meant 10-Pence Bet. "So what do you know?" I asked.

"He's a student."

"Loads of people are students these days. Your point?"

"He's *eighteen*."

Oh no, you must be joking. No one looks like that at eighteen. "You're having me on."

"First year at university, engineering something."

I frowned. I thought of 10-Pence Bet, how smooth and unlined his face was. And how polite. Bells started going off in my head: good-looking men don't stay nice for long. "Figures. There ought to be a law." I sighed. "They shouldn't build teenagers to adult spec. It's just not fair."

samedi, le 10 avril

"Have fun last night?" N asked. We were at the gym. I leant against the wall just outside the door of the men's changing room while he laced up a pair of sneakers. The announcement boards were crowded with fliers. Yoga, physiotherapy, five-a-side football. Something called Ultimate. Ultimate what? I wondered. Ultimate stretching? Ultimate watersports? Ooo, get the rubber mat.

"Okay," I said. Friday was A3's birthday. I wasn't going to go because I was afraid of the Boy turning up. When I had told N this, he said I'd be silly to let that stop me. So I fretted about what to wear, flirted with the idea of not going, then went anyway.

N started warming up on the treadmill. The machines on that side of the gym face a window. I can't imagine who thought the vista of illegally parked cars and staggering teenagers in the street below would be an inspirational view. "Was your ex there?"

"He was." The Boy turned up late, before the birthday party left the bar and went on to the club. I was talking to A3, we were eyeing up various people in the room and rating them on shagga-bility.

"Guy in the red shirt?"

"Only if drunk."

"Him or you?"

"Both."

Then A3, who was facing the door, caught sight of the Boy.

"Bloke in the blue checked shirt?" he asked.

I turned round, saw who it was, and shuddered involuntarily. "Fuck off," I said.

"Sorry, that was unfair," he said.

"No, it's okay."

"Did he say anything?" N upped his speed and broke into a jog.

"No, he kept a good distance." Not knowing whether or not the Boy would be there was by far the worst part of the evening. I found it difficult to keep up conversation with anyone, my eyes were scanning the room for him constantly. If I saw someone who resembled him, my mouth went dry and my words jumbled. But once I knew he was there, I relaxed.

The Boy didn't look at me, I didn't look at him. He hovered around the fringes of the large group talking to people we knew.

N and I were both at a slow run. Sweat started to prickle my collarbone. "Did you pick up?" he asked.

"Not really," I said. "There was one fellow in the bar, who came up out of nowhere. He pulled my hair hard and bit me on the neck, then walked away."

"Really? What did you do?"

"Nothing." My knees had gone to jelly. The stranger had held my hair for a long moment, staring at me. I stared back. He pulled harder. Our gaze didn't break. I knew probably all of my friends were watching. Fuck them. Then the man who bit me walked off back to his friends. He didn't say anything.

"What did he do?"

"Nothing."

"Really?" N ran on for a bit. "Maybe he was doing it for a bet. So how late were you out?"

"Late late." We went on to a club. I was talking to a friend of A3's from home, a very pretty short girl with spiky hair. I kind of fancied her and was aware that the Boy (whose voice I could hear behind me) was probably watching. We queued and went inside. The music was old-school, they even played Vanilla Ice. I couldn't stop dancing. The Boy stayed on the edge of the crowd.

I flopped into a chair, sweating heavily from the exertion on the dance floor. A3 picked up my feet and put them on his lap, massaging my instep in the open black stilettoes. Someone snapped a picture of us. I closed my eyes to the heat and haze of the club. Music has always had the power to change my mood. Or perhaps it was the drink. It was easy to forget everything around me.

N jumped off the treadmill and we went to stretch. "And that was it? You danced for a while and went home?"

"No—at least four men tried to chat me up." One of them knelt down while I was still sitting, eyes shut, enjoying the music. "I've never seen anyone look so happy," he said. Ha, I thought. "Thank you," I said. We started talking. He wanted to dance, I didn't.

"Get anyone's number?" N winced as he tried to urge more length out of his hamstrings.

"Just one worth noticing. A trolley dolly from British Airways."

"Male or female?"

"Male."

"Nice looking?"

"Aren't they all?" The Boy stuck around for a long time, but even he was gone by 3 a.m. There was still a hard core of us buying round after round in honor of the birthday boy. The flight steward was more persistent than the other men who'd come up during the night, and gave me his card. I waved him goodbye as we staggered out to find the night buses.

"Weights?" N said, edging toward the frightening bench apparatus in the corner.

"Go on then."

dimanche, le 11 avril

I retrieved my bag and brought out a box of condoms. He held the member in front of my face while I tore the corner of the wrapper open. I held the shaft and balanced the unrolled rubber on the tip of the cock.

"Do you have to do that?" the client asked.

"Afraid I must," I sighed. "Minimizes the risks involved."

"I trust you," he said.

"That's very kind," I said, and smiled. "Trouble is, I don't know where this thing"—and I gestured at the instrument he brandished before me—"has been."

"Oh," he said, and was quiet a moment. "It's just that, I really don't like the smell those things leave on it."

I thought. "I could give it a good hot-water-and-soap scrub in the bathroom instead of using a condom," I offered. "Would that do?" Against my policy, but it was low risk for him and almost none for me.

He sighed in relief. It was a big fleshy black dildo—his own cock stayed well zipped up. I took the dildo over to the sink, being careful to wash all the soap off carefully so he wouldn't taste any when he sucked my juices off it later.

lundi, le 12 avril

Went to a club. Saw Angel, who was wearing a skirt that was more of a glorified belt. The girl just has unbelievable legs. The music was loud, we didn't speak, I wouldn't have known what to say to her anyway. Danced together and jumped and sang along when the DJ spun The Jam's "That's Entertainment." Looked at the boys who were watching us—realized none of them were old enough to know the tune.

Fucking 'ell. They probably weren't even born then. I smiled evilly.

I picked out one young man, a tall, thin, and freckled lad. He looked like a stretched-out version of the Boy. Led him back toward the toilets, where we snogged. I pulled up his dark green shirt, licked his nipples. "Do you live close to here?" he asked, surprised. I shook my head no, asked if he did. He didn't. I pushed out the back exit and we fucked on the steps by the bins.

mardi, le 13 avril

It's widely circulated and well known that You Get What You Pay For. I don't agree. Some things come for free and some at a cost, but one isn't better than the other.

There are downsides to unpaid casual sex, of course. Aren't there always? By engaging in truly random, one-night attachments, you open yourself up to stalking, relationships, and all other manner of sexually transmitted ills. For some reason, we as a nation have collectively decided that a drunken snog in a crowded club is an acceptable overture to everlasting love. It isn't. So let us get that straight right away.

The men I have encountered in my working life can be charac-

terized by a single feature—timidity. Whether it's requesting watersports or going through the back door, by and large the clients
seem uncomfortable with demanding what they, as paying customers, are implicitly entitled to. If one thing can be predicted,
it's that the more exotic the request, the more times he will ring
the manager pre-appointment to discuss it. One-night men, on
the other hand, tend to just take.

Don't get me wrong. I find a client's sometime inability to express his inner desires charming. Sweet, even. But it's amusing
when I ask what a man would like to do, and he replies with
"Whatever you want to do."

You mean, go home and watch television while sipping hot
chocolate in my pajamas? I think he would feel my fee was somehow less than justified. But still better is the mumbled reply of
"Oh, you know, the usual."

No, I don't know. For you the usual might be open-air rope
bondage with a ring of ponygirls. I know it is for me.

Your typical club-stud, on the other hand, has a take-no-prisoners
approach to his needs that I find refreshing. You're there, he's
there, the DJ is playing *Carmina Burana*, which is definitely the signal to collect your coat and get out, and you're the only two people not playing find-my-tonsils in the taxi queue. It's a forgone
conclusion what will happen next, and the only guarantee is that
someone's wrinkly bits will make it to CCTV in the next half
hour. And to be honest I don't pick up random men because I
want a love match. Nothing less than a full cervical bruising will
do, and I am rarely disappointed.

Or as N puts it, when you know you're not going to see her
again anyway, why not push the boundaries?

Who else but a nonpaying stranger would insist that he would
only do the deed if my womanhood was partially lined with ice
chips first? Who else would try—unsuccessfully—to fist me
whilst driving (N.B.: not ideal in city traffic)? No client would

dare, for fear I would whip out a calculator and start totting up the additional cost of this service.

There's a lot of talk in escort circles of Girlfriend Experience (GFE). That's because it is by far the most requested thing we offer. I have been cuddled to within an inch of my life by well-meaning chaps whose only previous acquaintance with me was via a website. I've sipped red wine and watched telly with single gents until the taxi beeped its horn outside. And no pickup, to my recollection, has ever stretched out on the counterpane and told me stories of his childhood in Africa.

The last gentleman before the boy at the club—and I am rather stretching the meaning of the word "gentleman" here—who followed me home on a random stayed exactly ninety minutes. We did the deed, considered doing it again, then he fretted about his recent ex, dressed, and left. I was somewhat offended that he turned down the offer of a cup of tea. Still, I went to bed having gotten what I wanted out of the night, which was a good and forceful banging.

Clients are another species altogether. They have invited me on holiday, asked my opinion on the possibility of extraterrestrial life, and cleaned my shoes while waxing poetic on the proportions of my profile. The most upholstered compliment I ever received from a pickup, on the other hand, was something along the lines of "Coffee? A clean towel? This is great—staying at your place is like being in a hotel."

Ah, no. I've been in plenty of hotels. And the men aren't paying for fluffy towels.

jeudi, le 15 avril

The client was a revisit. He was in law enforcement, and the first time out he'd taken me to a semiformal work event. From the ratio of nubile cuties to paunchy detectives, I may not have been the only paid girl there. Or perhaps the Met's PR efforts are paying off in unexpected ways. I had been seated next to my date, while one of his colleagues, a Scottish youth, looked down the front of my top in a way that suggested it was meant more surreptitiously than it came off.

This time the customer met me at his flat and asked a lot of questions, probably because we were alone. This can be dicey: are they just curious or potential stalkers? As they say, the truth is like the sun, its benefit is entirely dependent on our distance from it.

So I have a manufactured history that is mostly, but not completely, true. Minor but plausible differences in hometown, university, degree, current home. Other questions are simpler to answer.

"Have you ever dominated?"

"Honey, that was how I started in the business." When I was a student and worked briefly as a domme, it was something I didn't especially enjoy and didn't want to do again. Largely because getting out of character was difficult for me. But maybe being more of a submissive in my private life led to some empathy for those who like to be dominated, because I've ended up doing it more than a few times in this job as well.

"Really?" The client nodded and pursed his lips. "Really." He was tall, well over six feet. Thick framed and strong. Probably mid-forties. Bald. And single, which is (from what I've seen) as likely in clients as not. "I find that . . . fascinating."

What is it about men who know seven ways to kill you with their bare hands who just want to be pussycats in the bedroom?

"Have you ever let someone take control?" I asked. He was sitting in a stuffy chair, and I was curled up at his feet drinking Shiraz and stroking the back of his legs.

"I always wanted to, but . . ."

"Sweetie," I said, and reached up to stroke his chin. "Don't be shy. That's what I'm here for."

A first-time submissive is usually easy to handle and eager to please. It takes months before they start trying to deviously control the action from below. I asked if he would let me tie him up, he said yes, what with? I wasn't prepared, so I asked for a handful of ties. He led me upstairs to the bedroom and produced them.

I told him to undress. He did, as I sat on the bed, cross-legged. I ordered him onto the bed. He hesitated a moment. "Get down, face up, legs and arms straight," I said abruptly. He did. I pulled my skirt up and crawled over him, heels still on. Straddling his chest, I tied his hands to the bed. At the foot of the bed there was nothing handy, so I looped the ends of the ties round the wheels of the bed-frame and hoped they would hold. I could feel him craning his neck, trying to get his mouth closer to my bottom. "Lie back," I barked. "If I want you to touch me, you'll know it."

It was standard S&M, nothing challenging. Tease and (extremely) light torture. But I did end up with the cleanest shoes outside of a Nine West.

dimanche, le 18 avril

N has taken a hiatus from his usual running commentary on sport and tits to focus on pussy.

His cat, that is.

Unlike my dearly departed feline, who would take to spring like a cat to a nest full of little flightless baby birds, using her cat-like reflexes to jump cattily from branch to branch and scaring the living kittens out of any and all tree dwellers, N's pussy has been dragging along, unable even to pull herself up the steps.

She came back from the veterinary clinic with a bandaged paw and a pinched look, as it was explained to me, having had a thorn

the size of another cat drawn out of her foot. It had formed an ab-
scess and—well, something too disgusting and technical to go
into, really. But I gather it involved "draining," which I presume
has nothing to do with kitchen sinks. N has been looking after her
with the tender mercy of a ward sister who missed her calling. It's
rather sweet.

Last night as we left the gym, he did not offer me a lift home,
nor suggest a drink or a meal somewhere. Mumbling something
about changing a dressing, he all but ran to the parking lot.

I smirked. "If I didn't know better, I'd say you were getting a little pussy on the side."

mardi, le 20 avril

Coffee with N and A1 for no better reason than to dissect my love
life. Again. "So what happened to that trolley dolly?" N asked, sipping an Americano.

"Could have been something. But he called it off, by phone, this
weekend," I reported. It was annoying. Admittedly, he was probably more often in the air than in town, but this should be no barrier. In my opinion some of the best relationships involve not
seeing each other.

"Did he have a reason?" N asked.

"Too busy with work. Couldn't be bothered."

"Did he actually say that second bit?" N looked puzzled.

"No, I'm paraphrasing." It is probably too great a leap of faith to
believe a man would be so guileless as to say that he was too busy
with work and for that to actually be the case.

A1 shrugged. "Well, here's hoping he realizes what he's missing."

"Doubtful. We never got past snogging." Three dates, lots of
conversation, a torrent of e-mail. Resulting in nothing more than

a couple of awkward hugs and a bit of tongue-tying before Cinderella had to drive home. Wary of what happened the last few times, I didn't think it right to push him too fast. But whatever his buttons were, I clearly was not pressing them.

"Really?" spluttered N. "I would have at least slept with you first."

"Cheers, darling," I said, blowing him an ironic kiss.

"I have a friend," A1 ventured. "A bit on the short side, though . . ."

"Is that a euphemism? I've already seen your little friend, thanks," I said, glancing at the crotch of his jeans.

"Ouch," A1 said, and turned to N. "She's getting angry," he said. "She's never this sharp when she has a regular shag."

mercredi, le 21 avril

I know a girl. A nice girl, a well-brought-up girl, whose vowels are all very round and correct and whose manners are exquisite.

This girl, I've known her a few years, since we both were students. Like me, her degree was mostly useless; like me, she'd moved to London to find her way. And found it mostly a drain on finances. Moving from temp job to temp job, or stringing two or three part-time and freelance projects together at a time to make enough money to keep the tiny, not-terribly-expensive flat she lives in.

And this girl doesn't really know what she wants. She might fancy the academic life, but really more as retreat from the rest of the world than a genuine love for the world of letters. When I see her in pubs with friends, every few weeks or so, she always looks like a slightly shabby librarian, but I've noticed the way she moves and she could be so much sexier than that. Her legs are fantastic. I also know she's been struggling with depression for some time, with—literally—the scars to prove it. And the men in her life are either abusive or doormats.

I buy her a pint, knowing it's too late in the evening for her to get the next round, but that's fine because she really couldn't afford it. The money she does spend freely goes on books. She loves reading, this one, and get her on the right subject and her milk-white arms will be flying about, lit fag in one hand, expounding this or that theory or proclaiming this or that writer an unsung genius.

More often, however, she'll mumble through a conversation and I will try twice as hard as I would with anyone else to keep it going. Because no matter what her better instincts, she always answers the question "So how are you keeping these days?" honestly. And it's always something depressing.

What might make her life better? Who knows. Chronic money shortage is one problem. Feeling intimidated by every woman who comes within a quarter-mile radius of her current boyfriend doesn't help. (Oh, yes, she's probably pulled that accidental pregnancy scheme once or twice. Not faking it, of course, but conveniently forgetting a pill or three here and there, when the leash had to be tugged on a bit.)

So maybe it occurs to me, well, it's no cure-all, but a few months in prostitution might do her the world of good. Have to primp and smile for once. Put the overdraft back in the black. Get her mind off herself every now and again.

But I can't say anything. She's waiting to hear on Ph.D. funding for this autumn. In a mostly useless subject.

jeudi, le 22 avril

RESULT

Etymology: from Latin *resultare* (to rebound)
Function: noun, intransitive verb

    1: to proceed or arise as a consequence, effect, or conclusion
    2: beneficial or tangible effect
    3: something obtained by calculation or investigation
    4: what I will say when I make N look like the fool he is.
    Because it's not about the money, it's about the principle.

N and I went out to a club he worked at a few years ago. They were playing the usual pop trash, but the doormen knew us and waved us through.

It was packed with the usual bodies. A few on the floor, shaking their moneymakers, more at the bar looking everyone over. A meat market but not unfriendly for it. I leaned on a white leather sofa and looked round. A familiar face in a small clutch of men. Ten-Pence Bet. I elbowed N and gestured at him.

"Told you," he said. Or would have said, but I couldn't hear him over the music. Mouthed. I knew what he meant. I shrugged. Being with other men is not ipso facto gay. And the bet stood, regardless.

I saw 10-Pence Bet detach from his group and spin out in the direction of the bar. Alone. Good, because I didn't think a confrontation would work in front of a crowd. I followed him.

Tapped him on the shoulder. "Yes?" He turned around, saw me, smiled.

"This is going to sound odd," I said apologetically. "But I win a 10-pence bet if you're not gay."

"Pardon?" The music in the club was loud; he bent his head very close to mine.

"I said I win a 10-pence bet if you're not gay."

"Who's the bet with?" he asked.

"I really mustn't say. Does it matter?"

He smiled. Thought a bit. Leaned forward and kissed me. His lips were soft, slightly moist, lingered a moment. "You win," he said. I smiled. We walked away in opposite directions.

I found N, leaned heavily on his arm. "I win," I shouted in his ear. "Do you hate me?"

"I'll prove you wrong," he said, digging through his pockets.

"Yes, well." I smirked. "Until then, hand over the coin."

vendredi, le 23 avril

ESCAPE HATCHES—A BRIEF CONSIDERATION

- *Kyle of Tongue.* Pros: favored by child molesters and lovers of cold weather. They clearly go for the fantastic scenery. Cons: bleak isn't the word. What can you say about a place where the incoming tide swallows up the main road?
- *Home Counties.* Pros: so soul-destroying, so boring, so obviously bad, that no one would think their new neighbor is me. Cons: so soul-destroying, so boring, so obviously bad, that no one would think their new neighbor is me.
- *West Country.* Pros: dairy products, moors, beaches. Pasties. Ponies. Dreamily gazing at bronzed surfers in summertime. Cons: while the trains go there, am not certain they come back.
- *North America.* Pros: charming accent might attract general goodwill, free drinks. Cons: am frightened by the concept of Texas.

- *South America.* Pros: sunshine, interesting food, mountains. Cons: rumored expatriate contingent of Nazis in hiding may prove constricting to social life.
- *Australia and Environs.* Pros: a few acquaintances, rumored good weather, decent confectionery. Cons: rumored expatriate contingent of Brits in hiding may prove constricting to social life.
- *The Med.* Pros: excellent weather, superlative food, inexpensive housing, reasonable entertainment possibilities, and not terribly far from home. Cons: Costa del Croydon is not quite the vibe I'm after.
- *Fulham, South London.* Pros: the transport links are decent. Cons: what does it say about a place if the ease of escaping is its highest selling point?
- *Israel.* Umm, no. Just . . . no. Not yet.
- *East Anglia.* Pros: good beer. Oh, I don't half fancy a pint of IPA on a sunny afternoon. Cons: aesthetically displeasing "bump" bit of map.
- *Africa.* Pros: no idea. Cons: once I had a client from Zimbabwe. It doesn't sound like a terribly nice place at the moment.
- *New York.* Pros: extremely menschy. Cons: if television is to be believed, pressure to meet and mate is all-consuming. I am the alpha stiletto-wearing, lingerie-obsessed, Pulitzer-reading female here and competition could be disheartening. Particularly if the quarry is an unemployed finance graduate still living at home in the Bronx.

Lately it feels I am spending more time out of town than in it. The current good weather in London is pleasant and welcome, but an unfortunate case of too little, too late. I am packing again— knickers (all varieties), books (*Dodsworth, My Name Is Asher Lev,* some silly crime thrillers, and the ever reliable *Princess Bride*), and sunblock.

In search of beaches. Will report back with detailed analysis of several of the locations discussed above.

dimanche, le 25 avril

We took a holiday every year when I was young. Never anywhere too exotic, and never with my father. He claimed exhaustion from his business, until he retired and couldn't use the excuse any longer. By the last year of school, my best friend was one of my male cousins. We have the same coloring, the same small sharp features and freckles. People think we are twins. We still acted like children, taunting and hitting each other. But that year there had been a new undercurrent of tension: we started to watch one another cautiously, for signs that one of us knew something the other didn't.

So, our mothers take all the kids on holiday together. We drive to Brighton. I've never been so far south. And six of us in the car, it's cramped, the journey feels a lot longer than it must have been. My mother's sister, my cousin's mother, has brought a bag of cassette tapes to keep us entertained.

Her taste in music is nothing like ours, but thankfully nowhere as antique as Mum's. We know all the lyrics to her tapes, and we sing loudly, car windows down. It's a sunny day. We think the holiday will be perfect.

When we get there, the beach is horrible, wet and windy. There's nothing to do for three days. The mothers stay in and watch telly; we kids go out looking for an amusement arcade. I beat all comers at air hockey until no one will play me any longer. We spend all of our money on cotton candy, penny arcades, and chips.

I come back to the hotel, the mothers are still watching television. My cousin is in the bathroom. He's singing, obviously unaware that the echo that makes singing in the shower sound so good also means everyone outside can hear him. He's singing a Madonna song, and the frankly sexual lyrics—not to mention his falsetto—disturb me somewhat. Without meaning to, I can imagine him imitating the dancers in the video.

The other thing I realize is only that morning I was in the shower too, while everyone sat inside poring over street maps and the papers, and I was singing the Divinyls' "I Touch Myself."

mardi, le 27 avril

I'm staying in a hotel right on a river in Spain; the river goes only a few miles until it reaches the sea. I take a walk by myself. Not far from the hotel—the spring is very warm and sunny, and I am distracted by the flowers. The air smells drier and cleaner here than in the UK.

My camera is low on batteries, but I manage to take pictures of some flowers. Violet bursts of bougainvillea, orange starburst-shaped blooms I've never seen, tiny pink flowers in a smooth-trunked tree's branches.

There are more sidewalk cafes than anything else. I sit at one, in a green plastic chair under an umbrella emblazoned with the name of the local brew, sip a sangria and feel like an obvious tourist. Men who pass sometimes comment to me, more often things to each other. From what they say, it seems like they notice a woman's hair before anything else.

Because I have worn the wrong shoes for any kind of walking, I have to turn back and go home early. But instead of retreading the same route along main roads, I loop through the cobble-paved back streets where white and yellow stucco crumbles off flat-faced buildings. There are two churches, their names spelled in gay tiles pressed into the plastered walls. I try to take a picture of one but the battery of the camera runs out. I could buy new ones, but I don't know the word for "battery," and am already acutely aware of my strangeness to the locals. The hotel is a cool refuge when I get back.

jeudi, le 29 avril

So I'm sixteen, or close to it. One day my cousin and I are at a swimming pool, treading water by the ladder at the deep end. He has been asking about some girls I know. I am vaguely dismayed that his taste in women is running to the obvious—tall blondes and dark-haired girls with chests everyone stares at. Plenty of the boys have received favors from these girls, but they wouldn't look at my cousin nor his geeky friends twice, and he knows it.

Our friendship is becoming uneasy. Because we are related, we can and do share everything. Because of our age, attraction is possible—but, obviously, off-limits. When the subject of sex does come up, being shy and clever as we are, we couch it in the most neutral terms possible.

"If I wasn't your cousin, and didn't know you, I'd probably be attracted to you."

"Me too. If I wasn't your cousin. And didn't know you." And we know what we mean. Then an awkward silence, usually followed by a simulated farting noise to bring things back to the mundane. These conversations foretell the sort of relationships I will have with men through university, a parade of pale, gentle boys who are too shy to admit their desire until they are too drunk to care. A lot like the few people I dated at school, really, but with better access to alcohol. Sometimes my cousin's friends express an interest in me; he fends them off with protestations of my tomboyishness

("She would break you in half if she heard that") or maturity ("She wouldn't look twice at a child like you"). I was terribly mature; I'd even tossed a boy off in a cinema, don't you know.

There are other things as well. We don't know it for a year yet, but I'll be going to university, my cousin won't. His A levels were good, and he had offers, but he didn't follow through and his mother didn't press. He thinks he wants to be a Royal Marine or a mechanic. I think he's crazy. A decade later he ends up working prep in a commercial kitchen.

I pull myself up the side of the pool and scramble out in the direction of our towels, grab them both, walk back to the water.

"Hey," he says, a little louder than absolutely necessary. "You're walking differently. Does that mean you're not a virgin anymore?"

"Yes," I say, straight-faced. He starts to get out of the pool, and I throw his towel in the water. This is how he knows I care about him.

He's not sure whether I'm kidding or not, and doesn't press for details. I prepare a fake story anyway, just in case. When his mum comes to collect us, we both sit in the back of the car, and he just whispers names.

"Marc?"

"No." Marc was in my year, and taller than the rest of the boys. He also spits when he speaks without realizing it and follows me around too often.

"Justin?"

"No." I have a crush on Justin; my cousin is the only person I've ever told; I hope he doesn't tell anyone else. Before leaving for university, I will tell Justin all this in a letter, and he will never speak to me again.

He senses my discomfort. "Eric. Has to be."

The joke candidate. "No way!" I say, but refrain from giving him a nipple-twister, because to do so would compromise the new air of maturity this lie has conferred.

It doesn't matter much anyway. Within a month it happens for real, with my cousin's best friend. While I flinched, I didn't make a noise. And as far as I can tell, my gait was no different the day after than it was the day before.

vendredi, le 30 avril

I fly east, to Italy, to meet friends. The plane is small and crowded and the heavily made-up flight attendant screams at a child who keeps running up and down the aisle, even when the plane is taking off and landing. It's not clear whom he belongs to; his parents are making no effort to stop him.

The first thing I do after setting my bags in the cool tile hallway is go to check e-mail. And there's a small surprise, a message from Dr. C over in San Diego, who must have gleaned my e-mail address from A2. It's a short but affectionate note dating from two days previously. I reply with an equally short and cheerful message.

Mai

Belle's A-Z of London Sex Work

~

T-V

T is for Taxis

I usually ring a minicab for the way out and find a black cab on the way home. Minicabs will not necessarily know where you're going, and I've ended up reading their maps more often than not. Black cabs will get you somewhere smoothly, but might try to take you on a scenic tour to push up the price. Sometimes I hail a black cab on the way out, but can't count on finding one near home except on weekends.

Collecting local minicab cards is useful; it wouldn't do to always get the same drivers.

T is also for Timewasters

Theoretically, working through an agency should prevent ghost bookings: the people who express interest in your services and even go so far as to reserve a time and agree on a price. Only to find that they have meetings later than they thought, or the wife did come along after all, or he forgot the phone number (my personal favorite—this is what mobiles are good for, no?). So sometimes you will go through all the prep and end up on the shelf. At least you can reassure yourself that unlike in real relationships, it's not you, it really is them.

U is for Underwear

Matching underwear, sexy and luxe. For looks, not for comfort. Early on, the manager emphasized the particular look she likes the girls to have: big, expensive, lacy pants. No thongs. More is more. Garter belts are clichéd but a nice touch. Don't invest in anything that will be difficult to get in and out of. It must be clean and well fitting; there's nothing more unattractive than rolls of back fat or the dreaded double cleavage from an ill-fitting bra.

V is for Vagina

Keep it clean. If you don't wax or shave clean, keep the hair trimmed. Look out for any odd swelling, redness, discharge, or discoloration, and if you notice these symptoms, get yourself to a clinic as soon as. Do those squeezy tightening exercises gynecologists are always on about. Men love that.

samedi, le 1ᵉʳ mai

The flat I'm staying in is within smelling distance of the city's fish market. This in itself is not a problem. No cracks about whores and fish smell, please.

The major drawback to the location is the trucks that rumble in at 4 a.m. to drop off the day's catch. The men standing off the backs of the trucks, shouting to each other, unloading. Then it goes quiet for an hour or so before the first customers start coming to market.

Still, it's probably about time I started learning what rising with the sun is good for. Nabbing the best fish, for one thing.

dimanche, le 2 mai

I went to the beach with a small group. There was me and one other girl; the boys sat slightly separate from us on the pebble shore as everyone stripped down and tanned on their towels.

The other girl is not a close acquaintance. A few days ago we were talking, and she asked my age.

"Twenty-five," I said, knocking a couple of years off. She is nineteen at the oldest.

"Wow!" she said, looking genuinely surprised. "I never would have guessed." I shrugged. When I was younger, everyone thought I was far older; now, the situation is reversing itself. "You know, you don't have to tell people your age," she said helpfully. "You could probably say you were twenty and people would believe it."

Only if said people were teenagers. Bless her, though.

I was reading. One boy, a blond, was listening to music and singing loudly—and tunelessly—along. You couldn't help but smile. Some of the other boys threw a Frisbee around and splashed in the shallow water. When they got bored with that, they came back to where we were lying.

The other girl, who was flipping through a magazine and listening to music, turned toward me. "Are my sunglasses very dark?" she asked under her breath.

"Yes, they're quite dark," I said.

"So if I was looking somewhere, you couldn't see my eyes, right?" she asked.

"I couldn't, no."

"Good," she said, and turned away again, facing the boys, her head propped on one hand. Gazing, I noticed, in the direction of a particular young man. Her own boyfriend had stayed at home.

lundi, le 3 mai

The first girl I ever slept with was a friend's girlfriend.

One of my close mates at university was a shortish, thinnish, good-looking ginger boy who loved *Doctor Who* and was a complete sex bomb with the ladies. I can't explain why. He just was, and we loved him.

We called him "the Jew Boy with the Moves," because this guy could cut up your brother's bar-mitzvah-party dance floor like a hot knife through butter. He was all slinky hips and sultry looks, and by Jove, I had an almighty crush on him. I'd never had a go, though in the first year he made his way through every single one of the women in our group. It just seemed a boundary destined never to be crossed.

Eventually he settled down with one girl. And I couldn't resent losing out, because his girlfriend, Jessica, was an über-desirable petite vixen with caramel-colored shoulders and dark blonde hair that was always in perfect curls.

One night JB and Jessica invited me and my then-boyfriend to a club. It was a place I didn't know in a part of town I didn't go to. I didn't know what to wear, and met the other three at a pub in jeans, flip-flops, and a thin black satin shirt, no bra. Jessica and I stood in the middle of the room while the men fetched our drinks, and I was suddenly aware that everyone was looking at us.

We sank pints and moved on to our destination. The club was a gay club. My first. It was a mixed crowd, being a Saturday night in a medium-sized city where the staff couldn't be too picky with the door policy. There were boy couples and girl couples, gangs of students, old single boys looking hangdog at the bar and men dressed like women dressing like men's fantasies of women. There were gold-painted cages, but no one dancing in them. I didn't know where to look. My boyfriend, alas, did—at his feet. All night.

The music was not good, but it was frantic and loud, like all club music was then. JB and Jessica spun me out on the dance floor. They were, together, an incredible couple to watch. Just too tiny and cool for words. Her slightly bony shoulders wriggled suggestively—her back was bare in a sleeveless tie-on shirt. I'd been attracted to girls before, but never felt so free to just stare at one. It wasn't out of place here.

JB took me to one side. "You know, she wants you," he said. Was he kidding? This wee goddess? But as soon as he said it, I knew it was true, and it was like a switch had been flipped. I could imagine taking her to the toilets, tonguing her as she laughed and sat atop the cistern. I could imagine putting things in her, my fingers, the end of a beer bottle.

"She's your girlfriend," I said, aware as the words came out how whiny and awful they sounded.

He shrugged. He said he'd take care of my boyfriend. He said he did this for her a lot—picked up girls for her. I was stunned.

JB drove us all home. My boyfriend lived closest, thank goodness. Then we went around to Jessica's house. Her parents were away somewhere, or asleep, or didn't care, I never knew. She held my hand and we walked through her door, plain as anything. Her boyfriend waited until she waved back to him from the doorway, then drove away. Her neck was the most slender, tenderest I'd ever seen. Her lips were softer than any I'd ever kissed.

mardi, le 4 mai

I walked into a shop in the late morning. The Sicilian sun was already high, driving people to seek out shady spots.

Colorfully wrapped Easter cakes sat on a shelf. I reached up to take one down, but even on tiptoe the sweet was just out of my reach. A man came up behind me. "May I help you?"

"Can I have one of these?" I asked him.

"It depends," he replied. "Can I have one of you?"

jeudi, le 6 mai

We sailed on to Croatia and I bought a paper for the first time in a fortnight. They are full of disturbing images, the sort that lead one to think about politics, war, and the politics of war, and how these acts have always happened except we could never see them before. How righteous indignation and backlash sometimes seem products of ignorance, because who could not have guessed this would happen? Did we really need pictures in order to know? Are we truly angry at governments for doing what we knew they would do?

And you think, perhaps, there is one guarantee in life (that it ends) and one fairly safe bet as well (that it is painful), and freedom and property are illusions that can only exist in the mind. And that cleverer people have already thought these thoughts and discarded them and why don't I stop this rubbish philosophizing already? Oh, look, a woman in a stripey hat walking a champagne poodle.

I don't mean to make light of these events, but I'm hoping for a little pickup in the terror-sex department at work when I get home. It would do me the world of good.

vendredi, le 7 mai

It's a chalk-bright afternoon and I've been walking, listening to music all day the last few days. This helps—no one assumes you can hear them, with the headphones on, so no one speaks to you. This is good. I don't understand the language very well. When I want to hear the sounds around me, I switch the player off but leave the headphones on. I smile a lot. People smile back. Are people happier everywhere else in the world? Sure seems so.

But I know it's not the truth. I was in a bar, talking to a man my age. He'd been through three wars before he was twenty-one. Why are men so horrible to each other?" I asked, naive.

"In my experience all people are horrible."

"So why are we this way?"

"We don't know how else to be." And we were quiet. He finished a drink, smiled at my guidebook. It was a smile that said, "Where do you want to go? You know you won't find it in there."

Not that I've used it very much anyway—I like to choose a direction and keep going. In this way I found the Jewish quarter, decimated and abandoned forever ago, like a forgotten film set, and the edge of the water, which I hadn't figured as being quite so close. His smile, it was so understanding, so accepting, I could feel the waves of goodwill just pouring off him, mixed with a little pity for me.

That, or he may have just been trying to pick me up. We girls have an absolutely appalling reputation abroad. Was there a pamphlet distributed in the last decade to men in foreign countries saying that the small islanders are simply gagging for it?

(I mean, I *am*, but yo, I'm on holiday, creep. So lay off.)

samedi, le 8 mai

Holiday sex is always the best sex. I've had it everywhere—Poole, Blackpool, swimming pools.

Someone else makes the bed afterward, empties the bin of spent condoms, even picks up your wet and smelly towels from the floor. If the people below are kept up all night with the noises above, odds are they either won't know which people were responsible, or they'll be away the next morning anyway, or you can get away with a mild blush and a sheepish giggle, because you're on holiday, and only the sourest of pusses could deny anyone a healthy and vigorous bit of holiday exercise.

Al always took me to the beach when my spirits were flagging. He didn't enjoy the experience at all—sand gets everywhere, which is anathema to a man as fastidious as he is, and he burns easily, which meant most of the outing would be spent reapplying sun cream to the parts of his back he couldn't reach. One time we went away and he forgot to put sunblock on his feet, and they burned. For the entire week afterward he couldn't wear socks or shoes.

But he did it for me, so I could recharge my batteries, he always said. And because he knew he'd be rewarded with an almighty screw in whatever bed-and-breakfast we were staying in that evening.

A2 loved the act of getting to his destination better than the holiday itself. He would drive and drive, and we would cover the entire country in a week, making stops wherever the spirit took us. If we spent the night in the Highlands, you could almost lay money on the fact that within twenty-four hours we'd be holed up in a shabby guesthouse in Devon. He also liked taking pictures out the window of a moving car, which always made me laugh and dive for the steering wheel as he did so.

We stopped and posed by abandoned buildings, funny road signs, and large trees. We laid blankets in stands of trees and had sex as the mosquitoes attacked his backside. I sucked him off in Friday-afternoon bank-holiday traffic going north.

I thought in all our trips we probably never stayed in the same place twice. Until we booked into a hotel one night in the back end of nowhere, attracted by its slightly antique signs. The woman at registration greeted us familiarly. We'd stayed there only three nights before and completely forgotten it.

A3 and I took a trip together once, to look at caves. In the complete dark of underground, in the complete silence in the middle of the earth, he held my hand for the first time. It is difficult to think of a time before or since when I've been so thrilled.

A4 and I went on a beach holiday almost the first week we met. His housemate's girlfriend wanted cockles. We didn't buy any, but we went to three beaches looking for someone selling them. It was a very hot morning. At the first place we stopped, the water was in a shallow bay and the beach was more like a pile of shells.

We walked into the water, which was exactly as warm as the air. It felt like bathing in sweat. We drove on.

At the second village, there was nowhere to park. We pulled off the road and looked at the beach and the water. We were still unsure around each other and didn't have many topics of conversation yet.

The third beach was perfect, sandy and deserted. It was somewhere Al had been with me often. The wind was coming up and the heat had gone from the day. The water was open for miles and came in strong waves. A4 stripped down to his bathing shorts—I was in awe of his beauty then, and couldn't stop staring at his body. He dove into the surf and flopped around happily. I walked out to the water's edge and put a foot in. It was freezing! I jumped back.

"Are you mad?" I yelled out to his bobbing head. "Aren't you cold?"

"It's bracing!" he yelled back, and even at that distance I could hear his teeth chattering. I laughed and laughed. On the way home, we went past endless farms and looked at the pigs rooting in the last light of the day. A DJ on the radio was playing old songs, swing jazz, and we listened in happy silence. Sometimes to make me laugh he'd say, "Bracing!"

But the best holiday with him, and we went on many together, was camping. We set up a large tent in the woods next to a cold-water spring and stayed several days. The water was icy in the very hot summer and we bathed naked. A giant dead tree slanted out of the water, and balancing on that, he had me over and over. It felt so wonderfully primal. Until a naturist came along and paddled in the shallow water as if we weren't even there.

Holiday sex is the best. No one to answer to, no work, no neighbors. And if you're lucky, no phone reception. Pure sensation. It's probably exactly what the clients at work are after.

lundi, le 10 mai

There were no direct flights back. Spent one night in Rome at a large, central hostel.

The shop around the corner must have been the only one open in the early evening, as it was crowded. Bought bread, tomatoes, ricotta *al forno*. The markets of other countries are fascinating to me. Walking the aisles slowly, seeing what is given pride of place on the shelves. Single-serving meat pastes in the Czech Republic, screw-top bottles of sangria in Spain sold as if they were soda, the odd variety of things offered in the supermarket queues in North America. Razors, balloons, and dried meat especially.

The kitchen of the hostel was large and well equipped, with loud groups of young people at the tables. I sat on the corner of one, eating sandwiches and reading a newspaper. Wrapped two rolls and some cheese in a bit of paper to save for breakfast.

A few people sat nearby. They were English, but not traveling in a group together. I asked one where he was from. Cheddar, he said. Ah, I said. I knew someone from there a long time ago. Asked what he was doing in Rome. Not much, he said. Meeting a friend but she had gone on elsewhere. Did he like Italy? Yes. He showed me a map of all the places he'd walked in Rome. Someone had left a sweet bread, a loaf of *colomba*, in the communal food cupboard. We tore it to bits. The buttery flesh was sticky on top with crystallized sugar and candied peel. One of the others asked if we wanted to go for ice cream.

"Which flavor?" I asked.

"They have every flavor," he said. The boy from Cheddar agreed. It was late, but they were open late, apparently.

We walked for almost an hour. The city was waking up, groups of men and women everywhere. I was pleased to be in the company of these men. They were each funny and clever, though I took a shine to the one from Cheddar. "Is it that one?" I asked as we walked past yet another *gelateria*. "No, not yet," he said. "It's better than that."

It was. I couldn't help but laugh, when we finally reached our destination. The large bright store had every flavor imaginable. I mean that. They had Nutella flavor, Ferrero Rocher. Peanut butter. Fruits I'd never heard of. They had more flavors of chocolate ice cream alone than most places had altogether. I was delighted, ordered a cone with one scoop of coconut and one of mango. The three of us nibbled from each other's, then bought more, different flavors.

We stood outside in a little plaza. The other boy disappeared, I don't know where to. The bit from Cheddar and I were talking about twins, and sex, and twins he'd wanted to have sex with, the sort of things that really only drunk people discuss, except we weren't drunk. Perhaps high on ice cream. I asked what he did. He was a student, he said. Some variant of chemistry. Poor, of course. Though someone had once offered him a job as a stripper.

"Didn't you take it?" I asked.

"No," he said.

"Pity. I did it for a while, once. When I was a student."

"Really?" he asked. I nodded. The other one came back. We dropped the subject.

They wanted to see the Trevi Fountain. Actually, both of them had seen it before. They wanted me to see it. "How many times have you been to Rome?" Incredulous. "And you've never seen the fountain?" We walked and walked. Well-dressed couples were going in to lamplit restaurants.

At the fountain there were groups of tourists, though it must have been about midnight. People selling cheap electronics. Short Asian girls with rosebuds who would stand almost in your armpit. The water was full of coins and rubbish. They say throwing money into the fountain ensures your safe return to Rome someday; I wonder what disposing of your candy wrappers there signifies. We left.

Walked along the river, crossed a bridge. On both sides were statues of angels; we stopped, talked about sculpture, talked about Titian. How the male form looks better in stone but the female looks better painted.

We looked at the map, turned down a road toward the Vatican. Stood outside St. Peter's. There is an obelisk there, a single needle point into the sky. There's another obelisk in London. Strange how we moderns have moved them around the world singly, when the Egyptians put them up in pairs. It would be like erecting half a minaret or just the nave of a church. You can go up in the dome of St. Peter's, I said. From the roof there is a gift shop staffed by nuns, you can buy a postcard of the Vatican and post it from the roof. That, in my opinion, is the finest thing in the religion, which has no shortage of amazing things.

We walked back. We circled round ruins, pillars of the Romans fallen into piles of stone discs. Something—I can't remember what—reminded me of a poem, and I told it to them. The boys talked about children's television. Cheddar told us about *The Singing Ringing Tree*. We others could not remember it. Neither of them had ever read *The Little Prince* as children, so I told them that story.

"That's terrible," Cheddar said. "What a story to tell a child."

I shrugged. We saw a scooter that had silk flowers glued all over it parked outside a restaurant. We bought and shared a terrible, overpriced slice of pizza with an artichoke topping.

Back at the hostel the other boy went to bed. Cheddar and I stayed up, talked and talked, mostly about Brighton. I drew nonsensical things on a paper napkin, he kept it. He talked about going back to the Vatican to see the Pope in the morning first thing. Stand in queues for the confessionals that stand also in long rows, organized by the language the priest inside speaks. Asked if I would go.

"My flight is at eight," I said. "I need to get some sleep." It was about five.

"I think I'll stay up," he said.

"You should nap first, you'll die at this rate."

"I haven't written in my journal yet," he said. "I'll sleep when I'm dead." He walked me to my floor, we exchanged e-mail addresses, touched lips on the stairs.

mardi, le 11 mai

Only just awake enough to check e-mail when I finally arrived home. A note from Dr. C, who is visiting the UK soon. And wants to see me. Must go sleep on it, as if I had a choice.

dimanche, le 16 mai

A few days ago, before going to Rome, I had a missed call from the agency and a text from the manager, confirming a client at half nine.

I rang her back. "Terribly sorry, you'll have to cancel, I'm still away."

"Ah, right, darling. You see, this man, he is so nice. . . ."

"No—I'm actually away. Out of the country. I'm not back until late Tuesday." As I told her, in several calls and e-mails through the last few weeks.

"Are you certain? Because he asked specifically for you."

Am I certain I'm not home? Yes, fairly sure of that. Unless North London has suddenly turned into a sunny seaside locale full of flowering plants. It could happen. "Yes, I'm afraid so."

"Can I ask him if he would be willing to book you for tomorrow instead?"

Lady, are you deaf? "I can't do tomorrow. I'm not back until Tuesday."

She sighed. For the love of . . . It's not as if the man wants to marry me. Someone else from the agency would probably do just as well. I said so, as gently as possible. "I think perhaps you should take this job less casually," she said tartly and hung up. Ten minutes later a text came through:

LOST BOOKING.

I texted her on returning, but have not heard back yet.

mardi, le 18 mai

Ah. I must look like the world's largest mug, as I was just approached by three fundraising youths from the very same charity, all on the same street. Sorry lads—did you not see me brushing off the last one?

Fundraiser 1: "Where are you from?"

Me: "Guess."

"Barnsley."

"Sorry, no. Where are you from?"

"Barnsley."

Fundraiser 2: "What's your name?"

Me: "Linda." (obviously, not my real name)

"Fantastic, Lucy. Have you ever thought about how many people will be afflicted with mental illness in their lifetimes?"

"No, but I understand short-term memory is a growing problem."

Fundraiser 3: "Can you guess what proportion of the UK will suffer mental illness at some time in their lives?"

Me: "One out of three. I just heard all this thirty seconds ago, thank you."

mercredi, le 19 mai

There is one client with my real name and phone number. He rang to ask why I wasn't seeing anyone. Being a regular, after all, shouldn't he be the first to know if I was off the market?

"I'm not," I said. "Have you heard otherwise?"

He said he'd rung a couple weeks ago and the manager said I was on holiday.

"Ah, yes, that's because I was," I apologized.

"Then I rang yesterday," he said. "And she said you were away indefinitely and offered me someone else."

Have I been not-so-subtly dropped? I checked the website and the profile's still there, though rather lower in the listing than before. No matter. He offered to book with me privately for next week. I said I'd think about it.

jeudi, le 20 mai

Things you may not have needed, but perhaps were curious to, although there are perhaps a few people who already, know about Belle.

- I love to sing.
- When alone, I am usually listening to music or singing. The As and N are cruelly and repeatedly subjected to this. I always sing in the shower. Once, I forgot myself and started

singing in a client's toilet—when I came out, he was laughing. I love to sing, but am not a very good singer, alas.

- I love perfume.

Especially if it smells of citrus or lavender. I love smelling it (in small doses) on other people, as well.

- I prefer the texture of food to the taste.

Raw mushrooms, cherry tomatoes, sandwich pickle, and fudge all feel good to the tongue. Pasta, peanut butter, and cooked carrots do not.

- I can tell edible mushrooms from poisonous ones. Usually.

Admittedly, this is not a skill that comes into use very often. I can also identify most of the speedwell (genus *Veronica*) wildflowers. This is of no use to man nor beast.

- The day of my birth was predicted by my mum's best friend.

Spooky.

- My dream dinner party would include . . .

William Styron, Katharine Hepburn, flip-flops, Noel Coward, Iman, cashew nuts, Alan Turing, Margaret Mead, Dan Savage, fruity cocktails, Ryan Philippe, and a dungeon.

- I don't really want to work independent of an agency.

Regardless of what happens. The clients are vetted through them and (most) never even get so much as my phone number. I spend enough time on the phone as it is, and I've seen the manager having to take inquiries in public. I do actually have other avocations besides what is reported here. Managing my own appointments would cut into that.

• I still haven't heard from the manager.

You would think she'd at least have the decency to ignore me on a sunny weekend.

• *Je ne regrette rien.*

If the textbooks are to be believed, this makes me a psychopath. If the glossy magazines are to be believed, this makes me an independent modern woman.

dimanche, le 23 mai

The manager and I are still at apparent loggerheads. She hasn't rung, and I haven't tried to ring her. While I appreciate this sort of treatment may be a mainstay of all madames' arsenals, I don't half feel like calling her up to say, "Pardon me, but do you know who I am?"

Must resist the urge to smack-down, though. I always wondered why the profiles on the website were occasionally shuffled to put some girls above others. Now I suppose I know.

Ahh, the (relative) freedom. No particular desire to make or keep manicure/waxing/any other appointments. Though I daresay if the sun comes out and I go into the garden in a bikini, someone may be forgiven for coming at me with a lawn-trimmer.

Walking last night from a A3's house to the tube station, I passed a shop festooned in the most horrible things ever: little plaster babies' feet. Painted in pastel colors. Sticking out of the wall. Someone please assure me that the biological desire to reproduce does not signal the end of taste. It's enough to put a girl off her vibrator for fear of being impregnated with jelly babies.

mardi, le 25 mai

And still no word.

"I want out," I groaned to N. The manager's cold shoulder is beginning to wear on me. There are plenty of other outfits around, but the thought of going through another agency seems like another dead end. I've even gone so far as to pull out an ancient CV, think how it might be updated so the gaps in employment don't look Grand Canyon–wide.

"Okay, but don't leave just to sell out."

I rolled my eyes. Aren't we past the age where authenticity matters more than solvency? Everyone I know has a career, spouse, property, or retirement fund. Or several of the above. I questioned his choice of words.

"What is the definition of selling out?" he said. "Never do anything for money that you wouldn't do for free."

"I spend a lot of time picking at my nails." It came out sharper than I expected. "Don't think there's a chance of a career in that."

"Don't be sarcastic," N said. "It never suited you."

There is, in the end, only one place for a woman to turn in her hour of desperation. When all else has failed, when the bank accounts are running from black to red to overdraft limit to carefully worded letters from the bank. She has to draw on every nerve she has and steel herself for the inevitable.

The job pages.

I started with the administrative positions. General knowledge of computers? Check. Organizational skills? Plenty. Self-motivated and hardworking? Sort of. Dedicated?

To what, scheduling meetings and faxing letters? Being able to seal envelopes and transfer incoming calls requires dedication now?

Maybe not for me. I perused academic posts instead.

Depressing. It would seem the higher the degree, the lower the corresponding starting salary. A2 and A4 are academics, and confirm my suspicion that research grants are a convoluted plan by the powers that be to keep clever people from thinking about things like world affairs. Why pay attention to politics and other matters of import when there is a £5,000 grant to be fighting tooth and claw over?

jeudi, le 27 mai

I am determined not to give up, in spite of the fact that papers and websites suggest the London economy is based on exactly three things:

1. Copywriting and copyediting. Been there, done that . . . actually, I haven't as such. Tried to be there and do that, and been turned down by everyone from scientific journals to *World Walrus Weekly*. The country's finer philately organs did not even honor me with a rejection letter.

2. Temping and PAs (personal assistants). Definitely been there and don't ever, ever want to do that again. Revisiting calloused fingertips from sealing billing envelopes at a stockbroker's is a fate too depressing to contemplate. The abject degradation of having to collect someone's

daughter's school uniforms from the dry cleaner makes scat play look a doddle.

3. Prostitution. Damnation.

I could stay in the business and go independent. It would mean never having to give up a third of my earnings to an agency again. On the other hand, it would mean vetting my own clients, taking calls all hours of the day and night, maintaining a portfolio, organizing security and . . . oh. Too much work for me on my own. There'd barely be time for scheduling waxes, let alone any other essential maintenance operations.

samedi, le 29 mai

Letters. Applications. Download, print, fill in. Envelopes and stamps on letters I'll probably never have replies to. And then, late yesterday afternoon, a call from a personnel department. They want to see me for an interview. A position I would love to have.

Shortlisted. And I know the list is extremely short. My chances are good.

That's it—I'm off the game.

From the profiles on my agency's website, it's apparent that a lot of the girls—maybe not the majority, but a large proportion— are not from the UK. Eastern Europe, North Africa, Asia. Britain is doing a roaring trade in importing sex workers.

I don't ask about their motivations for doing the job. It's not my business. I wasn't forced into working for the agency and hope they weren't either. If the agency was really a stable of illegal workers under the thumb of an abusive pimp, they wouldn't hire so many local girls.

Would they?

I realize that all that aside, I'm not really in a very different position from those Jordanian and Polish girls right now. Maybe they're over on student visas and in extreme debt. Somewhere along the way, it was implied—not guaranteed, I understand that, but implied—that the reward for working hard at school and completing a degree was a reasonable career. Now here I am wondering whether a six-month appointment color-correcting magazine illustrations or assistant managing at a high-street retailer would be a better career move. And competing with hundreds of other graduates for the same paltry pickings.

But for now, I have shirts to iron and interview questions to worry about.

lundi, le 31 mai

I rose early to catch a train. This was a London I had only heard rumors of: suited men and women crowding the platforms, waiting for a place on a packed carriage. Most looked slightly dazed, not quite awake; others had clearly risen early and had their schedule down to a science. I wondered whether some of the freshly made-up women had to rise at half four to look so pulled together by eight.

The train arrived on time, but it took less walking than I expected to find the offices. I went round the corner for a cup of tea and to waste time beforehand. A woman whose grasp of English was remedial at best prepared my drink, pouring in the milk long before the tea was steeped and before I could stop her. I sat at a small table facing a window on the street. Everyone around me, builders to executives, was bent over a newspaper. I had none, and looked out on the human traffic.

When I arrived, the other two interviewees were already there. We introduced ourselves, talked briefly about the social and professional connections that joined us. Then we filed into a room and, with a group of interviewers, watched each other's brief presentations. We were directed back to the first room afterward, and called in one at a time for the interview proper.

A dark-blonde, pudding-faced girl was the first candidate. When she left for her grilling, the other interviewee smiled wanly at me. "I knew when I saw you I didn't have a chance," he said. I had thought something similar, since while my degrees and references were better, his experience was enviable.

"Don't be silly," I said. "It could be any of us." Either, I corrected silently, since it was fairly certain the other girl didn't have a chance. Her degree was only tangentially related, her graduate experience nonexistent, and she had mumbled and dragged through her presentation, the content of which was not terribly impressive.

The second candidate went for his interview and must have left straight after, as he didn't come back to the room.

I entered the room for my interview already sweating. Don't walk into the table, I thought. Don't drop anything. There were three people on the other side: a tall, thin man, an elderly gentleman with glasses, and a thirtyish woman with short dark hair.

They took their questions in turns. The division of labor soon became clear: the older man asked very little and was clearly more senior. The thin man asked questions relating to personality—the usual things, such as what I thought my weaknesses were and where I saw my career in five years' time. The younger woman was left the technical questions, and these scared me the most, but I thought before starting to answer each. At some points I was aware that composing an answer left them hanging for the start of my sentences, but I thought it better to get it right than to amble aimlessly.

When the interview concluded, the three stood with me. The selection should be made fairly quickly, they said, since they wanted someone to start as soon as possible. I could expect a phone call or letter in the next few days. Since I was the last candidate, they left the room as well. The elderly man and the young woman turned down the hall one way, to walk to their offices. The tall man offered to walk me through to the lobby.

We stood quietly in the elevator together. I smiled. "I remember you from a conference three years ago," he said. "Impressive presentation."

"Thank you," I said. Crud. Most of the presentation I'd given earlier in the day had been recycled from that one.

We walked through the quiet carpeted hallways. He started talking about his own work, something he was clearly passionate about. I like people with passion. I asked him leading questions, argued the devil's advocate while making it clear I actually agreed with his side, and in the end he stood with me at a taxi queue until the cab came to take me to the station. He shook my hand warmly and closed the door for me. As the taxi pulled away, I could see him still standing at the curb.

My heart was beating fast. That was good, I thought. Now I have someone on my side.

Juin

W - Z

W is for Whore

Working girl, prostitute, call girl, woman of negotiable affection, ho. I don't think any one term is any more or less degrading than another. It's simply a label, go with it, have fun with it. Indignation at someone else's moniker for a whore is so outdated. So politically correct, so nineties. You sell sex for a living—what did you expect, to be billed as an "erotic entertainments consultant"?

"Sex therapist" wouldn't be too bad, though.

X is for Xerxes

Xerxes was a great king of Persia in the fifth century BC.

(I couldn't think of a good topic that started with X.)

Y is for Youth

Younger is better in the business. This is an ironclad rule—unless you're over forty, in which case the agency will probably add a robust decade to increase the naughty-granny factor. Expect that your profile will not tell your age accurately. If actresses can continue to play ingenues well into their thirties, why can't you? But it's up to you to remember which lie you told whom and keep up the facade. The client is paying for an illusion, and letting slip that you were old enough to keep John Major in his constituency is not a good idea. Doubly so if he is a Labour backbencher.

Z is for Zippers

Someone once asked me to undress him using only my teeth. While in principle this sounds like an interesting task, there is one thing that cannot be undone with the mouth alone, and that is the zipper of a man's trousers. You know how you have to hold them taut at the top when you unzip your own? You can't do that without hands. It took about eight minutes just to get his trousers down and completely killed the mood.

mardi, le 1ᵉʳ juin

Angel rang. It was a bit of a surprise; I hadn't heard from her in ages, only caught a glimpse of her from time to time, and had really not thought I'd hear from her again.

She was crying. I was in a taxi and couldn't really hear her due to the noise of the cab, but it sounded like she was somewhere noisy as well, on a street or by a tube entrance. I told her I was on the way to meet a friend, and she could ring me later or drop by for coffee if she wanted a chat.

She did drop by. She smiled and breezed in, looking calmer and pulled together, but I knew it was only a matter of time until she broke down. Which she did, magnificently. Someone had just dumped her. A relationship—I had to confess ignorance that she was seeing anyone at all—had ended. By e-mail.

I was shocked. "No way to treat you, no matter what happened," I cooed. I poured boiling water into a *cafetière*, let it steep probably too long, pushed the plunger, and poured her a beaker of steaming brew. "So who was it?" I asked, out of mild curiosity.

"Didn't you know?" she asked, looking up, tearstained face. "You'll laugh." It was First Date.

Bloody hell.

"And the worst part of it all, he is still carrying a torch for you."

Bloodier hell. How do you comfort someone who has just been chucked for, among other reasons undoubtedly, a memory, and a pretty insubstantial one at that? "I'm so sorry," I whispered.

"You're good at things, you're talented," she moaned. "I just don't know, I disappoint people."

"You can't take that personally. Someone else being disappointed in you is their problem." Cruddy way to soothe someone, I know, but I didn't know what to say. This woman was more acquaintance than friend, and a stressful one at that. But I felt for her. I've been on both sides of that equation.

jeudi, le 3 juin

An invitation came through the post a few weeks ago. I haven't replied yet for not knowing what to do.

It's a weekend in the country to celebrate a friend's engagement, and promises to be a good time, with garden parties and drunken sing-alongs round a bonfire. And I would ordinarily be there like a shot, but for one thing. The Boy.

The odds that he was not invited are slender. With most exes, I would not mind, but I haven't heard so much as a word from him since the near-miss at that birthday party some time back, there's been no sign of the mystery car at all, and I therefore have no idea whether he still pines, or hates me, or has forgotten about me altogether. And I can't decide which outcome would be the worst.

It would take only a minute to ring the bride-to-be and ask, but that would flag my concern, and if I know this couple at all, I know that other people's discomfort is their sport. So best not say anything at all.

I could certainly use a weekend out of town, though, and it's the best option going so far.

samedi, le 5 juin

N and A3 and I dissected the interview. N has no real idea what I studied, but was unfailingly supportive and convinced the job will be mine. A3, on the other hand, works in a similar field and is, it must be noted, grumpy at best.

I've my own personal angel and devil figures, just as in cartoons. Though the idea of carrying their combined thirty-odd stone on my shoulders is laughable.

mardi, le 8 juin

"They must at least be considering you," N said. "I went for an interview in Newcastle once, and they rang up to reject me before I even got to the train to come home."

"What were you going to Newcastle for?" I asked.

N gave me an odd look. "Never you mind," he said. "Point is, you have to be more patient. They'll let you know in due time."

He's probably right, but it doesn't stop me fretting. Could I have given a better presentation, I wonder, or answered their questions more professionally? Did something about my clothes or manner put them off? How did I stand up against the others? If I get the job, will I fit in, will I disappoint them? Do any fit men work there?

mercredi, le 9 juin

As near as I can figure, possible reasons I have not been contacted yet about the interview include:

- They have decided to hire someone else, and neglected to tell me.
- They have decided to hire me, and neglected to tell me.
- They are making an offer to someone else first and waiting for a response before rejecting the other applicants.
- They are rejecting the other applicants before contacting the successful candidate (i.e., me).
- The letter has been lost in the post.
- The letter has not been lost in the post, but was delivered to the wrong house.
- The letter was delivered to the wrong house, and the occupant died suddenly on the way to the door, and no one has found him or the letter yet.
- The letter was delivered to the wrong house, and the occupant has a dog, who ate the letter.
- The letter was delivered to me, but as a test of my mental acumen, cunningly disguised as one of the thousands of circulars that come through my door daily, and I mistakenly threw it away.
- The letter was delivered to me, and rapidly disintegrated.
- The letter was delivered to me, and soon thereafter I suffered acute head trauma, erasing my memory of either the letter or the trauma.
- And my memory has filled in the erased portions, so not only do I not remember any of this, I do not have any mysterious gaps in my recollection.
- I dreamt the interview.
- The letter has not been sent yet.
- They haven't made a decision yet.

jeudi, le 10 juin

I couldn't take waiting any longer. I rang the personnel department. The woman on the other end of the call was kind-voiced, slightly dappy—I had to give her the job reference number three times. She apologized—apparently there had been problems with the internal mail and the letters hadn't been posted yet, though a decision had been made. I gnawed the fingers of my left hand while she looked for the information.

"Ah, here you are," she said. "It looks like you've gotten it."

My heart leapt. I grinned. "Really?"

"You are Louise, right?"

And just as quickly, it fell back to the pit of my stomach. "Er, no." The pudding-faced girl. How had they chosen her over me?

"Oh, sorry!" she tittered. "I'm afraid you haven't been successful, then." I thanked her and rang off.

Phone call from Dr. C, who is visiting his parents and wants to drive up and visit next week. I suppose the current situation gives me some free time at least. Silver linings and all that. And I am definitely going to that engagement party. Nothing hath charms to soothe the wounded ego quite like alcohol and flirtation.

So I should be away all weekend. Sod's Law: if in the city with no escape, the days will be blazing hot and sunny; the minute I step foot outside this urban sphere, it will chuck it down endlessly. And I will be wearing open-toed shoes with white trousers. If you experience unpleasant weather this weekend, be assured that it is my fault entirely.

dimanche, le 13 juin

The benefits of sex with an ex:

- No chance of being shocked by what he looks like naked the first time. That horrible mole is right where you left it.
- Not having to awkwardly ask for contact details after. If you don't have them, it's not by accident.
- He knows where your buttons are, how many there are, how long they need to be pressed, and whether they should go side-to-side, up and down, or in little circles.

And the drawbacks:

- There's probably a good reason you're not together anymore. A very good reason.
- One of you will think this means the relationship is back on.
- There is absolutely no way you can tell any of your friends without coming off as the world's biggest prat. After all, they had to live with you post-breakup, right?

Cripes. I'm going to commence a head/wall interface now. Back later when I have knocked some sense into myself.

lundi, le 14 juin

So, yes. Sex. With someone I honestly expected never to have sex with again.

The Boy. The effing Boy.

Still sorting it out. It's a mess. He gave me a lift back to London and now won't leave. But I would like to confirm that—at least before the slightly tipsy postcoital glowing phase ended and the horrible, horrible veil of Oh-Dear-Me-Not-Again descended—it was good.

Better than good. He sat on my chest and fucked my mouth; he took me from behind, above, and below. I smiled and asked how he'd gotten so good with his tongue, thinking there must be some genius tart showing him the ropes now. "I don't know," he said. "I just think about it a lot." I came harder, faster, and longer than usual, and for a brief moment I thought, If he never said anything stupid again, I could be quite happy with this.

Sod's Law Mark II: he will open his mouth and say something stupid within thirty seconds of thinking that. And it was raining outside so I couldn't make some excuse to vacate the flat, walk around for a bit, and come back when enough time had elapsed to be certain he'd gone.

mardi, le 15 juin

There's no why to ex sex, there's only the how (long it will last, soon it will be over, fast can I leave). Most of my exes are friends, and most of my friends are exes, and I don't fuck them afterward as a rule. But there are one or two who fall out of touch, usually because there was little in the relationship worth building a friendship on, and this was one.

The morning he left he offered me a lift to a meeting. Thank goodness, I thought, that means he'll be on his way, hopefully never to return. Before we could go, though, he asked if I had any money on me. I didn't. Except when working, I usually carry less spare change than the Queen.

He drove us via an ATM so I could make a withdrawal and pay him back for the tomatoes he had bought me. (N.B., these were replacing tomatoes I already had that he had helped himself to. So, I was paying for my own tomatoes twice. Nice.)

I emerged from the car shaking my head. Walked to the ATM. Withdrew a crisp tenner—the tomatoes hadn't cost that much, but who knows, maybe he was going to impose a surcharge on my own toilet paper, or something—and walked back to the car. Put the note in his hand.

Closed the door. Kept on walking.

A text came through a minute later:

Am just filling up with petrol if you still want a lift come back and meet me.

I didn't reply. He rang. Did I want a lift? he asked. "Yes, if you can act like a normal person," I said. I described the direction I was going, said if he wanted to drive me, he could pick me up. He rang again a minute later. Said he was at the end of the road now and didn't see me. I said it was because I was still walking. Hung up. He rang again, asked where I was. Described the road I was on, the building I had just passed, the route I was taking. Hung up.

He sent another text:

This is really stupid, I'm just 10 meters behind u the whole way. And as per usual, is exactly what I knew would happen.

A minute later, his car came up on my right. I stopped walking. He reached across and opened the passenger side door.

"I just got your text," I said.

"And?" he said.

"Goodbye." I shut the door firmly and walked on. His car lingered a minute until someone beeped a horn, and he drove up to the next roundabout and disappeared. And that was it. Put on headphones. The next song was about someone walking out the door, and I felt good, and smiled so hard it brought tears to my eyes.

mercredi, le 16 juin

Had a call late last night. Not work—A1 was having some sort of crisis and his woman was nowhere to be found. He left four missed calls and a garbled message. When I tried to ring, it went straight through to the answerphone. Boys. It was late, but I put myself at the mercy of the London Underground and went to his.

The tube route between my place and A1's involves two changes. And I worry that time of night about missing the last train and being stuck in Earl's Court with a Metrocard and distinct lack of clue.

The tube is, by far, the most antisocial mode of transport yet invented. On the bus, you can shield others from your germs by sneezing into the back of their heads. On the tube, you are forced to share breathing space with every phlegmy disease vector from here to Uxbridge. And in spite of being nose-to-armpit with complete strangers and mingling more viruses than a Crichton novel, you are Not Allowed to Stare.

In normal circumstances this would not be hard. City dwellers are masters of the Appraisal Glance, in which a person is sized up and dismissed in the split second they come into view. But when you're trapped in a hurtling canister on a bumpy track to Dollis Hill, the eyes literally have nowhere to go. You have to stare. But you're not allowed to. This is why paperbacks are so popular; it gives you a shield to hide behind as well as an excuse to not hold on to the rail and stumble over the snowdrift of *Metro*s cluttering the aisle.

Waiting for a District Line train, I was aware of someone looking at me. I pretended to check my watch and look up and down the track. Some youngish man, wearing a suit. Probably just idly checking out everyone on the platform. Fair enough. I needed a shower and some sleep and probably didn't merit a second glance.

The train arrived. I sat down. The man sat opposite me. Was that another look? No. Ignore it. I looked at his hand. It was a fine, well-shaped hand. Very attractive. I rested my forehead on a side handrail.

In peripheral vision I could see him looking me over a couple more times. Definitely more than necessary. But he didn't seem predatory. Probably just wondering why I'm out, as I do with people all the time. Probably drunk. Who rides the tube in a suit this time of night sober?

I looked up. His blue eyes were staring at me. Cool as. I couldn't help myself and grinned like a loon. He didn't crack a smile. We both looked away quickly.

Argh, I thought. Giddy moron. But I can't help it; if someone looks at me and I'm not expecting it, I smile. I must have seemed a complete idiot.

Two stops. His head turned back toward me. I looked at him. Smiled. Stuck out my tongue.

And he laughed. Looked away again.

Right. Two more stops. Both looking obviously in other directions. Quite obscene eye-avoidance, actually. My stop was approaching. I stretched. I could see him glance at me but refused to meet his gaze. What was he going to do? I could wave as I stepped off. I could say something.

I stood up. The train slid into the station. The doors opened. Go on, at least nod, I thought. Then: follow me off, follow me off. I stepped onto the platform. No, wait, don't. He didn't. Just some drunk lad in a suit, going home. The train moved into the night.

(A1 was fine, by the way. A bit tired and emotional is all. By which I mean drunk.)

samedi, le 19 juin

Was standing with a female friend, C, at the bar of a club. N was meant to be meeting us later, but had texted to say he would be late. We stood at the bar with our drinks, cooly avoiding eye contact and in complete denial of the terrible, cheesy music the DJ was pumping out.

A man careened in our direction. "Say, ladies," he said, and I thought, Isn't it a bit early for someone to be this drunk? "It's my friend's birthday, like, and he's just standing over there—" and he pointed into a crowd of disorganized faces.

C was already putting her polite-smile mask on. Wasn't it obvious we were not waiting to be chatted up?

But chatting up was not what the young squire had in mind. "And he was wondering, would you two show him your tits?"

C's mask didn't crack. "Sorry, no," she smiled politely, turning back to her cocktail. I smirked.

"You sure, ladies? It is his birthday and all."

"No," I said less politely, and turned away. C and I ordered more drinks. N was being very tardy. We tried to have a conversation over the music, which was much louder now, but could not, and ended up just smiling vaguely at each other. C toyed with the furry fringes of her exceptionally tactile sweater.

Two more men lurched in our direction. We only half-turned to acknowledge them. It was the same young man again, and another. "Hi, ladies," the second man said. It occurred to me that men only call women ladies in a mockery of chivalry. "It's my birthday tonight, and I was wondering, would you two please show me your tits?"

Well. At least he said "please." C's mask was impenetrable. "No."

"No," I echoed.

"Are you sure?" he asked, pulling a look of false pleading.

Does this ever work? I wondered. He didn't even offer money, for goodness' sake. So women are expected to act like whores for free, and this is considered being a good sport, while actual prostitutes are objects of mockery and revulsion. You have to wonder.

"No," a voice behind the boys said, and it was N, a head taller than either of them. The boys scarpered.

N gave me and C a lift. She's young, almost a teenager, really. Actually, she's in her mid-twenties but acts eighteen. In the nice sort of way.

We were talking about marriage. She was curious about N's situation, why he's still single. She asked if I wanted to marry and have children someday. I said no. She said she didn't, either.

"Oh, you'll cave," N said to her. "You'll find the right man and it will just happen."

She bristled but didn't argue with him. "So what do you think about my future, then?" I asked N. "Spinsterhood?"

He looked at the road. He was being careful with his words. "I think you've chosen your own path and don't want anyone to interfere with that," he said. "You value your freedom above everything else. So yes, I think that's what you will have if you want it. I'm not saying you'll never change your mind, but it would take a remarkable man, and I think you'll want to be single for a long time still."

dimanche, le 20 juin

I was flopped on my bed, reading. The phone buzzed. Dr. C.

"Top of the road, you said?"

"Bottom of the road." Actually, I'm never quite sure which is which, but if he didn't see the number, he was probably at the wrong end.

He tapped on the door a minute later. "Bottom of the road?" I grinned. His smile was nicer than I'd remembered. He had a single bag and an old blue car. His brother's, he said. I let him in.

He dropped his bag next to the sofa. Ack, I thought. Should have put some pillows and blankets out. Wouldn't want him to think I assumed he'd be sleeping with me. We faced each other, said nothing, just smiling.

"So."

"So. Go for a walk?"

"Walk it is."

We wandered for hours. I didn't even notice the time until the sun went behind the trees. He talked about his family, his work. He talked with his gorgeous mouth and his hands. We sat on a bench and watched round women walking their tiny, even rounder dogs.

"Home?"

"Home it is," he said.

I offered to cook something for him. "To be honest, I'm not really that hungry," he said. I wasn't either. He brought a large bottle of liqueur out of his bag. There must not have been room in there for much else. We sat at my kitchen table with a bowl of ice and finished the bottle.

I was tipsy, so was he, but in a nice way, like the night we were first together. When the glasses and bottle were finally empty, I took him up to my bedroom. We kissed and fondled each other through our clothes. "Your breasts look great in this," he said. "May I ask you something?"

Anything, I almost said. "What's that?"

"May I whip your breasts? Through the shirt, I mean."

I produced a rubber multitailed whip for him. He started with light taps at first. I laughed. "You can go harder than that," I said. He did. It hurt. It wasn't the hardest anyone had ever whipped me, but it felt like the most fun. I kept laughing. He didn't say anything, but he smiled too, it seemed so ludicrous. When he finished, he put the whip down and his hands under the shirt.

"The flesh is warm," he said. Lifted the shirt. I wasn't wearing a bra. "They're pink." He pushed me up against the wall and had me like that. Then we fell into bed and were almost instantly unconscious.

lundi, le 21 juin

The phone woke me. I was groggy and answered without looking to see who the call was from. "Hello?"

"Hello." It was the Boy. I shivered. I should have hung up. Didn't. "Where are you?" he asked.

"Umm, at home." No point lying. No time to think. "Where are you?"

"Outside."

"Oh." I put down the phone. Stretched, gently pushed the sleeping man beside me awake. "Um, I have a guest downstairs," I said.

He must have heard something in my voice. "Who is it?"

"My ex." A frown flickered across his face. He asked what I wanted to do. "Answer the door, I suppose." He said I didn't have to. That I could ring the police. I said I knew that. We dressed. He went down to the kitchen. I answered the door.

The Boy stood there. Shorts and a T-shirt. His car was pulled up opposite. He was alone. The street was quiet. He asked if he could come in. I let him.

He nodded at Dr. C in the kitchen. I introduced them. Asked if anyone wanted tea, breakfast. They said yes. I put the radio on. Everything seemed far too calm. I turned to the stove and scrambled eggs; put bread under the grill to toast. Made light chatter with both about the weather (pleasant) and what was on the radio (rubbish) and the news (depressing). I dished up and put plates of equal size in front of them.

The Boy dug straight in. His head bowed over the plate. It was odd to my eyes to see him sitting at the table after these few months.

"Aren't you having any eggs?" Dr. C asked.

"Just a slice of toast," I said.

"Lightweight fuel," he said, smiled, and ate. The two of them were quiet. I couldn't sit down, just paced lightly in front of the sink nibbling a crust. The Boy finished quickly and asked to use the toilet. I said he could. He had never had to ask before.

When he was out of the room Dr. C turned to me and whispered, "Why didn't you tell me about him?"

"Didn't think there was anything to tell," I whispered back. "Haven't seen him in months."

The Boy came back in. He asked if he could talk to me. I said he could. We stood there, in the kitchen, silent, Dr. C watching us. The Boy asked if he could speak to me in my room. I said yes. We went up the stairs. I left the door open. He sat on the bed, motioned for me to sit next to him. I sat. I knew we were within earshot of the kitchen.

"I have to ask you a question, I want you to be honest," he said.

I bristled. What right did he have to ask me anything? And when had I ever not told him the truth? "Yes?" I said.

"Are you sleeping with this man?"

"Yes."

"He slept here last night?"

"Yes," I said, and it occurred to me to wonder how long the Boy had been outside.

"I can't believe you would do this to me," he said. I was mystified. Was I supposed to be keeping a tally of lovers to recount for him? Was I still supposed to answer to him, care what he thought of me, care what anyone thought? I asked him to go.

He was calm. Oddly calm. Usually the Boy is fidgety and talk-ative, but he was silent and composed. He said he could let him-self out; I insisted on walking him down. To the door. Out the door. I stepped outside after him and pulled the door shut. Dr. C was still in the kitchen. Heard the lock close after me. I didn't have the key. Whatever the Boy was going to do, I wouldn't let him attack a stranger. He would have to get through me.

The Boy realized this. He turned, the color back in his cheeks. "I have to talk to him," he said with sudden urgency.

"No," I said, and crossed my arms.

"I have to talk to him," the Boy said. "He can have you, I just want him to know what . . . what he took from me."

"He took nothing. He doesn't even know who you are. Why should he? You let me go. Twice." The Boy asked to go inside. I re-fused. He asked again, several times; I refused. I knew it was beyond his code of conduct to hit me, but I didn't depend on that and I won-dered just where his breaking point would be. A few people were starting to come up and down the road in the course of normal morning business. I counted on that to save me, if I needed saving.

The Boy was clearly getting nowhere simply by asking to be let inside. "Come on," he whined. "The man's big enough. He can clearly take care of himself."

"You wouldn't touch him?" I asked.

"I wouldn't touch him."

"Liar." I could see his arms were crossed but his fists were clenching and unclenching over and over, turning the knuckles white then pink then white.

We stood. He looked at me. "Go to your car and drive away," I said. He stood unmoved. I repeated myself. He went. I followed him out of the garden gate. Watched him get in the car. He was slow to put the key in the ignition. I waited until he drove away. Went back to my door and knocked. Dr. C let me in. We went up to my room and fucked.

mardi, le 22 juin

In the morning Dr. C left. He had to drive back south. I smiled and made the bed as he packed his scant belongings. I didn't know if we'd see each other again; the bruises across my chest were already faint but may last longer than the two of us being together. I didn't know and didn't mind.

There was a car on the corner, could see it from my window, and he knew it too. The Boy. I walked Dr. C to his car and waved him off the street, went back inside, locking the door behind me. The phone was ringing. I didn't answer.

A few minutes later it rang again. "Hello," I said.

"May I come in?" the Boy asked. I said no, I'd meet him outside. I locked the door behind me and slipped the keys in my pocket. Kept the mobile in my hand, just in case. He walked out of his car and met me at the gate. Asked to come in again. I refused. Said we talked in his car or not at all. He tried again, saw I wasn't giving in, and I followed him back to where he was parked.

I sat in the passenger side and half-closed the door.

"I'm sorry, I know I've done so many things wrong, I'm so so sorry," he said. His eyes had gone red, and his shoulders turned in. I was struck with a pang of tenderness. I said nothing, though. He kept on apologizing, crying. I let him. I thought of all the times when we were dating when he hadn't apologized and it had torn me up, and of the few times he had and I'd hurried to soothe him and reassure him it wasn't his fault.

No interrupting this time. I just let him get it off his chest.

It was hard to watch. I knew I could lift him, end what he was feeling. I knew I could make the next ten minutes a lot easier for us both—maybe even the next ten days, if we were lucky, until we argued again—by saying I'd have him back. But I knew there would always be an argument waiting round the corner for us.

And whatever he said, people don't just change. Not that they can't change, but no one does overnight, and I had had enough.

And that's what I told him. I just whispered that I'd had enough. He sobbed but didn't keep begging.

This really is it, I thought. I thought about what N had said in the car. Was I dooming myself to the fate I'd chosen? Was this the last chance not just for him, but for me, forever?

"I loved you so much," he said finally.

"I loved you too," I said. Knew this really was the last time. And knew he knew it too.

jeudi, le 24 juin

Was just back from the gym, sweating and tired. Switched the kettle on more out of habit than a need for a hot drink. Still, they do say tea when you're hot.

The phone buzzed away on the kitchen counter. I looked at the screen. It was the manager.

I thought a moment, almost let it go to voice mail. Didn't. Answered.

"Darling, there is a booking for two hours. . . ."

Had I misheard? "Oh right." Weeks of silence and now a booking out of the blue? "How have you been?"

"Good, darling, good. Have I just woken you up?" Just back from the gym, I said. She approved. "Must keep in shape," she said, and moved on quickly. "Listen, this gentleman, he is staying at Claridge's, he has asked for you at ten o'clock." A two-hour booking with travel and all services. At the highest hourly rate we charge short of extras for odd requests.

I bit my lip. Gift horse, mouth, and all that. But I'd already said I was going to meet A3 at the pub later. And I hadn't gone for a wax in ages. Cutting the pubic hedge alone would take an hour.

And I was tired, and hadn't eaten yet, and a thousand things. "I'm sorry, I'm afraid I can't do it. I'm certain one of the other girls would be happy to?" I suggested softly.

"He liked your profile, wants you specifically, darling. I can make small lies, but not a big lie like sending another girl."

My goodness. Unheard-of honesty in a madame. Perhaps I'd just had the wrong end of the stick after all?

My voice grew stronger. "I so wish I could, but I have other plans," I said. I could have made it—just. The money would have been useful. But I didn't want to. A3 would be waiting, and I could imagine no better evening than letting him finish my pints and drone on about work.

"Okay, darling," she sang. "You are always such fun. I will speak to you soon?"

"Speak to you soon. Good night."

samedi, le 26 juin

As it's sunny, and because there is an outdoor portion of my home that is actually rather private but gives the thrilling illusion of public nudity, I have been kebabbing myself since the weekend.

Health professionals will tell you that only total abstinence is a guarantee to staying healthy, but I believe in the practice of safer sunbathing. When exposing delicate girlflesh to the sun's radiation, protection is always necessary.

Also, I wonder if the time has come to start considering working from home. The world, as they say, is my oyster.

Not that I've ever had an oyster. Kosher laws and whatnot. Perhaps instead:

The world, as they say, is my chopped liver.

dimanche, le 27 juin

"I'm an author," the client said. "Really," I said. "What kind?" "Genre fiction," he said. He quoted a *New York Times* bestseller standing and a familiar title. "Ah," I said. "Like Mickey Spillane." "That's right," he said. I said, "I always liked that part at the end of *My Gun Is Quick*, where Hammer tears the negligee off the heroine. Their single night of passion together."

I sat on his lap and he ran his hand over my thighs. "Feels like thigh-high stockings," he said. They were. "What do you want tonight?" I asked. "Simple man, simple pleasures," he said. "I just like to come in a naked woman's mouth." This transaction may seem expensive, but if you think about the money and effort you might spend on a business trip, trying to court someone just to get to the possible stage of her naked and you coming in her mouth before it's time to fly home, it's not so pricey. And the result is guaranteed.

We undressed each other and he lay on the bed. "You remind me of someone I was once in love with," I said. He looked doubtful. It was true—he had the same high waist and ascetic limbs of a fourteenth-century tempera saint. An identical form and face to A2. I tickled the high arch of his foot and kissed the inside of his thighs.

After sucking him for a few minutes, I asked what else he liked. Rimming, he said. "Giving or receiving?" Receiving, he said. I spread his legs wider and felt between the rounded cheeks of his arse. "Here, I think it will go better with a pillow under you." He obliged. The pucker was tender, pink, and hairless. Clean, it tasted slightly of soap. I put my lips back around his cock and tickled the hole with a damp finger. He came quickly and hard, filling my throat.

"It's only been thirty minutes," I said. He was paying for an hour. "I don't suppose you could manage again?"

"No, sorry," he said. "Too old. Too tired."

"Shall I stay and we can chat, or leave you, or you could turn over and I could pummel your back in a poor imitation of a massage."

"I'd be fine if you left. I'll just go to sleep happy and satisfied."

"I'd wish you luck with the books but it sounds like you don't need it," I said. "Must pick up a copy."

"Get one in paperback," he said. "See if you like them first."

I dressed, applied a fresh coat of lipstick. The money was in a hotel envelope. "Wasn't it Dashiell Hammett who said you don't pay a call girl to do what she does, you pay her to leave afterward?"

"Probably." He smiled drowsily. I closed the door softly behind me. There was only one taxi outside. I stepped in the back and was whisked home in the light and sound of a city evening.

This book would not have been possible without the support and patience of the following people: Patrick Walsh, Helen Garnons-Williams, and their staff and associates; Christy Fletcher, Emma Parry, and Melissa Chinchillo of Fletcher and Parry; and Amy Einhorn of Warner Books. All are owed many thanks.